Incidents of Travel
in Latin America

INCIDENTS OF TRAVEL IN
LATIN AMERICA

Lars Holger Holm

London
Arktos
2016

Copyright © 2016 by Arktos Media Ltd.

All rights reserved. No part of this book may be reproduced or utilised in any form or by any means (whether electronic or mechanical), including photocopying, recording or by any information storage and retrieval system, without permission in writing from the publisher.

Printed in the United Kingdom.

ISBN 978-1-910524-55-8

BIC-CLASSIFICATION

Travel writing (WTL)

Latin America (1KL)

EDITOR

Jonathan Paquette

LAYOUT AND COVER DESIGN

Tor Westman

ARKTOS MEDIA LTD.

www.arktos.com

Contents

At the Gate	1
Colombia	17
Parque de Tayrona	24
Medellín	48
Santa Fé de Antioquia	52
Never forget your hat!	61
Boca Chica	84
Galéras	88
You are in a Third World country *if*	103
Zauberberg	129
Capurganá	137
In Cielo	144
A trip to Panamá	147
La Coquéra	156
Aguacate	158
Triganá	161
San Juan del Sur and a return to the pleasure of crustaceans	178
Turbo	188
Necoclí	190
Bahía Soláno	204
Caracól, Tikál, Calakmúl	220
A season in Puerto Rico	233
A sailing trip in the Gulf of Honduras	247
Antígua	265
Lake Atitlán	273
The Bus	284
Hotel del Pacifico	308
Boca del Cielo	331
Taking to the heights	338
Yet another ascension	343
The ultimate ascension	351
Epilogue	357

Planetai (πλανῆται) means Wanderer.
This book is dedicated to all Lonely Planets.

The author at the top of *Cerro Tusa* (Venecia, Antioquia, Colombia) after a somewhat strenuous ascension! (Photo: Asíle)

At the Gate

My plane to Barranquilla, Colombia, wasn't delayed but it had proved impossible to prolong the car rental without paying through the nose. Since that would have been an ugly sight, I decided to return my stately vehicle hours before take-off. This left me with time to kill. I figured Las Olas Boulevard in downtown Fort Lauderdale would be the place, and entered the local bus servicing the Hollywood International Airport. Truly, it would have been easier to say hasta la vista to a Corolla. But this was a state-of-the-art American beauty, with all that goes with it. The reason I ever enjoyed the privilege to hang out with her for so long was the following.

As I arrived in Miami one month earlier, the compact cars were in such demand that the rental dealership didn't have enough of them available. To make up for the vehicle shortage they'd thrown in some Mercury Grand Marquises — a more elegant edition of the Ford Victoria preferred by police forces and cab drivers nationwide — in the lot, offering them at economy price. Generally unable, even under normal circumstances, to resist temptation, I jumped at it. My European heart made an extra beat at the mere thought of turning the key to an eight-cylinder monster with a 4.6 litre engine, knowing I was deliberately and willingly indulging in sin. Since Miami (or to be precise,

Miami Beach herself) is pretty much the emblem of it, there simply couldn't be a better way to arrive there.[1]

South Beach is a case in point. In the 1970s and 80s its population was up to 80 % Jewish and South Beach itself is practically still a ghetto. Before before World War II Jews, though allowed to buy property anywhere, could only settle south of 5th Street and this restriction on their activities was only suspended as late as in 1949. After that, South Beach became known as 'the waiting room of death' as increasingly older people found it desirable to retire there. At this time there was nothing really fancy or upscale about it. If designer perfumes nowadays permeate its atmosphere, back then the streets smelled of mildew and *gefilte fisch* and on a visit you would overhear a wild array of eastern European languages blending with Brooklyn twang and Yiddish — it's no coincidence that Michael Corleone in order to visit with businessman Hyman Roth in the second *Godfather* film has to go to Miami.

The Jewish scene was to remain relatively unchanged until the late 1970s, when Fidel Castro opened all of his prisons and mental asylums and poured their contents into clandestine boats destined for Miami, thereby creating a tsunami of crime inundating its beaches. South Beach quickly became one of the most dangerous places in all of North America and the Jews began to move northward. Then came the Art Deco renaissance, initiated by prominent Jews of the modern art scene determined to save the beach and restore it to pre-war glory. Some TV shows — pioneer among them had been the iconic *Jackie Gleason Show*, since the mid-1960s produced in Miami — and criminal series

---

[1] I think it's fair to say that this type of car still sits in a no-man's land between 'no longer modern' and 'still not classic' (the last models rolled out of the Detroit factory as late as 2011). As of today it primarily appeals to Latinos and Afro-Americans as the epitome of the American Dream within reach even for the not very rich. It is indeed a well-manufactured vehicle in the grand tradition of full-size sedans that takes on the long, straight US Interstate Highways in the same manner as a mature Côte-du-Rhône takes on a ripe Roquefort cheese — it's a marriage made in heaven!

(*Miami Vice*, followed by the contemporary *CSI Miami*) helped to put it back on the map, and in the 1990s it began to be hyped up to its present level of mediatised hysteria. Although today in many ways synonymous with Sodom, South Beach is simultaneously home to a large Orthodox Jewish community that has gradually come to supplant the original population of more liberally oriented Jews, and paradoxically seems to thrive in the shadow of its frivolous glitz. Or perhaps not so paradoxically, after all.

Besides, it isn't just Rabbi Rabinowich who knows how to profit from it, even if he occasionally gets caught with his pants down. We also have the heritage of pushers and dealers in the grand Cuban tradition of *Scarface*. We have Cuban Jews and Israelis mixing freely with Colombian, Venezuelan and Russian goy *mafiosi* distinguished by gold chains so heavy that they can hardly keep their necks straight. Their women, (as artificially big-chested as they are self-absorbed — that is, when they're not absorbed by their cell phones) prefer diamond rings and necklaces since their values never decrease. Add to these a set of modern day WASP retirees populating the entire Florida coastline, but in particular its south, as well as the steady coming and going of foreign tourists and well-to-do Europeans taking refuge there during the winter season.

If Asians don't make up any significant portion of Miami's population by and large, Latin families do, clustering around Calle Ocho (SW 8th Street), Little Havana and West Little Havana, with their rather picturesque mixture of small malls, cash only gas stations, restaurants, shops and Latin bakeries, seedy one-night stand motels with names like Venus, Stardust and Jamaica, strip joints, dry cleaners, PC repair shops, dollar stores and lawyers advertising for clients needing help to file for bankruptcy, divorce or to get off the hook for speeding or 'Drinking Under the Influence of Driving'.

Like an oasis appears to the south of mid Calle Ocho the wealthy and serene Coral Gables (by no means off limits for Latinos who have made it) with its lavish golf courses, long tree adorned alleys, manicured gardens, elegant mansions in a variety of colonial styles, streets with Spanish and Italian names marked in black print on whitewashed corner stones, a chic downtown and a *jeunesse dorée* pitching camp in the gardens of the Biltmore Hotel. It also, somewhat surprisingly, includes within its perimetre a token trailer park for people of considerably lesser means, symbolically located next to a funeral parlour and a cemetery.

The contrast is immediate and only announced by the drive-through archway and extended gable made from coral that have given the name to this town. Driving south on 49th street — which is another thoroughly Latino dominated residential backwater tucked in between the major traffic artery Route 836 (separating it from the airport), and 8th Street — you find yourself transported, once you have crossed over 8th Street into the Gables, by the fairy's magic wand. Here the rather inconspicuous SW 49th Avenue completely changes appearance, like Cinderella going to the ball, congenially assuming a new name resounding of saga and history: Granada Boulevard. Whereas the single plane villas to the north of 8th Street would no doubt announce a wealthy neighbourhood in Managua and Tegucigalpa, they are just plain ordinary in Miami. From the absence of barbed wire to protect the residents from unwanted intrusion you can tell you're actually not in Managua or Tegucigalpa, but doors and windows are indeed covered by iron bars, just as in those places.

Once you've entered Granada Boulevard on the other hand, bars in front of the windows would be an unpardonable faux pas, giving you away as a despicable nouveau riche from the Third World. Here we don't rely on iron bars but on the Coral Gables Police, discreet cameras, alarm systems and Neighbourhood Watch. The streets are clean — not a dog turd as far as an eagle's eye can see — and hardly frequented by pedestrians. Although there are perfectly maintained pavements in place everywhere, there are times of the day when the residences of

Coral Gables are akin to a vision of serene, golden America painted by a late Edward Hopper. The effect of its flowery gardens and long canopies of trees arching the streets for miles give a surrealistic impression: on a clear day the colours are overly vivid and, seen through a pair of good sunglasses, almost psychedelic. Adding to the enchantment is a full scale lighthouse in Moorish style overlooking the green sea of the golf course with its huge Banyan trees. I have sometimes remained motionless in front of the lighthouse thinking I'm the only witness to the world on Day One without humans. It's rather like the dream in which you wake up to a perfect world but there's nobody besides yourself in it. So, like a King Midas everything you touch does turn into gold, but you also starve to death by the means that made you rich. A memento to ponder for sure.

Add to Coral Gables the various Central and South-American nationalities populating communities such as Fontainebleau and the City of Doral. In the middle of it sits, as the heart of ultra-urban civilisation, Miami Airport set against the vibrating, silvery skyline of downtown. To the north of the airport is Latin Hialeah, and the predominantly Afro-American scene of Little Haiti, North Miami and Miami Gardens, which, in spite of its seducing name, features many a thorny, unkempt shrubbery. Some houses look more like abandoned tool sheds, flaunting rebar and naked concrete. Aluminium chairs litter the grass and loaded boat trailers clog up the driveways. There are entire blocks filled with military looking barracks (housing projects) with people aimlessly hanging in street corners, or drifting in and out of utility and second-hand stores — that is, when they're not actually pushing a department store trolley ahead containing all of their belongings, including a cardboard mattress custom made from a FedEx delivery box.

As a contrast there is the strange amalgamation of former hippie homes at the opposite end of town, tucked away in quaint Coconut Grove, with its vaguely bohemian younger generation and wealthy

Coral Gablers 'with a difference', living practically next door to the Bahamian ghetto around the intersection of Grand Avenue and Douglas Road, where rape, abuse, robbery and murder allegedly are still on the weekly menu and police cars are frequently transfixed, flashing their strobe lights for hours.[2]

The Miami University campus is further down, constituting Coral Gables' southwestern corner along the US 1, also called South Dixie Highway.[3] Continue down that main stretch and you reach South Miami with its interminable automobile showrooms and car sales parking lots. Off to either side, tranquil Pinecrest, Cutler and Palmetto Bays to the east, Kendall, Homestead to the west, and still more remote neighbourhoods which the imagination is keen to populate with alligators lurking in the swamps. Having passed these vast areas there remains only the frontier town of Florida City with its last call discount liquor stores still within the limits of Dade County, as well as the 18 mile long desolate causeway through crocodile infested mangroves

---

2 In this connection it might interest movie watchers that the marital comedy *Meet the Fockers* from 2004, featuring Dustin Hoffman and Barbara Streisand as the 'once' hippie couple, receiving in their charmingly rundown and luxuriously overgrown Miami home the ever so slightly stricter parents of the to-be-bride, congenially personified by Robert de Niro (who also produced the film) and Blythe Danner, is set in the Coconut Grove. The children to be married are played by Ben Stiller and Teri Polo.

3 To the newcomer in Miami it can be more than just a little confusing that some streets have up to four different names, so that although you're correct in assuming you should make a right turn onto *SW 22nd Street*, you won't find it because you're supposed to know in advance that at this particular junction it's marked out as *Coral Way*, and at another one as *The Miracle Mile*. Though you just might be able to figure out that the above mentioned *Calle Ocho* is identical with *SW 8th Street*, you also need to know that another synonym for it is the *Tamiami Trail*, as well as *Felipe Vals Road*. It goes without saying that *East 8th Avenue* is also and better known as *Le Jeune Road*, or simply as *42nd Avenue* and that *East 9th Street* is of course identical with *NW 62nd Street*, in turn identical with *Martin Luther King Jr. Boulevard*. Nothing could be simpler!

bringing the traveller to the endless Florida Keys, where a different story begins.

The very last of these is the liberal haven Key West where Papa Hemingway settled down in the 1930s in order to be as close to Cuba as possible without having to deal with the Cubans themselves. I have to admit that I belong to the non-negligible category of people that is more fascinated by the extravagant Papa Legend than by Papa's books. I wish I could say that I truly enjoy the latter, but to me Hemingway's prose, though so often praised precisely on this account, appears frugal and simplified to the point of sterility (the only one of his books that truly captivates me from the beginning to the end is *The old Man and the Sea*). I thus fail to fathom its hidden depths and underlying symbols, of which critics and connoisseurs have spoken so eloquently.

It's therefore all the more surprising, and indeed gratifying to be able to marvel at the titles of his books, since they are almost invariably (*A Movable Feast* is in my opinion a notable exception) charged with rich suggestion. I don't know if he made them all up by himself, if it was his editor, his wives, or some other person with a particular genius who invented them. Whatever the case: they're just perfect. Please do me the favour of listening to the inner reverberations of titles such as: *The Sun also Rises*; not 'Farewell to Arms', but precisely *A Farewell to Arms* and *For Whom the Bell Tolls*. Absolutely not 'The Snow of Kilimanjaro', which would have been trite and commonplace, but again, precisely, *The Snows of Kilimanjaro*; *The Old Man and the Sea*; and my personal favourite: *Across the River and into the Trees*. It's very possible that I shall one day have to change my appraisal of Hemingway's works, based on yes, unprejudiced, but also limited and, above all, face value reading. I do wish it would happen. For now I stay with the titles that have always haunted my imagination.

If Hemingway's prose sometimes, per chance, seems flat, this is even more accurate about the Florida ground he walked. From Jacksonville in the north to Key West in the south, Florida is not only thoroughly developed but also flat like a pancake — the only hills you'd come across are either made from landfill garbage or they are highway overpasses. South of Jupiter, to the north of West Palm Beach, palm trees, precisely, gradually come to dominate over and against various ferns. This is not just because of the latitude but has to do with the Mexican Gulf Stream which runs closely along the coast to this point and then branches off into the Atlantic Ocean, in this way ensuring South Florida's year round tropical climate. A predominant eastern trade wind, heated by the surrounding tropical waters, effectively shields off southeast Florida from the incursion of northern winter storms, making cold spells rare and almost relished as a temporary contrast.

Original nature scenery on the other hand — exception made for the inhospitable Everglades — is scarce in the southern part of Florida. Seen from the air, the immensity of Miami-Dade and Broward County's two-dimensional urban grid becomes apparent; it might even dawn on you that you don't need to be stranded in Alaska to realise how infinitesimally small your personal, physical existence really is. A look at this cityscape at night from an airplane reveals a geometrically precise system of highways and other thoroughfares lit up by endless rows of white and red light dots. There are myriads of cars on the roads even late into the evening. They meet, part and blare their horns in intersections enclosing square residential blocks, like the symmetrical arrangement of molecules as revealed by the electron microscope in quest of the vanishing point of matter.

What you don't always think about when you (a single ant within the entire colony) drive past one residential block after the other, which in any given neighbourhood, and in the absence of topographical land marks, all have a tendency to look the same, is that the number of villas and their adjacent gardens is not just accumulating numerically but by the square: what seemed to you a row of 15 houses enclosed within the intersections of main roads in reality is a cluster of 150 residences.

This exponential repetition *ad infinitum* adds an almost hallucinatory dimension to the city, as splendid and monotonous as the ocean surrounding it, and gives a vertiginous idea of the staggering number of humans in this once unforgiving marshland which, wherever asphalt and concrete subside, has an artificial tendency to transform into a tropical garden.

It really is an Eden of sorts. There are many Adams and many Eves. There might be a God-Father somewhere too, and an archangel announcing his will and ultimate condemnation of mankind. But the most conspicuous other character in this scenario remains the snake holding out his promise of the apple. Not only are there many explicit casinos and gambling spots. All of South Florida really is a gigantic money making machine. This is more paradoxical than it might seem at first glance. Some of the money is obviously made here, most notably by the commerce generated in the harbour area at the estuary of the Miami River. It's the first East Coast port of call for cheap Chinese merchandise to Wal-Mart and also home to an impressive fleet of Caribbean cruise ships. Next to it there is the Miami downtown, featuring a wealth of bank and corporate skyscrapers. Consequently there is a constant need of various kinds of maintenance crews — sun, wind and salt take a relentless toll on any man-made structure. Aspiring to be North America's only tropical Paradise, the place also is in constant need of gardening, gardening and more gardening. Finally there is the tourist trade of Miami Beach.

But apart from these evident sources of income, Miami-Dade County possesses no real industry. Conclusion: the vast middle class apparently thriving here must either have made enough money to be financially secure, and/or be engaged in the social service sector. A whole society built on providing services — for what, for whom? The inevitable question rears its head: what do all these people live off? The answer is probably akin to what I imagine applies to Los Angeles on the other side of the continent: there is a giant influx of money and investment from other places gathering and circulating in the internal economy of South Florida. Money that doesn't primarily come from the sales of local dairies, orange juice and avocados, but from all the peoples of the north who have saved throughout their lives to be able to buy a place in the sun, in the rays of which they now bask hoping to spend some more of their money. This said, in the wake of the 2007–2008 financial depression, an astonishing number of brand new condominium high rises still gape eerily empty all year round on the sandy eastern beaches, meaning someone must recently have lost tons of money by investing in them.

Back on the Beach, the city, north-bound, stretches into again Jewish dominated Surfside, Bal Harbour and thereafter reaches the strait over which a bridge carries pedestrians and motorists to the Utopian sounding Sunny Isles, fittingly beginning with a mile long nudist beach hidden behind a line of dense vegetation. Sunny Isles is also home to the City of Aventura, rife with huge condominium highrises and a gigantic shopping centre. This futuristic looking part of the coast in turn comes to an end at the Golden Beach, where greater Miami's most expensive and privately owned seaside (as opposed to lagoon-side) mansions are located — name says it all.

To the north of these luxury villas, many of which have been bought by industrial Venezuelan money, discreet Hallandale makes its entry — a silent and nostalgic memory of once roaring 1970s Hollywood, with its huge traffic circle and adjacent night life, and Dania Beach, even more secretive than Hallandale, and lost further into the shadows of time, provide the last landmarks on this coastal road, since at Dania it comes to an abrupt end. Before the inlet for heavy commercial maritime traffic and cruise ships to Fort Lauderdale, overlooked by the Hollywood International Airport, there is the Wilderness Beach, once the private property of a Mr. John U. Lloyd, who in his will bequeathed it to the state on the condition that nothing must ever be built or otherwise constructed on this stretch of virgin territory, protecting a narrow lagoon lined with huge industrial cranes on its opposite shores. It's the only stretch of original beach in this part of Florida, and whenever I walk its dunes I find myself watching out for the *Aleph*, hidden under a mangrove tree.[4]

All these facets of south Florida — as well as many others here unmentioned — had begun to sparkle in my mind as I was finally released by the infamous (sometimes downright obnoxious) Homeland Security and allowed to leave the airport. As soon as I found myself comfortably installed behind the wheel, I pressed the pedal of my Mercury Grand Marquis and was catapulted down the dusky I-95 in grand American style to become one with my experience. A week later, after having immersed myself to satiation in slow-flowing rivers of vehicles, I had to take leave of this rolling fortress only to again be assailed by outside reality.

When the local city bus began to move I was surrounded by returning day shift Haitian airport workers chatting exotically in their French-Creole vernacular. I was indeed on my way to the Las Olas Boulevard, but at only 4 PM, decorum suggested it was a fraction too early to start having drinks, so I stopped at Starbucks, which for once had a staff able to interpret 'a double espresso' without having to resort to the menu board naively asking if, per chance, I wanted a *doppio*? The initial 'Can I help you?' I couldn't get around. But I did put the clerk to the test by asking him what kind of help he had in mind. A tired smile semi-lit up his face as he pontificated: 'And what can I get for you, Sir?'

But you can only stretch a coffee for so long. Though I managed to bring a newspaper together with a cigarette outside, I discovered little in it worth glancing at, not to mention reading. Incidentally, southern Florida was just suffering its first cold spell for the winter. Newspapers and presumably (you would only witness their comments via the text

---

4 A first reference in passing to Jorge Luis Borges' short story *El aleph*, entailing the quest for a point (el aleph) that contains all other points.

machine on the TV screen) high-pitched news anchors warned owners that shivering crew cut rats on diamond leashes could catch cold if allowed outdoors after sunset. Dressed for the tropics I soon found myself in the street throwing apprehensive glances into warm and festively lit restaurants, where armies of waiters in black shirts swirled around the tables preparing the set for the night's performance. But something in me vaguely objected to the idea of being tied to the attention of six ostentatiously aftershaved men, all introducing themselves by first names, giving me odd compliments for my excellent choice of pizza toppings only to in the end expect huge tips for their trite jokes — it's a very common idea in the US that relieving you of your plate before you even finished eating while simultaneously throwing the bill on the table, is synonymous with excellent service, as though every second that half-empty plate is staring back at you would be an eyesore to you and a testimony to the laziness of the staff. Typically, if a couple dines out, and one of the two finishes before the other, the waiter will promptly remove the empty plate, as if indicating to the person taking his time that he'd better hurry up.

What finally drew me in to an establishment named Caffe Europa was the appearance around a high bar table, close to the window, of three immaculately manicured, and expensively enhanced Latina beauties. Routinely I gazed in their direction as I entered the premises; apparently they couldn't care less. So I modestly took a seat at the bar from where I could at least enjoy observing three women dressed to kill, pretending to converse with one another. Here I also met with Paul, a gentleman from New York about my own age, having dinner. He introduced me to the bartender, describing her as a friend of outstanding talents.

Now, you don't necessarily fancy your bartender to have a facial expression betraying a hundred years of boredom with human affairs. But there is also the other extreme: the female bartender who is your cheerful, ever so attentive, eye-blinking gal from the word go: 'What can I get for you — Honey?' 'We have the best pizzas in town', freely alternating with gossip, a little hutch-hutch, blink-blink, 'see what I mean', and 'would you like another glass of wine *Love*?' presented with such candid enthusiasm that you'd have to have a heart of stone to refuse such an offer at your own expense. To be both honest and kind, she actually was a pleasantly spontaneous, entertaining lady who in solidarity with her husband had spent part of her life locked up in what had been, by then, a US owned Venezuelan oil or mining town — one of those corporate islands guaranteeing the commodities of corned beef, watered down American beer and chewing gum, even in the midst of a Congolese jungle.

And what about Paul? A New York expat teaching journalism and mass communication at Miami University. He looked slightly haggard and pale, but it might just have been the habitual complexion and state of mind of an East Coast Jewish university professor in cultural, if not (God forbid!) ethnic exile. It transpired he was in a rather intricate parental situation. Apart from having fathered a now adult woman living in California, he had also more recently spread wild oats in South Africa, the consequence of which was a 14-year old girl living with her mother in Johannesburg. I believe he also mentioned having a relationship with another woman at present. He recommended the fish — steamed with fresh vegetables in aluminium foil — finished his glass of white wine and ended his meal with a dessert. It occurred to me that I might finally have met the other person in South Florida who ever reads anything beyond newspapers, fashion magazines, the TV Guide and this year's best sellers. He handed me his business card and encouraged me to get in touch whenever I'd be in town next.

With Paul gone, the two seats next to me were occupied by men of a quite different order, the older of them a teary-eyed crocodile dividing its hunting hours equally between business and business. He proudly flaunted his ring, a huge diamond in its midst, which he had allegedly obtained for twenty bucks at an auction many years ago while no one besides him had realised that the stone really was a genuine diamond.

The other man — from the interminable plains of an equally interminable Midwest — could just as well, and rather, have been a used car salesman, covering up any knowing dishonesty with a laughter a bit too loud and too long. It so happened that he was the local art dealer — we're talking Picasso and Warhol originals (not that I would know the difference between a genuine Warhol and a fake one, or be able to even see the relevance of such definition). His gallery was situated next door.

Mr. Diamond jested that he'd just bought a piece of art which would prevent him from buying another one over the next couple of weeks. He then switched the subject to real estate, wondering if the art dealer could help him find a two bedroom condo in Lauderdale with beach access. The art dealer assured me that both he and Ron — along with their presumably well-to-do mutual friends — were just a bunch of (and these were his exact words): 'nice, ordinary, hard-working people'. The two of them had a couple of glasses of red wine. They were paid for by the art dealer, apparently owing his client before going back to his store that would close at ten o'clock. He invited me to pop in for a look. I said I would, but then the next guest in the hot seat kept me posted.

My new neighbour was yet another distinct character. A Brazilian businessman from Sao Paolo, of the type that you would easily identify as the typical Latin playboy, though no longer one in his absolute prime: still mainly dark, wavy and curly hair; expensive accessories (including an impressive Patek Philippe wrist watch), clear, if a little roughly cut facial features. Matrimonial ties to a woman and two young sons in no way deterred him from throwing curious glances at all women in sight. 'I like poossi' he spelled with virile emphasis in my ear while eagerly searching the attention of two newly arrived gringas (the Latina models were gone by now), taking seats around the semi-circular bar.

He had ordered an entire bottle of Californian Riesling with his food but drank very little. Instead he offered me most of it. Time flew. Don Pedro, while giving the project a fair chance, seemed unable to lastingly catch the interest of the gringas, although I saw them eyeing him up and down whenever he looked the other way. 'American woman very different than Brazil', he frustratedly concluded, and left me alone with them as well as with the remains of the bottle.

I on the other hand knew better than trying to make an impression. Besides I too soon had to leave. Shirley, the bar maid, volunteered to get me a taxi but I told her I'd manage on my own. After having paid my dues (making it a point of honour not to exaggerate the tip, in fact keeping it ever so slightly under the suggested minimum) I entered the street, took a deep breath in the crisp air, hailed down a cab and set off to the airport.[5] A couple of hours later I again hit ground. This time

---

[5] It seems this kind of European stinginess has since been effectively counteracted by the management. On a recent revisit to the establishment I was surprised to learn that the cheque, without warning, included an added service charge amounting to 20 % of the grand total. As if this seemingly compulsory charge was not enough, even greater tip percentages were suggested in print. I was in the company of a lady whom I had invited for dinner and so would have embarrassed everybody had I protested against this outrage and asked to speak to the manager. But that's what I really wanted, because it wasn't mentioned anywhere on the menu that forcing the customer to tip was now standard practice. My first thought was: is this legal? The second one was: bastards! I know: Americans usually consider Europeans lousy tippers. Be that as it may. Please bear in mind, though, that it never occurred to us that the customer, as opposed to the employer, is responsible for hiring and paying the staff. Read me rightly. I certainly don't mind rewarding truly good service with a couple of extra bucks, but I don't want to be forced to do it. I find a 15 dollar extra fee — on top of the advertised price plus taxes — for being served exactly, and in order of appearance, a glass of wine, an ice tea, a chicken pasta, a pizza, and a Tiramisu a rip off. Besides that, I now have enough evidence to proclaim Caffe Europa the financial maelstrom of the entire city, the background being the following. I was at said Caffe Europa also some days before the event described above and managed to have my car ticketed although I was sitting six feet from it and only went inside to pay an es-

in a coastal Colombia where the night — if nothing else — was a good deal warmer than the one I had just left behind.

presso for 3.50 at the bar. During that brief absence 'someone' managed to paste a parking ticket to the amount of 32 dollars onto my windshield and disappear in the blink of an eye. Now, if that is not ominous, I don't know what would be. You'd probably say: Why on Earth do you keep returning to that damned place? My only answer is: The moth is attracted to the ever luring flame even if it will devour him and beautiful women seldom seem to mind all this bull since in the end somebody else is paying for their expenditures. To conclude: it's a nasty game, but someone's gotta play it!

Colombia

Barranquilla doesn't have much that recommends itself. In a sense it was quite merciful to arrive there in the wee hours. At 3 AM there were still a myriad of taxis lined up outside the airport terminal. This allowed me to name my price.

To know what a taxi from any given airport to the city centre should cost is a classical issue sometimes open to a debate ending with the tourist's overpaying — the question is only with by how much. It's often easy to understand why though. Let's say you arrive in the middle of the night (inconvenient departure and landing hours being part of the punishment for consorting with so-called low cost carriers) to a city you hardly even know how to spell the name of, in a country where murder, kidnapping and robbery supposedly lurk at every other street corner. Add the local crowd waiting for their family members to exit from the baggage claim area, eyeing you from top to toe, trying to decide for themselves whether you're the long awaited Quetzalcoatl, a B-film star on vacation or just something the cat brought in. What you see in most of their eyes is a tacit submission to the fact that you — no matter what kind of budget you're travelling on — have more money than they, but also that they won't have the time to get closer to it before you're surrounded by ten eager cab drivers, and this so quickly that you hardly even have the chance to verify that your luggage is still intact and where you last saw it.

The resistance you now face is identical to the cab driver's instinct to stick to a tourist price that he will only knock off provided he really has to in order to get you on board. (I'm speaking here of airports where a standard fee for transportation to and from the airport hasn't been imposed by the authorities, or where metres both exist and are set in motion as you enter the cab). Your best deal is often to confuse the situation by inviting local bystanders to participate in the discussion. Unless these happen to be secretly in cahoots with the taxi drivers, they will soon give you a realistic estimate. In other words, and in this particular case: what started out as an offer for me to be driven to a hotel considered decent and located in a better part of town for 30 dollars, ended in a settlement for 15 — remember, one salient argument not to lower the price is the 'inconvenient working hour', an exotic concept that the taxi drivers have learned plays an important role in an alien northern world wrapped in endless winters.

The driver was a local boy who at hallucinating speed brought me across the extensive urban grid. It was a fair distance but he did have a specific hotel in mind in the northern part of the city, considered safe for *gringos*. The hotel itself offered a discount to its officially advertised price as a consequence of a deal between the hotel management and the drivers, so that the latter would keep bringing tourists there. The curvy receptionist gave me one of these warm and sensual Colombian smiles, melting my jaded heart right away. I felt magnanimous and grateful too for having been brought through the menacing night to a safe haven and I let the cab driver, who made little effort to produce any change, keep the rest of the twenty dollars equalling a tip of 10,000 pesos, or five dollars — not bad.)

The room at the end of a narrow corridor was rather disenchanting. It had only one window facing a shaft that could perhaps be climbed in an emergency. But it was better to hope there would be no fire. As I went out to the reception to ask for an empty glass, I ran into a broadly smiling Colombian man roughly my age, carrying a plastic cup filled with rum in one hand and a cigarette in the other. I glanced over his shoulder into his room and beheld what I took to be one of his younger daughters. In fact they were newlyweds, and she must have been almost thirty years his junior. He offered me cocaine and booze, well, almost his wife as well. But I truly wasn't in the mood, knowing that cocaine has a most treacherous tendency to enable me to consume any amount of alcohol without feeling its effect — that night. The day after is a very different matter, heralding itself in a hermetically sealed frontal lobe and a view of the horizon not even able to inspire a sense of tired melancholy: it's just saturated with dread. It is as though time itself has come to a standstill under an eternally leaden sky. Though it might in reality be the most beautiful day in world history, I would be unable to enjoy it. Alas, on some not so memorable occasions in the past my body has forced me to learn the price to be paid for the temporary and artificial exuberance of my mind.

Instead I took a shower — it even had warm water — and turned on the TV. There were Boca Juniors receiving Estudiantes. Just as the match seemed to get a bit more interesting I discovered, through the corner of my eye, a huge cockroach insidiously trying to hide from me. I chased him from his hiding place behind the refrigerator, and he (why do I assume it must have been a he?), well aware of the fate awaiting him if caught, ran for his life. Apparently he got confused by discovering his own image in the mirror. I took advantage of his hesitation and smacked him dead against the cold glass with one of my shoes. The mirror held but he was squashed. I went to the bathroom to get some toilet paper and wiped the glass clean. I then scooped up his remains from the floor with the tissue and flushed them through the toilette, sermonising: 'Let that be a warning to all your family and friends!' Whereafter I poured myself a whisky.

Even though I gradually came under the influence of the benign Scottish fairy, I didn't fall asleep until around six in the morning. I woke up at the merciless knock from room service, feeling pretty miserable. The reception wanted to know if I had the intention of staying another day — it was one of those hotels where check-out is expected at 11 AM. At this time I was only able to interpret this as a wilful violation of my privacy and muttered something hardly intelligible and not too courteous. To my defence the following might be advanced: being a frequent guest at hotels I sometimes get the feeling that management would be the happiest if you could check-out before you actually check-in, in this way helping them to avoid the hustle of making a room ready for you and then having to remind you to leave it before you wake up.

It was the accumulated effect of general fatigue and some pretty irrigated evenings prior to my departure. I still felt unrested, but the idea of staying next to that shaft staring at the Jackson Pollockish painting they had suspended on the wall for the purpose of artistic decoration was even more revolting. I decided to get out of there. Luckily I had some idea of where I was headed.

When I mentioned the city of Santa-Marta to the receptionist (this one not as pretty as her colleague during the night shift) she offered to arrange a semi-private transportation over there for 30,000 pesos (15 dollars). Considering it was an almost two hour trip I figured taxi, local bus and then taxi again would round up to about the same, and accepted the offer. I then went out in the hot Caribbean sun to hopefully draw some pesos from a teller machine and then have breakfast.

Hitting the pavement I was immediately struck by the ugliness of the city as well as the lacklustre quality of its inhabitants — in reality they were probably no worse, or no more morose, than people anywhere else in the world. It was the dust in combination with the all-too hot sun, my hangover and my sleepiness, that contributed to produce in me a sensation of being a prisoner in a stuffy, smelly cage I shouldn't have stuck my head into in the first place. Nonetheless I did have the presence of mind to tell my weary self: 'This might be the only time of my life when you get to see something of Barranquilla: since your transport will not be before two o'clock, you better go for a walk all the same.'

This said, I walked one of the interminable avenues for three quarters of an hour. At this point the side streets offered me the optical relief of some colonial looking residences. They were not near the sea or any park, and the compulsory barbed wire, gates crowned with pointed steel and walls lined with crushed bottles, made even the best maintained garden, glimpsed at the end of a long hallway, seem a precarious refuge. But I was tired, and this circumstance might have prevented me from giving even the small part of the city I came to experience a fair appraisal.

Back at the hotel I was informed that the travel organiser had been unable to gather further passengers; in other words: the run had been cancelled. My remaining option was to take a regular taxi to a road crossing through which the local bus bound for Santa-Marta would pass. By now I was eager to get on my way. Next thing I knew I was dumped at a roadside littered with sheds selling anything from recycled baby diapers to cold beer. My bus was instantly hailed down by one of many self-appointed traffic directors.

It was a small bus but it did have the unexpected advantage of air conditioning and a seat to almost every passenger. I realized that the young mother across the aisle had some pretty rough hours ahead of her. By extension, I too was in for an ordeal. A cute baby, a little princess for sure, but already now impatiently stretching and bending over the seats, falling down on the floor, where she was finally picked up by the mother only to be given a little symbolic spanking on the butt. It didn't really help. On the contrary. Screams and tears alternated, in part and temporarily subdued by sweets or an intermittently captivating small object. In short: the little princess was inconsolable.

It was only all too typical. The mother was not a native Indian. My experience from countries like Peru and Guatemala, where the Indian element is predominant, is that even wet babies almost never scream or whine. Their mothers always seem capable of keeping their kids calm, even during the longest and most strenuous journeys. I think perseverance and mute endurance is just in their blood. But then again, Indian mothers don't listen to reggaeton and rap day in and day out.

The vistas as perceived through the side windows were hardly more inspiring. The winter rains (occurring in what northerners would identify as summer months) had been unusually heavy, resulting in extensive inundations of the tropical plains. Vast areas of the lowlands were flooded, and entire villages had been at least temporarily abandoned. The effect of the torrential rains was clearly visible on both sides of the road. Inundated fields and marshlands had turned into lagoons in which rickety sheds seemed to float freely in putrid water. I thought of all the poor people affected and wondered where they had all gone. Some were dead, no doubt; others had perhaps anchored their boats to the rooftops, waiting for the water to subside. Meanwhile there must be scarcity of food and fresh water, disease lurking everywhere.

At a distance, without previous warning, rose the hills and mountains of the Santa Marta region. The young mother, finally able to silence her toddler, kindly, and with some kind of relief, pointed out its summits to me. From having appeared desolate and abandoned the landscape shrouded itself in an aura of picturesqueness as intense as it was unexpected. Before I knew it we arrived. A taxi brought me to the city centre. I had asked the driver to take me to a hotel. So he did, and I decided the huge colonial and former administration building towering before us would have to do for the night. Even though the hotel as such had many rooms on no less than five floors, it had almost no guests, leaving me with the presentiment of a sojourn in Kafka's *Castle*. But I knew that if only the fan would work I'd be able to fall soundly asleep.

Close to the hotel there was a small plaza featuring the supposedly oldest cathedral — a white-washed building in traditional, rural Spanish style — in all of the South Americas (surprising really how many oldest-of-them-all-churches there can be in this part of the world), bespoken by some conquistador arriving in the Bahía in the year of our Lord 1528. Beyond the cathedral the crowd of street vendors could be seen gathering along the main business street. I passed a statue of the independence hero Simón Bolívar, who in 1830 was buried in the church, although it wasn't to be his final resting place. Twelve years later his remains were exhumed and transferred to Caracas. I asked one of the vendors for directions to a beer and was told how to reach the beach walk. Minutes later I sat down at a corner café shaded by parasols, furnished with chairs and tables in reddish wood. There was a steady and busy stream of traffic in the street and a multitude of people among lavish Christmas decorations — among them a number of white-bearded, larger-than-life Santa figures — as well as vendors on the beach walk. Behind it a stretch of sandy beach unfolded, ending to the east in the commercial harbour area; to the west it terminated in a couple of moderate high rises. A small island in the middle of the field of vision provided both platform for a lighthouse and a welcome barrier against the muddy Caribbean swell.

I strolled down the beach walk and found myself a restaurant allegedly specialising in seafood. But the shrimp in garlic, which I would have hoped to be in Spanish tapas style (gently simmering in olive oil, red pimiento etc.), was a disappointment: shrimp drenched in some yoghurt-like white sauce lacking even the relative merits of a Greek tzatziki. I decided to call it a night, paid my bill, found the hotel, crashed, and slept for at least ten hours. Almost surprised, and above all grateful, to find myself still alive I woke up the following morning, curious of what a new day, untainted by nocturnal debauchery, might have in store.

Parque de Tayrona

The new day come I decided to first of all change my residence. On my way back to the hotel the previous evening I had passed by a pension called Hotel Paisa. In Colombian Spanish *una paisa* signifies a woman from the mountainous region of Antioquia, containing a considerable portion of the countries' northwest, notably the western and central Cordilleras of the Colombian Andes. It was indeed a hotel ran by women. Although they were neither very nice in general, nor specifically accommodating in particular, and seemed to regard any simple demand (a drinking glass, an extra towel) as some kind of intrusion on their privacy, I felt strangely at home there and settled in a small room on the second floor with Wi-Fi, air conditioning (albeit quite noisy), a ventilator, some 100 TV channels and a minuscule, yet private bathroom with running (cold) water.

For nearly a week this was to be my home. I soon found reason to assume that the edgy attitude of what I took to be the owner, or at least the manager, probably stemmed from the fact that she was a die-hard lesbian. Though no longer quite young she had a nice set of boobs. But there was a chill in the tropical air telling me those knockers would not be up for grabs by any man, no matter how persuasive. She would typically be found — late at night and as I returned home from my own diversions — hanging out in the 1960s style hammock in the patio, smoking cigarettes, impassively verifying my intruding identity while continuing to conspiratorially converse with another female destiny hiding in the dark. From the beginning I had decided not in any way to let her manifest unfriendliness get in my way. But it wasn't all that easy: some of the other women on this particular scene were almost as hard to get along with.

I only saw the stern looking woman serving in the restaurant smile one single time. Well, she actually laughed, but it was because I had cracked her open by inadvertently hitting my head against a ceramic flower pot hanging down from the ceiling. In the end it was only the simpleminded cook and another woman, sometimes attending the reception, who would waste a smile on me for no good reason.

To the atmosphere of distrust was added the imperative that I pay for my room each and every single day in advance. In truth, I couldn't even order a cup of coffee without being charged and asked to pay for it right away — even after a week on the premises. They had a way of keeping track of every penny owed that made me think of hungry watch dogs. The food they served didn't look very appetizing either. I did have breakfast there the morning I arrived, but even though I thought it was quite cheap, it wasn't particularly good. Hence I decided to have my future breakfasts elsewhere. Maybe they took this as an insult. I don't know, and I don't care.

Strangest thing was I liked the place all the same. If I'd ever come back to Santa-Marta I wouldn't hesitate to take up quarters there again. Partly because accommodation was cheap for what I got. I appreciated that the sheets were often changed and the room kept clean (now I suddenly remember that the cleaning lady was pleasant too, and that I really should have slipped her a tip before I left). I guess some of the unfriendliness seemed pardonable because the ladies were all honest and hardworking. After many years of living in cities and travelling countries, I have learned not to get upset if people turn out — as they occasionally do — to lack a sense of humour. But then again, the lady who laughed so hard when I hit my head on the pot did indeed have a sense of humour, only it was at my expense. And I didn't find that very funny.

Once installed in a hotel room to my liking I decided to take my time and don't rush my visit to the natural reserve *Parque de Tayrona* — my pretext for coming to Santa Marta in the first place. For the time being the historical centre of the town was practically the only area where I made some sightseeing. The rest of the time I spent behind drawn curtains, contributing columns — in response to an invitation to do so — to a net forum for free thinkers.

On this platform I presented a theory, the bottom line of which is that nations (as opposed to tribes and other ethnic groups) are accidental social constructions — Israel perhaps being the most arbitrary of them all. A nation state, as we know it from present day political reality and historical antecedents, is the result of warfare and territorial conquest initiated and carried out by ambitious kings and princes.[6] Conversely, the modern, post-war definition of nation states as political entities, now and for all hypothetical futures, confined within static, non-expandable borders, spells the beginning to the end of the *raison d'être* for the nation state as such.

Nation states — and even less so empires — are very seldom ethnically homogeneous. They don't even necessarily comprise a linguistically unified area. For example, one of the oldest nation states of Europe is the Swiss Federation. Within its borders no less than four official languages are both spoken and written. Even though the French and Italian spoken within the country's borders are indistin-

---

6   I find the following quote from Hobbes's *Leviathan* pertinent to my argument: 'But though there had never been any time, wherein particular men were in a condition of warre one against another; yet in all times, Kings, and persons of Soveraigne authority, because of their Independency, are in continuall jealousies, and in the state and posture of Gladiators; having their weapons pointing, and their eyes fixed on one another; that is, their Forts, Garrisons, and Guns upon the Frontiers of their Kingdomes; and continuall Spyes upon their neighbours; which is a posture of War.'

guishable — abstraction made from the inflections of accents and local expressions — from the French and Italian spoken in France and Italy, these speakers have no problem in seeing themselves as Swiss, that is, as members of a political and social entity distinctly apart from France and Italy.

In addition, the local Germanic dialects spoken in the so-called German speaking part are so far removed from normative, official German that they merit to almost be considered a separate language, not just a dialect variation. Finally, a minority in parts of the eastern alpine region of the country speaks and writes an archaic derivative of Latin called Rhaeto-Romansch. Considering how natural obstacles have tended to demographically isolate one part of the country from the other, there are few tribal or racial ties uniting these populations. It's on the contrary clear that Italic, Latin, Ostrogoth and Lombard ethnic elements have over vast periods of time penetrated the south; Frankish and Gaul the northwest; Germanic and Celtic the northeast; and that Switzerland, from its formation in the Middle Ages as an integral part of the Holy Roman Empire, to this day has remained the big *carrefour* of Europe, remaining as ethnically mixed as it's linguistically diversified. Yet it is without doubt a nation state. Castilian Spain, with its near constant conflicts with its Basques and Catalan subjects, demanding political freedom in the form of separate statehoods, is another salient example of the arbitrariness of present national borders.

Likewise France — an almost archetypal nation state in the European context — could only be linguistically united as a French speaking nation at the expense of the suppression and marginalisation of other Latin vulgarisations, such as the *Provençal*, the *Langue d'Oc*, and the *Catalan*. Initially French (*la langue d'oeil*) was only the particular Latin dialect spoken in the region of *L'Isle de France*, today's greater Paris region. As for the racial cohesion of the French nation, the predominantly Germanic and Celtic north has relatively few ethnic characteristics in common with the Mediterranean type of the south.

The southern regions of Sweden, to give one concluding example, only remained Swedish by virtue of the military predominance imposed by the royal Vasa dynasty. After the death of Gustav III in 1793 (the last king of Vasa lineage) it could, and should indeed, have been expropriated by the Danes, but I guess they too had grown weary of war by then and lacked the necessary force. Nonetheless, geographically, as well as ethnically, the southern province of Skåne has more in common with Denmark than with Sweden; the particular Swedish dialect spoken among its inhabitants is to this day perceived by northerners as more alien to the general Swedish tongue than any other local dialect. Notwithstanding, it's my opinion that Swedish, Norwegian and Danish are only dialects of one and the same original Norse language, of which Icelandic remains emblematic insofar as it has kept many archaic forms and refused the modernisation and grammatical simplification so typical of other Scandinavian tongues. Alone on linguistic grounds, Scandinavia should have been united under one single crown already in the Middle Ages. It's an ironic fact that no Swedish or Danish king was ever powerful enough to lastingly bring about such a union. Post Viking Norway, historically speaking, was always a province annexed to either the Swedish or the Danish crown; the country acquired full national independence as late as in 1905.

My argument follows the premise that a will to expansion is the imperative inherent in all territorial power. Lilliputian 'nations' like Andorra, Liechtenstein, Luxembourg and Monaco are historical fossils that have only been allowed continued existence because they provide bigger countries with some indispensable commodities, such as tax relief for all too rich citizens, cheap booze, weapon hideouts, casinos and brothels.

Any budding nation obtaining a modicum of wealth and power instinctively strives to enlarge its territory. This leads to *inter-national* warfare in the course of which disputes over territory are finally (after many centuries) settled in such manner as to finally make the whole concept of nation states obsolete. In this situation massive immigration from outside, as well as regional claims to relative independence, are only some of the aspects of the dissolution of nation states at the behest of even larger political organisations, such as the modern empire of China, the federal union of the United States of America and the European Union.

If we agree that an empire — by one of many possible definitions — is a nation state infatuated by delusions of grandeur, it follows that it must be driven by an even greater will to ingest neighbouring countries and territories (China's relation to Tibet would form a case in point). The United States has not for a long time shown any apparent will to officially expand its geographical territory. By the definition given it is consequently doubtful whether the U.S. can be described as an empire. However, if financial expansion (war by economic means), military infiltration, political control over territories, (nominally remaining independent countries), can be considered imperialistic traits, then the U.S. too most certainly falls into this category.

Let's assume that we maintain the definition of a modern nation state as a democratic, open society in which the citizens are both accustomed to and know how to responsibly enjoy their freedom. Let's also assume that we affirm the ideal that such sovereignty should never have to fear being the victim of aggression from outside its own legal perimetre, since it has signed international treaties under common law with all its neighbours to respect their territorial claims, just as much as it thereby has ascertained its own right to administrative control of its own 'once and for all' given geographical area. Well then.

Jean-Jacques Rousseau, in his *Discourse on the Origins and the Foundation of Inequality among Men*, envisaged more than 250 years ago a Utopian ideal that with the present day political and legislative unification of Europe has become a positive reality. I quote from his 'Dedication', addressed to the unnamed representatives of the Republic of Geneva: 'I would have liked to choose a country [*to live in*] that, forced by a fortuitous incapacity, has turned away from the ferocious love of conquests, and, by a still more fortuitous position, has been spared the fear of becoming attached to another state.'

Just as much as Rousseau imagined this to be a single, independent country, the fact is that in the larger Europe of today such guarantee to peacefully exist within the confines of a democratic nation state, exempt of the fear of being invaded by a neighbouring state coveting its riches, has only recently been created. It's precisely the supra-national character of the EU which guarantees that no member state will be left to its own devices in case of being attacked from the outside. The national price to be paid for this security is the handing over of parts of the legislative power to a central, federal government, consisting of representatives for each and every member state in proportion to demographic density and industrial/financial importance.

In my articles, though, I wasn't trying to advance Jean-Jacques' view to back up my argument, since nothing would have helped me gain popularity among the participants of the forum for as long as my conclusion remained, that the centralisation of power to a supra-national legislative body is a necessary price to pay for national security in the event of an exterior military aggression — whereby it should be kept in mind that the particular country they have in mind (Sweden) has long since scrapped its army and, although not formally a member of NATO, put its entire defence, in case it ever be needed, in the hands of the very same military organisation. Nor did I care to enumerate the advantages of no longer having to deal with elaborate customs and border controls, different currencies and national tolls to travel within Europe, since, unfortunately, to advocate such evident benefits of a European Union would have been in vain over and against a readership that to some extent actually seems to prefer seeing Sweden invaded by and integrated into Russia rather than tolerating a NATO presence on Swedish soil!

In my opinion such conviction can at best only be regarded as a naiveté among members of a population that hasn't suffered the immediate consequences of a war in over 200 years. Thus realistically, if also a bit pessimistically: in the name of a *Pax Europaea* (to be compared to the *Pax Romana* which inaugurated the drawn out decline of the Roman civilisation, as well as the *Pax Americana* upon which the current European model is ultimately based), I feel compelled to defend the integration into, and the eventual dissolution of European nation states within, the all-pervasive organisation of a United States of Europe, even if such union necessarily also entails common laws, taxes, budgets, as well as the social, racial, spiritual standardisation, homogenisation and nivellation of the European civilisation as a whole. (With hindsight it's easy to see that, had it not been for the perseverance of American federalists, the U.S. would never have been able to successfully break its traditional isolationist stance. On the contrary, America's role in international affairs would have been sorely limited, and it's doubtful if she would have been able to even come to the rescue of the allied European countries in two world wars.)

Hence my bottom line: it's still up to anyone to enjoy the cultural particularities of any given European region because these, if encouraged to do so, will remain intact for some time to come. The price to be paid, however, for the continued internal peace of Europe is an '*ave imperator*' in the direction of Brussels. The hypothetical dissolution of the parliament there would bring about a rapid annihilation of the already scattered remains of old Europe, even the dismantling of modern civilisation as we think we know it. To those who inversely, and quite justifiably, object that freedom of speech and press is presently compromised in many European countries — notably in some of those that fought the hardest to obtain it, such as England and France — I object that this has little to do with national policies *per se*, and much more with the influence and pressure which post World War II Jewish and Israeli interest organisations and lobby groups exert on European politics and legislation.

My position — besides being fiercely individualistic and politically independent — has the awkwardness of being broadly 'anti-Semitic', since I regard even mainstream Islam (and not just its radicalised 'elites') as a political and cultural danger to the rest of the world.[7] This stance, on the other hand, does not provide me with recourse to some parochial wish dream for national resurrection, ethnic purity and the like. Notwithstanding that ignorance is bliss, and that blondes presumably have more fun, You and I — taken as symbols of men without money and power — will always be regarded as non-entities by those who rule. The best we can ever hope for is for the dragon to continue feeding itself elsewhere and leave us to modestly pursue our self-imposed quest in the hope that other lonely souls will find a source of inspiration (perhaps even comfort and dialogue) in us, and thence gain the strength necessary to seek out an individual path worth travelling through the spiritual and emotional wasteland of our contemporary, technically perfected civilisation.

I am, alas, painfully aware of the incompetence, egotism and wickedness of our politicians, making a single honest man or woman in this context the exception that confirms the rule. By personal experience I know politicians to be nearly the worst kind of people imaginable, but that's why they are politicians and not something inherently more respectable, which is also why they will always be around no matter how we toss and turn the coins. In view of this, the present European Union — though far from being an ideal assembly — is at least a reasonably realistic attempt at keeping Europe socially, financially and politically together. Notwithstanding the enormous difficulties associated with such an undertaking, the alternatives are most likely even

---

7   Not to worry dear reader: by the same token I'm also anti-Swedish, anti-English, anti-Russian, anti-Chinese, anti-American, anti-French, at times, even anti-German. Last but not least: I'm always anti-Norwegian!

worse. For the European nations to once again relapse into petty rivalry, skirmishing, or even war, would spell the beginning of the end of a Europe trying to assume its rightful place as a diplomatic mediator (dictated not the least by its geographical location) and to exert a stabilising, even civilising, influence on the political giant powers of the United States, Russia, and China.

Having this opinion doesn't prevent me from being an inveterate individualist in many other respects. All my life I have felt an aversion against arbitrary authority, as well as against rules and regulations aiming, in the name of security, at a limitation of my personal responsibility and freedom. My happiness always consisted in being able to slip through the cracks of the system, to stay away from the blinded Polyphemus as he fumbles after a new victim in the opening to the cave where he keeps us all imprisoned. Riding out undetected under the belly of an innocent sheep has often been my proudest act of chivalry, and I have — sometimes grudgingly but in the end with relief — preferred the anonymity and modesty of an itinerant and lonely, publicly unacknowledged existence, to the wicked compromise and life-long hypocrisy that so often has turned out to be the prerequisite of a life in the public eye.

My solitary way of life has furthermore entrusted me with complete responsibility for my own actions, which also means I'm constantly exposed not only to the sweet fruits, but also to the very real dangers of freedom. I have the jealous conscience of a philosopher; jealous of every external being or circumstance infringing upon my freedom, mental deliberations and peace of mind. I don't like too many comments on my habits, even when dictated by the best intentions and aimed at my potentially worst tendencies. And although to cautiously avoid getting mixed up with riches, men in power and treacherous women does not as such make anyone a grand philosopher, it certainly is the beginning of wisdom.

As far as the European Union goes, I don't like the idea of parking tickets and tax reports being freely exchanged between countries. I — who don't even like to pay for parking garages and always, if I stand a reasonable chance to get away with it, tailgate other cars for free exit — still hope that language and other cultural barriers will make this exchange of personal data and infractions so difficult that it becomes impracticable. Inversely, I really cherish the idea of national populations remaining as eccentric and indomitable as they in reality are, or ought to be. Even so, my reason prompts me to remain a confirmed unionist, at least in theory.

So far as political opinions go, and again in theory, I probably come closest to being some kind of Libertarian. In reality and practical life I'm an Anarchist, but I don't like to boast of this in any way, since anarchy is only a good thing for the chosen few who naturally treat other people with courtesy and respect and in social intercourse are guided by a benevolent common sense. Although I never had a say regarding the formulation of the laws and their applications, I can go as far as to acknowledge that they seem intended, at best, to be the same for everyone. However, I do reserve the right to break against these same rules and laws on occasion, and to my own benefit, if it can be done without harm to anyone and, above all, go unnoticed and unpunished. But the main reason I don't want to publicly advocate Anarchism, is that although it's an appropriate political persuasion for a spiritually endowed man aspiring to be just and noble in his dealings with other people, it's a weapon of mass destruction in the hands of an envious and resentful person. Adopted as a political ideology on behalf of the masses it would simply wreak havoc within society and end with the utter destruction of the same. Anarchism must be practiced as an individual regime. Only as such can it be successfully reconciled with a gentlemanly disposition.

It follows that I have an instinctive and deep seated aversion against the unprovoked intervention of the state in the private life of citizens, and hold the opinion that the power of the state should never be allowed to exceed a certain limit. But there has to be some state surveillance, in particular as regards the present financial and industrial system, in which individuals are crushed anyway, and would be so even easier if there were no regulations at all — our recent so-called recessions and capitalistic crises should provide more than ample proof of the necessity for state vigilance on behalf of the majority of the population suffering at the hands of ruthlessly greedy banks and corporations.

What I fear the most, however, as far as the European Union is concerned, is that the Swedish political model combining unlimited immigration from culturally backward Arab and African countries with widespread social fear and repressive tolerance — I spent my entire childhood and youth in its stifling atmosphere — will be allowed to unduly influence the rest of Europe. Socially speaking the Swedish society is a nightmare come true, dominated by a monumental officially sanctioned hypocrisy, requiring any man participating in public life to line up — as in the ancient Near Eastern cult of the great Mother goddess Cybele — to have his balls cut off before being allowed to join the choir. My hope was always that Sweden, influenced by the rest of Europe, was going to experience an enforced change for the better. Meanwhile I have sincerely wished for all important general decisions regarding the future of the country to be taken in Brussels, since no such decision can possibly be any worse than the insane political policies carried out to this date by our nationally appointed representatives.

I can hardly think of anything so utterly horrifying as a 'Made in Sweden' feminist worldview on export to the rest of the world. For this reason I prefer to underscore my *European* heritage and lineage, realising that this same old Europe, notwithstanding centuries of wars, crises and convulsions, culturally, if not actually politically, has striven to become one and indivisible practically since the fall of the Roman Empire. With hindsight, the nation states were the stepping stones to reach this supreme realisation, the profound significance of which, in spite of many previous auguries, is only beginning to be grasped in our day and age. As mentioned above, a nation state with once and for all fixed geographical borders is a *horror vacui*, even a contradiction in terms. Sooner or later it has to seek to merge with a larger political body, and that's why the now allegedly peace loving nation states of Europe, at their present stage of development, are in real need of some kind of Pan-European Union to be able to influence the political, social and economic evolution of our planet.

Inversely, my critique of the existing European Union is that it's not European enough, meaning that it simply doesn't make enough to defend the individual European citizen against his enemies — external or internal, whereby I consider many national governments, hiding behind the non-committal tern 'EU-regulation' in order to cover up their local banditry, to be some of our worst oppressors. For example, the reckless admittance into the European Union of countries such as Romania and Bulgaria has become yet another unwarranted social and financial burden for the taxpayers in more efficiently organised unionised countries. It's no less than scandalous that Romania and Bulgaria are unable, even unwilling, to deal with their own widespread social misery. Instead they appear relieved to see their beggars and social pariahs migrate to the richer countries of the north, where they subsequently become entitled to all kinds of support and subsidies thanks to well-developed social security systems based on a willingness, and a capacity, on an individual level to actually pay taxes — the present grave financial crisis of the Greek society is mainly due to its maintaining of the most generous pension system in all of Europe for state employees without sufficient tax money to back it up. If alone letting Greece into the club finally appears to have been a mistake, what then about Romania and Bulgaria — possibly the next European nations to declare bankruptcy — not to speak of the frivolous idea of extending an invitation to join the EU to Serbia, Kosovo, Albania, Macedonia and Turkey?

The 'original' EU, the one I truly respected, was conceived of primarily as a defensive military strategy (the original coal-steel union between Germany and France specifically served that purpose) with possible economic and social benefits as a secondary effect. With a vainglorious contemporary France being what it is, and a Germany comparatively recently risen from the dead and at present seemingly determined to accept any amount of Arab and African 'refugees', it's of course inevitable that the present EU, while governing us is in turn 'governed' by still mightier forces. Among these one might casually mention the Federal Reserve, Wall Street, the International Monetary Fund (IMF), the Bilderberg Group, the Rothschilds and their many financial affiliates, as well as the Economic Consultative Committee (ECC) of the Bank for International Settlements (BIS). What this means in practice, is that the national politicians of the Parliament in Brussels are in the end perhaps little more than puppets dangling in the strings of global high finance.

Notwithstanding that the domestic interests and needs of individual EU member states and their populations have been seriously compromised by multi-national corporations and financial institutions, it's important to remind ourselves that the influence of these wouldn't just begin to wane because some European country ostentatiously exits the EU and again proudly proclaims itself a free and independent nation state, now closing its borders around the poor devils caught inside it.

There is no guarantee that a so-called 'nationalist government' would in the long run be any better for the citizens of any given country. In addition, it's highly unlikely that any nationalist European party, once in power, would actually realise its often repeated threat of taking the country it represents out of the European Union. That would be to jeopardise the future of the entire nation. Instead it would be much wiser for any such national polity to work towards a change of our dependency on the international high finance through the institutions and inroads provided by an already existing EU. The changing of the name of the game is not the prerogative of an individual nation but requires worldwide reform, not to say global upheaval and revolution, and this is not going to happen from one day to the next. The gains and losses at stake are simply too enormous to allow for a smooth transition from the dictatorship of the filthy rich to an empowerment of the filthy poor. As matters stand right now, you can't even point your finger in the general direction of the masterminds behind the global casino without incurring the wrath and vindication of its owners.

That said, I'm just as worried as many other earnestly thinking Europeans at the alarming incursions made upon our freedom of action, thought and speech, as well as at the concomitant and seemingly inexorable advance of the Muslim anti-civilisation into Europe. Although I do believe that the days of independent nation states fighting for territorial expansion are numbered, this still remains an intermediate to long-term prophecy. In the long run we can only question or rebel against this destiny at our own detriment and against better knowledge. But this development — perhaps as inevitable historically as the advance of glaciers is in an ice age are geologically speaking — shouldn't be hastened by our giving in to the basest of democratic and socialist instincts, by the token of which the primitive and fanaticised Arab is seen as the embodiment of the underdog, a symbol, if you will, of the eternally oppressed individual throughout history (slaves, women, workers, colonised and coloured people, etc.), and therefore in intense need of all our resources in order to state and exercise his present 'right' against our past 'wrong'.

No matter how desirable the idea of 'complete human equality' may seem to friends of democracy, history, over and over again, has shown that the breakdown of any social hierarchy is foreboding a chaos where that which was formerly at the bottom is temporarily carried to the top, only to quickly give way to ruthless individual tyrants imposing totalitarian measures. If the Islamic expansion continues at the present rate in Europe, Muslims will soon be able vote their way to power in order to dismantle democracy altogether. Adolf Hitler held two separate referendums to make sure, and demonstrate, that it was in accordance with the will of the German people to bestow extraordinary power on himself and thus ratify the radicalism of his political measures. Inversely, we can be absolutely sure that any Muslim political leader in Europe will not ask the people twice once he has gained power. Such event would simply seal the fate of our present European civilisation.

*

But what on Earth did these elaborate, if also quite interesting, considerations have to do with the fact that I was now in Santa Marta, and isn't this text supposed to be a written record of my travels? Well, I do regard the mental perspectives and vistas that travelling offers has the possibility to open up in each and every one as an integral part of the journey itself. Digression is part of the road. What I think about while travelling is often of greater importance to me than the mere moving from one location to another, notwithstanding the sensation and thrill that the seeing of something new entails. But I have never looked upon travelling as a vacation, because in that case I would have to admit that I'm practically always on vacation. I consider myself at work: studying, observing, living, reflecting, enjoying my own self-appointed, paradoxical work as a man of letters, in a time when letters in a traditional sense no longer exist. I could thus easily, and of course, have been somewhere else. For the time being, however, I was in Santa Marta, and it was here that I had these thoughts in relation to the political scene in a Europe that already seemed quite far away.

My eventual visit to *Parque de Tayrona* was memorable primarily insofar as it involved trekking through the mud for the better part of five hours. The weather had looked promising and I very smoothly transited from one bus to the other to arrive an hour later at the gates of the park. But here, even though I had already paid a substantial entrance fee (three or four times higher than the one demanded from locals) the driver of the van, destined to take us up to the beginning of the actual trail, took his sweet time. For half an hour I had little better to do than to follow how a charming young three-fingered sloth was handed over from one person to the other, while bottles of beer, water and soft drinks were loaded onto the bus.

It was already past midday when we finally set off. Arriving at the local eco-tourist village (call yourself ECO-something today and you can charge three times as much for the same sewers, — oh that? that's eco-manure!), I asked the local stable boys for directions to 'the playas'. Had I been only slightly better informed beforehand (and it was primarily my own fault that I wasn't), I'd known the name of the particular playa I wished to visit (there really was one the virtual image of which had captured my interest) and it really was close by. Feeling that I was already lagging behind in time, I instead eagerly rushed ahead into the jungle, since that was the direction in which the cowboys pointed. It was around 100 metres of a pleasant walk before the muddy water began to make a mockery of any attempt on my part to consider this a nice afternoon stroll in 'the park'.

The heavy rains hadn't spared the Tayrona Nature Reserve. After sliding for an hour up and down through the mud I arrived at the first tourist centre in front of a stretch of beach called Recife. It was only now it occurred to me that one doesn't actually visit the Tayrona over the afternoon, but in order to hang out there for at least a couple of days. Needless to add I hadn't prepared for that. So I quickly left the bungalow area and came out on the beach. Only to discover that to continue I'd have to wade across a river emptying into the sea. Luckily I had brought my trunks. While strapping my *mochila*, containing the rest of my clothes, to the head, I braved the current. It really was only a rifle and some crocs, basking in the sun on the opposite bank, missing to complete the image of a 'Dr. Holm I presume' in close encounter with the wilderness. Well, maybe I exaggerate — but only just a little! A 100 % truth on the other hand is that there were several wooden signs on the beach declaring that more than 200 (!) people had drowned in the treacherous waters off the beach. The message ended in the admonition: 'Please don't contribute to these sad statistics'. I was determined not to, and tried as best I could to avoid being swept along the currents into the boiling sea girdled with a long line of mostly submerged, craggy and dangerous looking rocks — hence its name: *Recife*.

The petrified land formations consisted of more rounded boulders, spectacular in their own right, but in my opinion not quite as impressive as for instance the rock formations of Nicaragua's Pacific side *Playa de Coco*, from which the silhouette of northern Costa Rica is clearly visible past a number of natural 'Indian heads' picturesquely dotting the coast line. I have to admit though that the rocks of Tayrona too were eminently sculptural, lending themselves to all kinds of anthropomorphic fantasies (e.g. seeing images of faces, profiles, beasts, gods, monsters etc. in the very living rock).

Knowing that I'd probably have to make it back out of the jungle before nightfall, I didn't have that much time to spend and soon found myself beating a new trail, allegedly taking me to the Piscina, so-called because swimming here is safe thanks to the continuous visible reef that transforms the small horseshoe bay into an intimate enclosure. It was only the water itself that didn't look so inviting. After all the rains the colour of the water was far from the alluring turquoise you'd encounter in tourist brochures. Even though there must be times when the water is clearer, making snorkelling and diving a potentially rewarding experience, this was not the case when yours truly paid it a visit. Consequently there were only the most incurably romantic native elements who took visible pleasure in embracing each other in the turbid swell.

Next to the beach I found a girl offering freshly squeezed orange juice, which at this point was more worth than a kiss from the immaculate virgin herself — in all honesty, I don't think orange juice has ever tasted better in the history of man! Thus strengthened I continued my path to the last station on this particular trail: *el Cabo*.

El Cabo really is an impressive little place with even more suggestive figure heads sculpted in stone — unsurprisingly, both the *Cabo* and the *Piscina* have in the past been consecrated sites of indigenous worship. So this is of course where I should have stayed — at least that's what everybody else who had taken the pains to walk two hours through the mud wisely had in mind. But since I and all my clothes were wet through and through, the idea of crashing in a hammock with dry mud sticking to my body seemed a last resort in case there really was no other alternative (I told you, I'm not that adventurous!). I thus decided to try to make the best of the opportunity in very short time.

I walked up to the man-made shelter on top of the minuscule peninsula that forms a natural barrier against the aquatic element. From this promontory I had a panoramic view, the sea occupying 180 degrees of my field of vision, the jungle the rest. It was wilderness alright. The weather had begun to look menacing (another reason I felt not to hang around for too long). Over distant peaks of rain forest hung heavy clouds interspersed by feathered scavengers; lightning ripped the horizon while an estimated $2^{1/2}$ hours remained of the day. It was high time to start turning back to base, I thought, expecting myself to be quite alone on the trail. But then again I hadn't counted with the fact that there are still some die-hard Germans left in this world.

Holger was born in a village somewhere between Hannover and Braunschweig, at that time part of a German Democratic Republic. From which both the notions Democratic and Republic can be omitted without doing eastern Germany's name and reputation injustice. Holger still vividly remembered his narrowly constricted youth and showed a gratefulness towards the present world, and everything in it, that would probably seem touchingly naïve to most contemporary westerners: to him the mere fact that he could now actually both afford and be allowed to travel the world was a source of pure joy.

He worked (and had done so all his adult life) in a German steel factory, and had joined a travel group for a three week's holiday tour through Colombia. It was now his last day before the group must return to Bogota for departure back to Germany. As the nature lover he confessed to be, he had decided to take a good walk to round things off. He must have hiked almost twice as long as I that day, but I took his stamina, considering he was German, to be a matter of course. We began to talk. Soon realising we were both trying to reach the same target before dark, we didn't even have to agree on keeping each other company. Still, considering that nightfall was only two hours away and we had a considerable portion of slippery trail to cover, I was surprised at how leisurely he estimated the time needed. He wanted to stop and take photos, then take a swim (it was his first visit to the coast during the entire trip). I thought: what the hell, and jumped in as well. When we finally arrived at the tourist station Recife we decided to sit down and have a couple beers (normally I would have been on my way, possibly with a can in my hand, but definitely on my way). Meanwhile it wasn't getting any brighter around us, and when we finally hit the trail for our last leg it started to rain cats and dogs.

Under the wide canopy of the rain forest there was some protection against the deluge, but it was also darker, and the only people we met on the trail were the last enduring Indians eager to make it safely to Recife for the night. Even in these circumstances Holger had a tendency to lag behind. I began to feel it wasn't such a great idea playing around so freely with the little daylight we still enjoyed, and urged him on from time to time. Holger was cool, I admit, but truth told: we only just barely made it before the gates of utter and humid darkness were slammed and chained shut with impenetrable twigs and branches behind us. We could no longer see two steps ahead when a series of white plastic sacks, somewhat phosphorescent and thus still visible in the dark, indicated a bifurcation in the trail. None of us had a flashlight and none of us was too sure what direction to follow, but if we would have entered the wrong one, we'd probably spend the rest of the night in the jungle as well. I was relieved to see a small light, like a diminutive distant star, detach itself from the massive darkness. It grew in size and luminosity as we advanced towards it. We had, at last, arrived at the horse stables from where I had embarked (Holger had taken a different route from another access point in the reserve).

Once arrived we were lucky again. A young couple from Santa Marta was returning home in their four-wheel. I hailed down their car in the darkness, knowing this might be our one and only chance to get out of the park and reach the entrance gates. It turned out I needed to worry no more. They generously offered us a lift. We were soaked to the bones, and graciously offered to sit and drip off on towels in the back seat. Holger got off close to where his eco-lodge was located, while Pablo and his newly wedded wife Linda (with a so far unnamed bun in the oven) brought me back to my hotel. I was exhausted and grateful to have access to the following commodities: a shower, some aspirin and a bottle of whisky. There was a soccer game on TV. But that didn't in the end prevent me from going out to have some dinner: a tender, juicy steak with *papas a la francesa* and half a bottle of Argentinian red wine in a steak house ran by a Spaniard from Catalunya and a Belgian from, well, Flanders.

The last thing I remember from that evening is a Champion's League qualification game glimpsed through a dense curtain of snow enveloping a bitterly cold arena in Romania, or was it Ukraine? 'Snow, what an exotic concept', I murmured, turning to the wall, faintly smiling, while dreams, sweet dreams, entered my mind through the gates of Oblivion.

＊

Even after my visit to Tayrona I stayed in Santa-Marta for another couple of days. A pleasant discovery was the bay directly to the east of the city. Not more than a hill separates the town Santa Marta and the village of Catanga from one another. But they are really worlds apart.

Catanga is a tranquil fishing village that has realised its potential as a tourist attraction. The developments nonetheless are still modest and the place remains laid back, principally accommodating scuba divers and the motley crew of tattooed European backpackers. The trail along the eastern coast line took me to the next little bay, this one exclusively catering to local and foreign tourists. From the hill top I discovered 'my own beach' on the opposite side of the bay, and went for it. Access to this beautiful sandy spot seemed relatively easy by way of a small ravine leading down to the waterfront. I was eager to get there before someone else would have the same bright idea. Once arrived I found swimming a great deal more gratifying than in Tayrona. The water was clear and calm, the sun warm and embracing. Thus it was here I finally had my *Faun's Afternoon*, indulging in one of my favourite pastimes: watching the hours go by to the accompaniment of gentle waves and rustling palm leaves.

One evening, believe it or not, I ran into some girls who took some interest in my humble person. I was sitting on the outdoor patio of a restaurant when I noticed a woman impassively staring at me. She was sharing beers with her female friend. To break the spell I cheered at her. It worked and I found myself invited to their table. The one who had stared so intently at me revealed herself as a behavioural psychologist (which could have explained the staring: she was studying me!). Her friend on the other hand worked as a nurse at the local hospital — guess who was the prettier!

Both of them had half-grown children with more or less absent men. We eventually went out dancing together. In order to do so I had to subdue my instinctive aversion for reggaeton and turn my attention to the girls themselves, visibly very happy with this kind of acoustic junk—I believe it even turned them on. I'm reasonably convinced even the pretty one would in the end have fallen victim to my devastating charm, not to speak of my irresistible dancing, but as the evening progressed and I began to take more and more interest in her at the expense of the other, the psychologist (at first inciting me to dance with her friend, quite erroneously assuming I wasn't too interested in her) only too willingly grew in the role as her chaperone.

But there was an opening for some future fun: they both wanted me to go with them to a *finca*, supposedly belonging to the psychologist. We agreed they should come to the hotel around ten in the morning the following day. I never found out whether they came to look for me, because I overslept. Though they knew where to find me they hadn't left any message in the lobby (or perhaps the lesbian manager was withholding this information just to spite me). In the end that suited me fine. I was actually relieved that the excursion to the finca never came to happen, since I had some presentiment of future possible complications of an emotional nature: though both girls were apparently looking for male company, it was the psychologist who had seemed the needier of the two. But since she was not as pretty as the other one, the scene was practically set for a triangle drama, or comedy. Regardless of which way the play would go, I no longer felt the same enthusiasm for it as I had done the night before: '*And thus the native hue of resolution is sicklied o'er with the pale cast of thought*'…

A week before Christmas I boarded a flight from Santa Marta to Medellín. The ticket with Copa Airlines was surprisingly cheap. Included in the modest sixty-five US dollars was a sight-seeing from the air as the flight was scheduled for a short layover in Bogotá. My choice to go by air was probably very wise. Even under normal circumstances a bus ride to Medellín from Santa Marta would take many hours and end up costing about the same as the flight ticket.

Considering the present state of the roads, though, it could be a matter of several days to get there. In what kind of mood and physical condition would I be in by then?

I have seen some idyllic-looking airports in my days. One in particular has stayed in my memory: it's the airport in the southeastern Thai province of Trat, where the whole airport staff had gathered on the tarmac before take-off and then waved farewell to us, the passengers, with lavish flower arrangements in their hands as the afternoon Bangkok flight took off. Although there is no such extravagant courtesy offered at the Santa Marta airport, it does have another very endearing feature: the bar/restaurant inside the terminal has an outdoor terrace directly overlooking a wide bay in the Caribbean Sea. It's perhaps not the most exotic looking beach in the world, but it does have one very interesting feature. In the shallow waters there is a multitude of huge man-made cranes. I'm sure they dig into the sediments for an industrial and financial reason, but from a purely artistic point of view, they look like giant prehistoric birds, looking for baby whales to eat.

Medellín

The city of Medellín is an enormous pile of red bricks spread out over an Andean valley and its adjacent hills. Depending on your mood and the time of day you arrive it can seem either a dream or a nightmare — which is not to say that the city is necessarily more nightmarish at night time. Like in all major Latin American cities traffic and pollution are impressive. Medellín's climate on the other hand is benign. Although the solar zenith is right above you, the average day temperature is more that of a perpetual Mediterranean spring, and in the night it can be wise at times to have a jacket or sweater at hand. Vegetation in between and around tenant areas is lush and there are hundreds of small rivers making their way down the hillsides into the river bed of the valley, creating here and there moments of pure natural magic in the midst of the urban sprawl.

Being dispersed over such a vast area, to go from one end of the city to the other can be quite a project even though the city has an effective metro system. However, there is one particular part of the city where most of the tourists usually end up, and that is the Poblado in the Zona Rosa, centred around the miniscule Parque de Lleras — not much bigger than a tennis court really — where hotels, hostels, restaurants and bars abound (as for myself I nowadays prefer to hang out in the restaurant district around the 70th Avenue in the Estadio).

On weekends the establishments lining the park are jam packed and this is where you will come face to face with the famous Medellín beauties who love to appear on this stage, financed by fathers, husbands and boyfriends, to show off their fabulous bodies. There is live music in every other place and every local man or woman knows how to dance, so the scene is really festive and many of the girls, as I will not get tired to repeat, are just staggeringly beautiful. Supposedly there are more boob, butt and lip jobs carried out per capita here than anywhere else in the world, including Hollywood and Miami Beach. One can hardly turn on a Colombian TV without finding at least some channels showing beauty and dance contests, as ubiquitous as the *telenovelas* featuring the same Colombian upper class enmeshed in melodramatic conflict, teary-eyed love, betrayals and never ending jealousies.

The whole thing might of course be written off as superlatively superficial, a hopelessly banal Vanity Fair of tropic dimensions, *un teatro de muñecas*, pulled by cynic corporations and a showbiz world gone bonkers. But judging it from a secure distance and being in the midst of it are two very different things, and I must admit that I have always wished I was a better dancer when I see these girls swing, because if you're gringo, and can dance for real, you're the King even if you're a hundred years old! Last but not least it should be remembered that these people love their music and their dance, and the whole nation, with the president as its prime spokesperson, never get tired of underscoring the both natural resource and cultural asset the nation possesses in its 'beautiful women'. And believe me, there is nobody around to regard that 'objectification' of women as an expression of male prejudice, condescension or patriarchal oppression.

Which brings us to the next attenuating circumstance: Colombia, in spite of its rampant urban cult of youth and beauty, is still very much, and perhaps even more so, a country for old men. You will not find here the open feminine disdain for older blokes so typical of Northern Europe and North America. On the contrary, these girls are still much depending on their sugar daddies, whether real daddies or symbols of the same. You will also, beyond the world of glittering fashion shows and urban glamour nights, see thousands and again thousands of younger beautiful girls who are very traditional in their outlook on life and find absolutely nothing strange in catering loyally to an older guy who, in turn, takes care of and provides for them. One might even say it's tradition here; it's reflected even in the *telenovelas*, where you will sometimes see an older, hairy, corpulent, bald guy — pretty unattractive by today's media standards — lay in bed together with a smashing young beauty, talking to her in the same casual way as though she'd been his daughter.

Apparently the vast audiences of telenovelas, notably the younger crowds, see nothing appalling in this. As for myself I recall recently seeing the Colombian film *Amor en el tiempo de cholera* (Love in the Time of Cholera), based on Garcia Marquez's eponymous bestseller. Supposedly this story is partly autobiographical, and even the older Marquez, who was born and grew up in the area around the colonial jewel Cartagena, never seems to have suffered any shortage of young, fresh new girls to enliven his nights and siestas — famous writer and Nobel laureate that he was!

Notwithstanding, my first visit to Medellín only lasted a couple of days. During that time I managed to pay a visit to the city's Fine Arts Museum with its comprehensive Botéro collection. It was donated by the artist to the museum on the condition that it would consecrate a whole floor as his own private gallery. The square outside the building is full of his sculptures cast in bronze, and the children love to climb them. I'm not a Botéro fan and have never really understood his particular idea of deformation of the human body — persistently turning naivistically conceived personages into giant Michelin figures, with huge, stocky legs, balloon shaped bodies, round heads coupled with miniscule mouths, hands and feet. Perhaps a bit surprisingly, Botéro himself says he has never been aware of any such deformation. This bewildering statement hasn't made me understand him any better, but it was impressive to see so many of his big canvases collected in one place.

After the visit I had at least become a bit more interested in his work than I had been before, understanding what a seminal figure he has been in his country's art history over the last half of a century. To be honest, though, I was more impressed with a couple of very fine aquarellists, the names and works of whom are today probably only familiar to a handful connoisseurs worldwide. I also saw a series of impressive social realist paintings in the expressive and dramatic style of that place and era. The museum restaurant too was very nice with a terrace from which one had commanding view of the Botéro square.

Santa Fé de Antioquia

After having done the compulsory night scene — even in the company of what luckily turned out to be trustworthy locals who drove me round at night time and showed me their preferred hangouts — I felt enough was enough and began to long for the relative tranquillity of a village tucked away somewhere in the Andes. This is how I ended up in Santa Fé de Antioquia. It's only slightly more than an hour's drive away from Medellín, yet a world apart.

For almost three centuries Santa Fé was the ancient capital of the mountainous administrative region of Antioquia, perched right above the confluent of the Cauca and Tonusca river valleys, the former winding from south to north through the central of the three Andean cordilleras making up the Colombian highlands. It's a colonial town in the best of Hispanic tradition. Sitting at only 500 metres' elevation above the sea (as compared to Medellín's central valley levelling out around 1500 metres) its climate is predominantly dry and hot. Although there are months considered as belonging to winter (meaning they should be predominantly rainy), precipitation is typically sparse and mostly confined to late afternoon squalls. In some periods of the year, for example in January-February, the central plaza, covered in black cobble stones, from midday to early evening turns into a veritable furnace.

There are a few interesting churches as well as some old manors and private properties worth visiting. But it's above all the stylistic coherence of the original architecture, predominantly tinted white and red, of the central village, that remains the main attraction and furnishes me with one important reason to feel at home inside its symmetric street grid, where the streets running south to north are by far the longer, since the town has been constructed on an oblong hillside, gently ascending towards the north. Although agriculture from all the nearby fields has always been a main source of income, tourism, national and international, is nowadays another important factor in the local economy. The typical tourist would not be a foreigner however, but a couple, or family, from Medellín intent on taking a break from the incessant hustle and bustle of the nearby metropolis.

But if peace and quiet was what I too was primarily looking for, this was not really the place to visit at this time of the year. My very first three weeks in Santa Fé came to straddle the *Fiesta de la Virgen Immaculata*, *La Navidad* and the New Year's celebrations, that is, nearly a month of practically uninterrupted folklore, boisterous Colombian gaiety and the resultant partial straining of my nerves.

I can honestly say that I wouldn't have made it there many days if it weren't for the fact that I found a place to stay in town that was perfect for my needs. As a matter of fact, I'm writing these words on the very same premises, separated from my old room by only a wall. I'm happy to be back in this spot which now, with hindsight, has grown very special to me. But now is now and then was then. Two years ago, when I first came to town, I had no idea what to expect. After one night spent in the hostel next door I ended up moving to the *Hotel Caseron Plaza*, the former patrician mansion of the *Gubernador*, opposite the rococo cathedral on the town's main square. I say 'rococo' cathedral, though it's really only the outer facade of it that might me be labelled as a primitive such. The original church is older and really very beautiful in its combination of solid stone and slender brick construction. From an aesthetic point of view it's a pity that later architects and renovators haven't continued to envisage additions in harmony with the original building. No intelligible architectural relation whatsoever exists between the original building and its present white washed gable, but this, unfortunately, is very common not only in Latin America, but in the Old World too, where buildings with impressive and beautiful bare stones are painted over with lifeless stucco.

Former Palace of the Gubernador, present day Hotel Caseron Plaza — all that may sound quite fancy. In reality this is a family run establishment visibly headed by the capricious and not always very easy to charm Doña Piedad (I swear, that's her name!). I always try to catch Doña Piedad when she appears to be in a good mood and prefer, given the choice, to solicit her staff for minor needs such as towels, ice bowls and wine glasses. Doña Piedad is often on the computer and doesn't look like she very much wants to be distracted from her activities by even a mildly irrelevant question. One such, it appeared to me, was my annoyingly recurrent question as to whether the Wi-Fi would soon be up and working again. The fact that the Internet hadn't stopped working on her computer (although it had stopped working in three out of four computers lined up in a separate room to the benefit of the guests, as well as in all portable devices carried by the guests themselves) made three full days pass before a technician was finally summoned. He was here this morning, supposedly fixing the problem, which now, at 3 PM persists. However, I still don't dare to ask Doña Piedad about it. Over time I have learned that no matter how many times the technician comes around, the problem will always be back. And nobody seems to be either interested or capable of doing anything about it.

As I arrived to the hotel this time around (that is, only three days ago as of the moment of writing), I vividly recalled the heated debate we had had last time I was about to check out. I consequently took the precaution to ask Doña personally if she could give me a package deal for five days, since I know room prices on the weekend (and that's where we're headed for on a Friday afternoon) to be considerably higher than on regular week days. She said she would have to talk to someone (looking like her father but in reality being her husband) about this and would return to me regarding this as soon as possible. So far I haven't heard a mouse squeak in this direction, but I did repeat the request to Laura in the reception who said she would pass it on to Doña Piedad, whom I just saw again, behind her desk, scrutinizing me with her inquisitorial eyes. Although she well knows that I would like answers to my two questions, she wouldn't make the slightest visible effort to give them to me.

Add to this that her injured, and at this time incapacitated husband, who also happens to be the owner of the hotel, inhabits the room closest to the reception and that she has to take care of him — as well. The old man has a nasty fresh scar all the way from the middle of his upper foot half way up to his knee, the result of an unfortunate collision with a motorcycle, and he spends most of his time reading or watching TV in bed. He does have a wheelchair parked outside his room though in case he would like to get around.

With Doña Piedad in charge of daily operations the atmosphere is at times a bit heavy around the reception and I tend to pass it by as quickly as I can, sometimes being obliged to drop my half-square foot wooden key holder there or otherwise carry it around with me in town. I believe this has proven quite beneficial to my working discipline as I now often find myself confined to the deliberate obscurity of my room and its rotating ceiling fan. Once here I feel the best thing I can do during the hot hours of the afternoon is to write. And that's what I'm doing. Not that the pool is not kept clean and offers pleasant cooling, but the sun chairs are of a dark green hue and hot as furnaces in the sun. Besides I only like to sunbath for moments, not hours. And then, a writer's got to do what a writer's got to do — write, right?

Over the last couple of years it has become something of a habit of mine trying to survive the so-called 'Holiday Season' as effectively as possible in some remote part of the world. To me the enduring attraction at the Caseron, and that which kept me posted, was and is the hotel's wooden deck beyond the pool area. It offers a panoramic view of the surrounding landscape. It presents the sun in spectacular skies; it shows stars and moons, mountains in all different shades of and sizes and a distant confluence of rivers. My favourite moment here is the blue hour, just after the sun has disappeared behind the western hill and left the stones around the pool to slowly give off their accumulated heat into the perfectly tempered night. Reclining on a sun chair, a glass in my hand, I enjoy the, albeit, fugitive sensation of perfection, and thank my lucky star to have been brought this far in life. It is true that a tall nearby radio mast in red and white does its best to scatter the illusion of Nirvana, but one gets used to it, secretly remarking to oneself that nothing *sub luna* must be too perfect, since otherwise we would be forced to regard our mortality as just a horrible calamity, and not, as God wants us to believe, the promise of ultimate liberation.

The single room I was offered on a weekly basis was situated next to the pool area, from which a small wooden bridge leads to the above mentioned terrace. It was a solace during so many evenings to bring a bottle of chilled wine up there and observe the sunsets beyond the western mountains: the sun's corona spreading like a peacock's feather across the sky, followed by the silky, smooth curtain of the night. Dry air at perfect temperature, the sounds of crickets among the trees and bats whizzing through the air. Then the zodiacal procession, unfolding night after night while the locals enjoy their more mundane parades in the square.

Sheltered by the Colonial Spanish style hotel complex, blissfully blocking out the glaring disco lights and the intense cacophony, I was able, night after night, to spend hours in the company of my old friend Orion, his dog, as well as the bull the former is hunting and the hare the latter is after. Castor and Pollux, the celestial twins were invited along with my special companion Regulus, the brightest star in the constellation of Leo and prominent in my astrological birth chart in so far as it was in conjunction with Sol at the moment of my birth. Moreover, Regulus, traditionally associated with the three wise men, the Magi of the East, is celebrated at Twelfth-Night, a week into the new born year.

At ten o'clock on New Year's Eve I nonetheless felt it would be a shame not to participate in the general celebrations. I went out in the square to have a couple of drinks, and ended up spending the rest of the evening with Alvaro, the landlord of the neighbouring hotel, rustic and charming in its own right, although for obvious reasons also a bit cheaper than the Caseron. Most importantly, it didn't have a terrace from which the entire galaxy could be studied. I did indeed spend my first night in town in Alvaro's hotel, but then moved to the bigger one next door, completely taken in by the prospect of privileged solitary nights under the stars.

Just before midnight this last day of the year our conversation had moved out to a table in the plaza, and it was here, having endured the fateful bell of midnight and the incessant fireworks, that I finally got so tired of listening in on the repeated vulgarities of an ugly German lesbian, that I decided to retire as discreetly as possible to my quarters. What I didn't realise was that I had just as discreetly left my suede Peruvian backpack, containing my passport, under the table, where it apparently stayed all night without being spotted by anyone. It was discovered by the hotel staff in the morning. I hadn't even noticed that the bag was gone when the cleaning lady knocked at my door, saying a gentleman wished to meet with me in the lobby. It was Alvaro's sympathetic son, to whom I had been introduced the previous evening. He came to deliver the *mochila* before heading back to Medellín. I never had the time to worry about the loss. But apparently Destiny had considered I wasn't appreciative enough of the fact that the bag had both been found and piously brought back to me. For this reason He had to come back in the same matter weeks later and teach me another, even starker lesson, the subtext of which I could no longer afford to ignore. However, of these future complications to my life I was still unaware while gazing at the stars and drinking wine on the eve of a new era.

In between my first and second visit to Santa Fe de Antioquia (over the years I think I've been there four or five times) an entire condominium complex with two major pool areas have grown up in the valley below the hotel. But none of these condos has the view of the landscape that the external terrace of the Caseron Plaza offers. Who, I always ask myself, wants to have a balcony in a location where the view is abruptly cut off by a neighbouring building? Since the complex is not built in terraces this is the case with all the condos in the second or third line seen from the pool. Still, Santa Fé is located at near commuter distance from Medellín. This kind of community thus is a kind of investment for affluent middle class citizens: professionals, lawyers, medical doctors, etc. who typically would buy a time share unit here, combining the setting of a 'country house' with the amenities and guarded security of the city. I'm not envious of their vacation village. I know my sunset view to be so far undisturbed — since colonial Santa Fé is perched on a comparatively gently ascending hill — and that's the only thing I really care about, then and now.

However, when I first arrived in Santa Fé de Antioquia in mid-December some years ago, the activity in its central Plaza was hectic to say the least. There were podiums being erected and, in one place, an entire small arena with two spectator gradients for the traditional stand-off between man and bull. The spectacle, though not a blood drenched corrida, is dangerous enough as it is. As soon as the young bull has been disentangled from the ropes keeping him tied down, the game is to come as close as possible to him, preferably to pull him by his tail without ending up being skewered on one or even both of his horns. And there are some guys who don't hesitate to attempt this feat after substantial quantities of *aguardente*, a beer can in one hand and a lit cigarette in the other — every time the bulls seems to get the better of a challenger the audience, children of the fearless fathers, scream in horror mixed with joy.

The merchants around the square have the advantage of being able to store their merchandise in the same stands they use to display them in. The stand itself, with all its hanging goods, folds back up like a small house the roof of which can be closed and secured with padlocks. All the merchants need is for somebody to collectively watch over these little huts overnight. Clothes, hats, candy, food, drinks, and all kinds of handicraft are in this way easily presented and stashed away every night

In the middle of the Plaza in Santa Fé towers the statue of Don Juan del Corral, who perhaps looks a bit older in bronze than he did in real life. He carried the title of dictator but only lived to be thirty-five. During the Napoleonic era he successfully fought against the Spanish and relieved the sons of slaves in Antioquia from further serfdom. A hero of some standing, no doubt, and one whose claim to fame might have been even more solid had he been granted a longer career. His statuesque presence is like the calm eye of the storm as the fierce winds of the fiesta begin to rush in from all the side streets and set the plaza ablaze. Music played out so loudly as the individual sound systems allow, creating an auditive pandemonium in the plaza that is matched only by the shrill voices of vendors, announcers, performing artists and the whistles of the police paving the way for the procession: hundreds of children dressed up as Madonnas and angels, accompanied by slightly elder folks in animal, dragon or demon shapes. In the midst of the procession there are heavily armed soldiers — one small kiss from one of those automatic guns and there'd be a heap of 50 dead people right on the spot. Young women make their way through the thicket of holy kids and enthusiastically pull the helmets off the soldiers' heads, only to mount behind them on the motorcycles and put the helmets on their own heads, waving limbs, cheering, drinking, shouting in ecstasy!

After the procession has passed through the square, a male transvestite with huge, spherical knockers protruding over his bra, enters one of the platforms and begins to present the folklore show featuring innocent boys and girls from nearby villages, dressed up in their traditional colourful costumes and dancing more elegantly than you have ever seen youngsters do before. In another corner there is a karaoke variety and song contest for pre-teen girls who try their very best to imitate all the lascivious gestures of the older girls in the business as presented by Latino MTV. Meanwhile there is a religious ceremony going on in the cathedral and the nuns together carry the newly restored remonstrance up the central nave. From under his white robe the priest pulls out his cell phone and begins to take flash pictures of the altarpiece as it is being carried forward and reinstated in its pre-designated niche. Most of the subsequent Mass, on the day of the *Virgin Immaculata*, is consecrated to fundraising for other objects of the church, allegedly in dire need of renovation.

The incense mixes with oil vapour from the many food stands outside to form the all-encompassing *quinta essentia* of the fiesta's electrically charged atmosphere. Above, the stars inexorably move from east to west in their predetermined paths, while the Moon, cloaked in silvery gauze, abides full tide. Far out in the dry, nocturnal landscape an owl takes advantage of the noise of humans to cover up the fluttering of her wings as she sets out to hunt. Still farther out, well beyond the perimetre of festively lit haciendas, fireworks, gun shots, aguardente, salsa and merengue, the silent puma stalks his prey, one careful step after the other.

And this, dear reader, was only the very beginning of the festivities leading up to Christmas and culminating in the New Year's celebrations, which yours truly duly and patiently lived through, although on some evenings he would deservedly take refuge in the relative calm of his favoured terrace, where the sounds from the square, though still overheard, didn't completely overpower the subtle music of the spheres, now and henceforth humming in his inner ear.

Never forget your hat!

But the gods were obviously jealous of my bliss and felt the need of sending Nemesis my way. The first loss and miraculous recuperation of the backpack containing my passport at the fiesta of Saint Silvester really should have kept me on the alert. But weeks passed and I became oblivious of the gratitude owed. So there I was one day checking in into a hotel in the city of Manizales in the Caldas Province. Routinely asked to show my passport, I was forced to conclude that it had simply gone missing.

I had reached Manizales from the Antioquian village of Andes. An hour into the trip the bus came to a permanent halt because 200 metres of road had been undermined by an inadequate drainage system that had collapsed into the receding ground. The repair work carried out while traffic on both sides waited would have stunned any road engineer from more northern countries. A few heaps of gravel had been dotted on the ground, while a crane moved back and forth spreading it in wider circles, only to afterwards, and rather capriciously, hammer them as flat as possible. The entire procedure took about 45 minutes. Since the heat inside the small bus had become unbearable when there no longer was the slightest draft from the windows, most of the passenger seized the opportunity to step outside to catch a breath of fresh, if also hot, air.

When traffic was on again I couldn't see that the road had changed much from before, but the gravel obviously had made a difference to someone in position of authority, because the vehicles were allowed again to pass in both directions as best they could. Back on the bumping bus I resumed my conversation with a Dutch couple who had come to Colombia to enjoy its unique bird life. It was the first time I spoke English for a month, and I had a lot to tell. A bit too much really. As sometimes happens I got carried away by my own eloquence and my need for entertainment. Of course, I don't accuse these perfectly innocent and endearing people, but hadn't it been for them I probably wouldn't have lost my passport. Unless it really was Destiny that this should happen.

The critical situation arose as I, on our final half hour ride from nearby Chinchina to the bus terminal in Manizales, suggested we'd split a taxi to the city centre. In principal it was a good idea, particularly if we would have ended up going in the same direction. But whereas I thought I wanted to stay in the city centre (I soon but nevertheless too late realised I didn't), they had recommendations for a hostel in the general vicinity of the soccer stadium and the best 'night life' in town — which they were not interested in anyway. I on the other hand had been in the countryside for a month and could do with some action. To me names like Mountain Inn and the The Stadium suggested establishments located on the outskirts of the city. With hindsight, I was extremely lucky to somehow, at the back of my brain, have retained the name of their hostel. Subsequently my ability to recognise the name, once I had seen it, was to save me a lot of trouble. Here's how it happened.

The cab ride had been preceded by my interrogation as to the best hotel options for the night (see Chapter II, 'Colombia', above for an elucidation of the notorious inability of taxi drivers all over the world to take you to a hotel where you really would like to stay!). As a consequence I wasn't quite attentive when the rather bulky luggage of the Dutch folks was squeezed through practically all orifices of the small taxi. Normally I rarely allow myself to lose sight of my Peruvian backpack, but for some reason it was stowed by someone else, out of my sight and supervision. With the consequence that when I subsequently jumped out of the car to leave the good couple to their own devices, I was handed the backpack with the commentary: 'It's open, I hope it doesn't matter'. That alone should have alarmed me and prompted an inspection while the cab was still holding. But I was eager to be on my own again and fell victim to a familiar character flaw: my innate impatience. I thus assumed that nothing could have happened to the contents of the bag, although it seemed odd to me that it should have been open since I know I would not have allowed it to ride on my back without having made sure it was securely closed. Alas, it's only all too easy to know in retrospect what one should have done in advance to avoid an accident.

An armed city guard insisted on following me while I was looking for a hotel to my liking. Facing a reception desk I finally discovered that the little bag of cloth which had travelled inside the mochila was gone. It had also contained my watercolours and brushes, not irreplaceable by any means. A missing passport was an altogether different matter. Understandably I was quite upset — with myself. It immediately struck me as an unforgivable naiveté on my part having left it to the taxi driver and all those 'helpful hands' that eagerly stretch out towards you as soon as you arrive in a new place, to storage my precious bag inside the car. Naturally I hadn't noticed the cab driver's name, let alone his taxi registration number, or the license plate. I only vaguely remembered what he looked like through the rear mirror. And I didn't even know, or remember, the names of the Dutch man and woman I had been travelling with. To top it off, I had forgotten the name of the hostel he had shown me on a business card.

After having collectively, and profusely, cursed all presumptive Colombian thieves, I finally pulled myself together and went back to the hotel at which we had first stopped on the taxi driver's recommendation. The reason I never tried to check in there was the bright lights in the lobby. I had therefore initially asked the driver to keep going. On my request he dropped me off in the middle of a street a couple of blocks away. Coming back to the first place I did recall that the front desk manager had come out on the pavement to see if he was receiving new clients. Perhaps he would remember and be able to identify the cab driver? He wasn't. But he was helpful all the same. He called the taxi companies and asked them to call on the internal radio for a missing small bag of cloth with a passport in it. I waited in the lobby for an hour. As nobody made any further sign I decided to continue the search myself. I took a taxi back to the bus terminal—a steep ride since the city is built on a mountainside. Once there I tried to get hold of people from the bus companies I had been travelling with, to exclude the possibility that I had accidentally lost my passport on either of the two buses. But it was too late in the evening: both the bus drivers and the other personnel had gone home for the night.

Among the cab drivers now present outside the terminal there was nobody who recalled seeing me arrive, much less what taxi I had been in. I decided my best chance was to try to track down the Dutch couple and asked a driver to bring me to all hostels, one after the other, in the area around the soccer stadium. This he did—grudgingly. Why I don't understand since he ended up charging me 50 cents for every stop he made. We stopped at two hostels where I asked if a Dutch couple had checked in recently. No luck. But then the name Mountain Inn appeared in lit up letters outside a building. I suddenly recalled this name as the one the Dutchman had referred to. The Dutch themselves were not there, but that was easily explained by the fact that the hotel had possessed no available beds. The manager suggested I try another hostel nearby. There I actually found them, but to no avail. They could only confirm they had seen the bag and that it had indeed been open, but they hadn't noticed the name of the driver or any taxi license number.

That concluded the search for the evening. I was lucky to get a private room (the idea of having to share a dorm with the motley international crew frequenting these kind of places is just appalling to me) at the nearby Pit Stop Hostel, identifying myself with a maculated passport that contains my still valid Visa to the US and for that reason still travels with me. The next day I called the embassy in Bogotá and found out that I could either get a temporary passport, valid for seven months, on a 24-hours notice, or a regular one in about three weeks. The disadvantage with the former was that it would only be valid for travels in certain countries, the U.S. not being part of them. Since I knew I would have to return to Miami, this option was ruled out. Instead I began to prepare mentally for an eight hour winding bus ride to Bogotá and an early morning visit, the day after that, to my country's embassy in the capital.

After breakfast I went back to the bus station, waiting for the bus companies to make calls in search of my lost item. Confirmed in my suspicions I took the cable car two stops up the mountain to the *Sala de Denuncias* (the word denunciation obviously having a somewhat different connotation in Spanish) located at the city police headquarters. The friendly officer on duty helped me fill out the form the embassy would request to be able to process my application. While on the premises I also met with a very cheerful (!) psychiatrist who said he would take me to the local radio station, so that I could ask the people there to spread the news of my loss through the ether. This service was free of charge. The reason I knew about it was that I had run into some people the night before who invited me, to invite them, for a round of aguardiente and salsa in a private flat.

One of the young men of the party had recently moved into a new apartment. Although we were told to be silent while passing through the entry door of the building — there was a night guard on duty in a boot right next to the gate — the apartment door in turn was swung wide open in to the common corridor as soon as we arrived. There were no furniture in the Spartan, yellow-washed salon and hardly a glass to be found in the kitchen. But there was, of course, a huge stereo chain system with speakers that were quickly assembled and in traditional Colombian style made to rock the edifice like an earthquake. One neighbour actually did come by to ask the apartment owner to diminish the volume. His complaint was respectfully heard, but as soon as he'd gone, the volume was cranked up again and the party back on.

The small glass that most of us used was pushed back and forth over the floor. Being both the tourist and one of two backers of the bottle (which, since the alcohol store announced itself closed for the night, had been bought straight from a night guard in the street that these people apparently knew and trusted), I was offered to drink more often than I actually wanted. However, there was general consensus that I should get going, not the least on the part of 23-old Guillermo, a student of political science from Belgium, who was very pleased to converse with me in French. But even he gradually drifted more and more into the arms and lips of his young mistress.

His landlady on the other hand (of a more mature age, it goes without saying) was not all that bad looking but should have had her teeth braided at an early age since they were protruding from under her upper lips at a 45 degree angle. Also she was a bit broad over the hip and didn't really have any tits to speak of. Pretty otherwise, I should say, and sympathetic in that particular Colombian way that seems to blend passion, loyalty and friendship in a potentially lethal mix. Anyway, she was the one who told me to address myself to the local radio station with an announcement for a missing passport. 'You offer to pay 20. 000 pesos, 30.000 tops (roughly $15) for anyone who finds it and gives it back to you. That's the way things like this are done here in Colombia', she added with an impish smile happily flaunting her rebellious teeth.

It was on her recommendation that I the following day went to visit the radio station. Doctor Sanchez, the merry psychiatrist, after having made his own 'denunciation', asked me to accompany him to his car. In it there was a young beautiful lady patiently waiting behind the wheel. From the point of view of a foreign tourist, a common difficulty in Colombia is to determine whether the young lady presented to you is the daughter (which age-wise she could easily be) or the wife/mistress of the man you have just met. In this case the family situation was never clarified and I didn't have the time, or nerve, to ask. I was on the other hand graciously transported up and down the steepest streets I have ever seen to the radio station located on top of a hill in a part of town called Ciphre, where ever friendly Sanchez helped me to transmit the message to the guardian, who in turn promised to have it handed over to the radio announcers.

That was it. I now ceased to actively search for my passport and spent three days sightseeing and playing chess with the gentlemen gathering in the afternoons in the Parque de Caldas, so-called after the martyr of independence, Francisco José de Caldas, whose statue stands in the middle of the square (the same man gave name to the *departamento* of Caldas, of which Manizales is the capital). At the end of these days I summoned enough force to hit the road again. One rainy morning — the night had been full of lightning and thunder — I stood with my violin, my ominous Peruvian backpack and my travelling bag in the street hailing a cab, as I suddenly remembered that in the process of looking for the passport three days ago I had also lost my old Panama hat. Though no longer in mint condition it had served me well, and I recalled having removed it from my head while talking to the Dutch couple in their hostel. Since these premises were right around the corner, I asked the cab driver to take me there so that I could check for my hat — that would be the last thing before I was headed for Bogotá. 'No lost hat here', the young lady tending the reception emphatically assured me. 'On the other hand, somebody came with this', she said, and handed me a photocopy of my passport with a telephone number written on top of it.

Strangely I never met with the person who eventually returned my passport. I had told the young lady attending the reception at my hotel to give 30.000 pesos to whomever would turn up with it in case

I was out for breakfast or not in the lobby when he came around. As it happened I was in my room, on the Internet trying to reset my flight ticket to its original Florida destination (I had, believing I would stay at least for another three weeks in Colombia, changed my itinerary to a flight from Bogotá to Fort Lauderdale and duly paid the $100 changing fee) without incurring further costs. To this end I was now on the telephone with the Airline call centre and the transaction was actually successful — the $100 for the initial change I lost to the company though.

Nonetheless it must have been the original cab driver who turned up with the indispensable travel document, because he was the only one to know of the particular hostel where the Dutch couple had staid. In addition it was also the place where I had found the photocopy of my passport. He was obviously happy to get 30.000 (a sum covering six average taxi rides in the city) and must have given the little bag of cloth to his daughter, because it was still missing — I believe the reason he didn't hang around to clarify the circumstances to me was that he didn't want to explain how this particular item could be missing when the passport inside it had actually been found! Anyway, the finding of the travel document was well worth both the loss of the hat, the small bag, watercolours and brushes.

I was thus set straight on my trail again, played some more chess and waited for the next day, dreamingly watching the rain pour down over the city. Morning come, I hit the bus station and arrived in the early afternoon to the small town of Armenia, the airport of which is so small, (you may even want to call it intimate) that it doesn't even have a tax-free store. By check-in it was found that I had exceeded my allowed stay in Colombia for sixty days (which I erroneously had interpreted as a two months visa) with one (1!) day, and had to pay a $35 penalty.

Later it also turned out that the two reservations I had tried to make over the Internet for flights from Manizales to Bogotá — which had manifestly been refused by the airline reservation system, my bank, or both — had in fact allowed the airline company to charge me twice for a non-existing reservation. It would be natural to assume that all they needed to do, once I had called them and pointed out this anomaly, was to again access my credit card details and reimburse the account from which the money had been obtained. But when I finally got the English speaking Señor Fajardo over a rusty Skype line, I learned otherwise: 'Oh no, Señor Holm, it's not all that easy, but don't give up, we're all here to help you.' Checking out other passenger's experiences with the same airline over the Internet, I came to the alarming conclusion that the charging of foreign credit cards for non-issued tickets was more or less standard company practice.

There are in my view three possible explanations as to why Aires Airlines insists on throwing these obstacles in the way of gullible tourists reclaiming their money. First, it must be well known to the company that foreign credit cards have a notorious tendency to bounce every time they're applied towards a ticket reservation. With the result that there are more or less constantly, as well as primarily, foreign customers requesting a refund of money. To even be considered for this procedure, though, the customer, who in reality never became one, has to comply with a surprising number of mandatory requirements. In order to initiate a preliminary investigation the customer must (a must referred to as a 'company policy' and just as impervious to reasonable questioning as the dogma of the Holy Trinity, the Immaculate Conception and the Fall of Man), send scanned copies of his passport, his driving license and a bank statement showing that the money has actually been drawn from it by said company.

My first attempt at meeting these requirements failed because, according to Señor Fajardo, the registration numbers on my scanned documents were illegible. Although I told him I could easily read the numbers from the same scanned copies, he maintained they were not visible. I had to get a better camera and try again. This time (and it took me another week or so to get around to it) the result, as testified by an automated e-mail reply sent in this regard, appeared to be satisfactory. A week later, though, there was still no sign of returned money on my account. I again called Señor Fajardo.

This time he informed me that it would take a about a month, from the moment my request had been registered, for the money to be reimbursed. Or to be quite precise: Señor Fajardo didn't actually promise me that the money would be reinstated. I was only assured that it would take a month for me to be informed about the result of their investigation, involving contacting various 'credit institutions' to verify that the payment had really been made on my part. On my persistently repeated suggestion that all they needed to do was to verify their own transactions, Fajardo kept answering me in an evasive manner that invariably ended in the assurance that the customer service, he himself an edifying example, would always be there to assist me. Assist me with what, you may ask? Alas, that was also my question.

There might be different explanations as to why a public company behaves in this way. The first is that in a country like Colombia it can get away with it is because the law, in so far at it applies at all, is implicitly on their side. This inherent imbalance of powers follows the same logic as traffic circulation in this part of the world, where a pedestrian *a priori* has less right of way than a bicyclist, who has to look out for the scooter driver, who in turn is inferior to a motorcyclist, who in turn is obliged to yield to cars, in turn subject to the caprices of truck and bus drivers. At the very top of this food chain one finds airplanes and their owners.

In for example the US any legally registered company facing the kind of blatant evidence I was able to throw at Aires would probably have returned the money within the shortest possible delay for fear of being sued over a sum by far surpassing the one claimed — arguing about the bleeding obvious would simply be bad business. Not so in Colombia. Here the company management knows that my chances of getting to them legally are practically non-existent. For this reason they can allow the remuneration process to be so painstakingly slow that the customer hopefully loses heart and gives up fighting for his right. Add to this the not all too surprising circumstance that Aires Customer Service has a marked tendency to make itself inaccessible. On numerous occasions when I tried to call them on the number indicated on their homepage, the automated voice asked me to press 1 for English and 2 for Español. But as soon as I had made my choice (and believe me, I tried both options) the recorded voice just returned again urging me to make the choice I had already made. Consequently I spent hours and days just trying to reach the customer service switchboard. When I finally got hold of an Aires representative (via their chat line!) the only explanation I could wring out of her concerning this anomaly, was that my chances to actually reach the call centre were best either between eight and nine in the morning or between four and five in the afternoon — no explanation given as to why precisely these hours would be preferable.

The second explanation entails a gracious benefit of the doubt. It could be that the company actually wants to make sure the customer has not had his credit card stolen or its number copied. The knowledge that foreign credit cards are often refused by the company in connection with online ticket reservations could provide imaginative thieves with an easy way of receiving money for nothing. But since the money ideally would just be returned to the account from which it was drawn in the first place, why bother to waste it on non-forthcoming airline reservations in the first place (remember, I paid not once but twice for the same ticket)? The benefit of the doubt thus hangs by a thin thread covered by an impenetrable smokescreen.

A third explanation has the advantage of being the most plausible and realistic, since it implicitly combines 1 and 2. Their claim, stating that thorough protection of the customer's identity and credit card information is necessary, is a mere pretext for making it exceedingly difficult for the customer to get his money back. But if so, why didn't Señor Fajardo tell me that the prolonged procedure was in the interest of customer safety? As a matter of fact no representative to whom I spoke was ever able to explain why the remuneration process had to be this slow. It was like trying to argue with Destiny itself.

Several months later, when back in Europe, I contacted my bank hoping it would be able to deal more effectively with Señor Fajardo and his devious staff. To my surprise the bank quickly found out that the money had been credited to my account, and not one or two months after the original event. No, the money had been registered as returned even before it had been registered as drawn upon. I know it sounds paradoxical, but all this time I had only been spinning around my own tail. Countless hours, not to say days, spent contacting the airline suddenly vaporised into thin air. The reimbursed money, for some strange reason, had been transferred and registered to my account at a date prior to the date when the charges for the same transaction were made. Technically speaking I had actually got my money back before my account was charged.

Was this the end of the story? Yes it was. The only thing that still puzzles me is this: Why did Aires for several months keep up the illusion that they would eventually pay the money they supposedly owed me, never realising or caring to inform me, in spite of all their alleged investigations and lengthy correspondence, that the job had already been done?

I know I shall never receive an explanation of how this all came about. Likewise I shall never know why a bank in Santa Marta charged me with a grossly exaggerated exchange rate via their ATM-machine. Nor will I ever find out why another ATM at the Santo-Domingo airport in the Dominican Republic charged my account with the withdrawal of 12.000 pesos (US $300) without delivering the equivalent in bills in the slot. That said, I'm happy to conclude that my financial encounters with individual people and business owners in Latin America have been, on the whole, very positive. For example, during my last stay in Colombia, I can't recall a single instance in which any man or woman, to my knowledge, tried to short change or in any other way cheat me out of money. All would stick to deals made and not show sour faces when actually receiving the amount agreed. Change on bills in hotels, restaurants and bars were always correct too. Which gives me the opportunity to highlight the few occasions on which I have indeed been the actual or prospective victim of a deliberate scam.

In Nicaragua, a couple of years ago, one shady thing seemed to lead to the other. I remember having negotiated a taxi rate from Managua airport to Granada that was only half-heartedly accepted on the driver's part. For me on the other hand it was a small but symbolically important victory. But I did make the mistake of handing him the entire sum of money convened in advance as payment in connection with the compulsory stop at the gas station. I know I should have refused, or at least only given him enough money to fill the tank for our trip. In the event, having received full payment, he no longer felt obliged towards me and subsequently refused to take me to the city centre unless I agreed to pay him more. I refused, with the consequence that I had to walk the remaining distance into town from its outskirts. Once there I immediately looked for a cheap hotel — in my experience it's often a good idea to get settled in as soon as possible upon late arrival in a new place, and relay to the next day the adventure of finding a hotel to one's actual liking. I found one close to the main square. In the court yard it offered rooms with a bed, a miniscule bathroom, a light bulb in the ceiling and a ventilator on the wall. That was it. The family lived and cooked food right in the lobby.

In the hotel patio I ran into Chris, a flamboyant gay staying at the hotel. He made no secret of his agenda — finding young boys — and proudly boasted of how, with his employer's Rolls Royce, he would pick up cute guys in Beverly Hills and bring them to the mansion with their pants down. Six months out of the year Chris worked as a butler for some unimaginably rich couple who had one estate in Los Angeles, another in New Zealand and a third in Lake Tahoe. The remaining six months he was off and, for better or worse, on his own. He told me he was on his way from Nicaragua to India, or was it Ceylon, pretexting some disappointment with the local prostitution in Granada. Or else it was just plain habit for him to go to Sri Lanka, because he claimed to have been there many times before. To me he seemed an unabashed and inveterate pervert. Probably for the same reason he was also quite entertaining, albeit in a characteristic gay manner. But although he was indeed depraved he didn't drink. This limited the fun we could possibly have together. Unable to persuade him to have a glass with me, I left him in the hotel to explore the night life of Granada by myself.

Not before long I ran into a smiling young man offering me anything money could buy. His specialty was drugs, and he insisted he could get me whatever I wanted. I cheerfully responded that I didn't need anything from that department and I left him to carry on business as best he could. But then I saw him again next day and we started to chit-chat. He told me about his university studies. I don't know what I answered, but I remember talking a lot since he seemed reasonably interested in keeping a dialogue. I also bought him a cup of coffee, later a beer, and then another one. Before we parted he once again asked me if I wanted to buy drugs. I said: 'perhaps some other day, but don't make it a priority.' The next day he again spotted me across the main square and I invited him to come and have a coffee or a beer, knowing guys like him don't usually have that much money to spend.

This kind of socialising between the two of us went on for a couple of days. By now I had come to accept as normal that he stalked me in order to get a free beer. As a matter of fact, I felt his presence to be quite agreeable even though he had a somewhat oblique smile and squinting eyes. However, as my time in colonial Granada was coming to an end — I was about to take a ferry boat on the adjacent Lake Cocibolca to get to the twin-volcano island of Ometepe — I saw him again in what turned out to be the last time. We sat down as usual and I bought him something to drink.

Here I finally got tired of hearing him repeat his standing offer. So I said 'OK, do you have it on you?' 'No, he replied, but I can get it for you in no time'. When we finally split from the cafe he told me to wait for him in the street. After no more than two minutes he turned up, quickly handing over a small, tightly sealed parcel that appeared to contain a pretty solid amount of the good stuff. I gave him the 20 dollars he had asked for: 'And how do I know you're not just fooling me with a bunch of not even dry seaweed?' I asked jestingly. He squinted impishly and replied: 'Naaoo, why I would I do such a thing?' Since I couldn't see any reason for this either, I laughed, pocketed the parcel, bid him farewell and set off down the street to seek shelter from indiscreet regards in my room. Having made sure the door was securely locked behind me I attacked the parcel with a pen knife. Suddenly I had a bunch of weed in my hand. But not just any kind of weed: a good handful of juicy seaweed!

I was amazed. For almost a week this young guy had diligently and convincingly played the role of a local friend and conversational partner only to finally be able to draw 20 dollars out of my pocket for nothing. It just seemed so incredibly petty, even though 20 dollars of course meant considerably more to him than to me. Our many conversations now revealed themselves as one long preparation for the decisive moment when he had earned my confidence to such a degree that I would no longer bother to ask him to show the actual goods before I paid for it. Still today, when I think about it, I admire him for his endurance and patience, notwithstanding that he did get a couple of beers along the road as well. What surprised me the most, though, is that I simply didn't see it coming. I really was his dupe. Still, what an effort for a mere twenty dollars and the inconvenience of then having to disappear in the crowd, because believe me: I kept looking for this guy in every street corner. And not only that day and the following, but also when I returned there a couple of weeks later. But he had vanished and I never saw him again.

Here the antipode to the story above. Santo-Domingo, the capital of the Dominican Republic, has officially around two million inhabitants, but the real figure — when all orphans, homeless or otherwise unregistered citizens and clandestine Haitians have been hypothetically counted — might well be three million, there is no way of knowing for sure. As can be expected in such circumstances there are a lot of people desperately seeking to make their services profitable. One of them is a lively, short man who habitually hangs around Hotel Barcelo presenting himself as a tour guide with bright prospects on practically anything from mountain biking to prostitutes — concertina-like their pictures fall out of his hands as soon as he opens his folder, and he's more than happy to give you a quote, since some of the girls, depending on quality, are more expensive than others.

This agile man, with a kind if somewhat toothless smile, caught me in the right moment. I had spent the better part of the hot afternoon searching for a shoemaker who could fix my Italian designer sandals. But the one I had been referred to had recently moved to an unknown address. As I was getting pressed for time, while asking around for alternatives — I had a rehearsal with the Dominican Symphony Orchestra that same evening and they were the ones paying for the fancy hotel — he offered me to bring the shoes to a place where they would be instantly repaired. Well knowing that I shouldn't take the risk, I gave him not only the shoes but also advanced the money he asked for to cover expenses. We agreed to meet later in the evening on the same spot, across the crowded highway from the hotel and casino complex towering in the background. But although he did indeed turn up at ten o'clock, as agreed, he didn't have the shoes with him. This anomaly didn't prevent him from asking for more money in order to cover for a taxi trip he wasn't supposed to be taking in the first place. I don't know what got into my mind at this point, but for some reason

I gave him even more than he had asked for. Whereafter he disappeared, promising to bring the shoes directly to my hotel first thing in the morning.

Morning come there were no signs of neither shoes nor man. The day passed. In the evening I had the concert with the Symphony Orchestra. Returning late, I again inquired at the hotel lobby about the shoes, but no one there had received or seen them. Next day I had to check out, by now clearly aware that shoes and money were gone. I cursed myself for being such a fool but it didn't make the situation better. I simply would have to leave without them. Brushing past the doorman behind his tall desk, I was halted by the same. I suspected more trouble in the making, since the check-out procedure so far had been anything but a bona fide operation. When I approached the desk crowned with the sign Check Out, the staff on duty had begun to eye me suspiciously. No 'Good Morning', no 'Good day', not even a 'Hello'. Only a pair of immutable eyes and three laconic words heightened by an ominous question mark: 'Your room number?'

Before she had even had the time to type my name, so far still hidden inside the computer, the girl attending to my business grabbed a microphone. I heard her icy voice echo simultaneously through the cool air of the lobby, from the restaurants, the casino, the pool area and throughout all the eleven floors: 'Number 427 is checking out, number 427 is checking out'. That was me: number 427 (an Orwellian scene in the tropics).

As soon as the alarm had sounded, there was, for the first time since my arrival, immediate room service. Seconds later a bottle of water was reported as being missing from the mini bar and, even more gravely, the glass covering a table was found to have a crack in it. I was informed that it was my duty to pay for this reckless destruction of hotel property. But I was not in the mood for it and asked her to get me the general manager. To him I explained that the crack had not occurred as a result of wanton violence, but from my posing a bottle of rum on it. This explanation, having the minor merit of also being true (although it technically speaking was my friend Hector who carried out the actual deed), eventually got me off the hook. I maintained that it was the deficient quality of the glass that was to blame for the accident. After some deliberation the manager decided not to press charges against me — 'this time'. I was relieved, paid the rest of my dues (mini bar, restaurant etc.) and wished the princess on the glass mountain a good morning. The last thing I now wanted was to once again be held back by a 'Señor, por favor!'. But this was exactly what happened. Unwillingly I readied myself to face yet another insidious challenge to my purse. I slowly turned round: 'Are these yours?' The doorman held out a plastic bag, urging me to peep inside it. There they were, my Italian designer sandals, repaired, even cleaned.

It came as a complete surprise. Although I had paid the man more than well, I had been so convinced that he had left without a trace that I could hardly believe my eyes. I felt a vague trust in humankind regain foothold inside me. Exhilarated I threw the bag over my shoulder and stepped out into the traffic, as always hectic on this thoroughfare. Among its many ramshackle vehicles the city taxis are in a league of their own. You'd be lucky to come across one where the doors are still hanging onto their hinges and where all tires are of the same dimension — that they are never of the same brand goes without saying, not even the caps are. Typically, the provisional, tiny spare tire will never come off the wheel either unless it too goes flat. The indention these cars have sustained, while still rolling, are impressive. They don't just look like wrecks. They are. Which doesn't prevent them from serving as collective transportation, accommodating up to ten people at the time. Each of them usually consists of so many different pieces, in so many different colours, that they look as though they were wearing military camouflage. Indeed, they blend in perfectly with their natural environment.

Eager to get out of this dusty city, in which I had spent almost three weeks intermittently playing the violin in the city's orchestra, I turned to the next pedestrian, asking him if he knew where I could catch a bus headed for the Zona Colonial — I didn't feel like spending money on a cab. He indicated the way while at the same time seizing the opportunity to introduce himself. He was a haggard man in his fifties, with dark, but not really black skin, and wavy hair. He had a searching regard, as though he were preoccupied with assessing my credibility and divining my wishes. His voice was raucous, more like a harsh whispering really. I noticed that he was dressed in a striped business suit, although it struck me as not being of absolute apex quality. His shoes too seemed just a bit too rustic and simple to accompany a business suit. In all it was a very hot ensemble to wear under the Caribbean sun.

He presented himself as a lawyer of civil law but did not hand over a card, explaining that he had forgotten them in his office. Instead he began telling me all about his family, his wife, his daughters, even his mistresses, emphasizing that he was a Latin man in natural need of the diversions such could provide. Meanwhile he considered himself blessed by God and was grateful for the health of his family and the success he had enjoyed in his professional life. Every now and then he looked me deep into my eyes as though he wanted to make sure I understood that he really was my friend. He asked me where I was off to. I truthfully answered that I hadn't quite made up my mind. He told me he had his roots in a central region of the island and recommended me to visit its capital. 'The people are honest and kind there, not like here,' he added with a tired smile. He even criticised my choice to stop by in the local Colonial Zone, which he considered good only for gullible tourists and pick-pockets. After having found out that I intended to take a bus to get out of town altogether, he came up with an idea.

He had a friend running a car rental company. If I wanted, he could find out how much it would cost me to rent a car for the remaining ten days of my stay in the country. Why not, I said, thinking I had nothing to lose by hearing him out. He asked how much I was willing to pay per day, and I said: give me an offer I can't refuse. He answered he might be able to provide me with a car for as little as $10 a day, insurance included. But for this deal to come through he needed, technically speaking, to be the one renting the car, thereby assuming full legal responsibility for it, although I would be the one actually driving it. I said it'd be okay with me provided he made sure the vehicle was properly insured and that we had a contract to that effect. In fact, I could hardly even believe my good luck: on this fine day I first got my shoes back, then this good man had nothing better to do than strolling up and down the road trying by all means to help me to a car deal that would enable me to visit the entire island at my leisure.

But not only had he forgotten his business cards in the office. His cell phone was also there. So he needed to find a telephone booth — I didn't have a phone either. We found one and he placed a call. I heard him saying that I seemed to him a quite trustworthy gentleman and it almost made my heart swell for pride to have my humble self described in such flattering terms. In between his own comments, he mouthed 'nine dollars', to me, that is, even less than he had predicted. It all seemed too good to be true.

After hanging up, he told me he needed to call back in half an hour to verify that a car was available. So we went for a stroll and sat down at a cafe to talk. He wanted to pay for our drinks, but I felt that the least I could do for him was to take care of that, and I told him so. He responded, saying he valued above all friendship and kindness in life, and that he was sure that I, given the opportunity, would do the same for a foreigner in need of something in my country. I wasn't quite sure what he meant by that, but before I was able to find out, the half hour had elapsed, and we went back to the phone boot from which I could hear him finalise the deal. He then invited me to cross the main road. Some money dealers offered us an exchange of dollars for pesos. I said we had everything we needed, but I could see they kept watching us intently as we paced up the street. We went through a small university campus. He pointed towards a building and said that he was lecturing there on civil law twice a week. We ended up in a MacDonald's where the brisk air conditioning allowed us to cool off. He was perspiring profusely from having kept his jacket on in the heat. I asked him if he wouldn't be more comfortable hanging it on the chair. He took it off. At this point I wasn't quite sure what we were still waiting for, and downright bewildered as to why we had entered a MacDonald's restaurant, but I went with the flow, confident that I would eventually be able to figure out what was going on.

While walking he had explained to me the intricacies of the deal that included a 130 dollar security deposit on top of the 90 dollars rent for ten days. He assured me he would pay this deposit himself so that I only would have to pay the remaining 90 bucks. Problem was that his cash was also at the office, while the car itself was just around the corner. If I could only give him the 230 dollars, he'd be able to conclude the deal in no time and bring the car to me: 'Did you say you wanted an automatic or one with a manual gearbox?'

I believe, that for a second or two, I saw nothing objectionable in giving him the money needed, because by now I had already begun to picture myself behind the wheel, steering into adventure land. Two hours had gone since we met and the time it had taken to bring the whole thing together started to wear on my patience. I was anxious to get it over and done with. But then, once that euphoric second had passed, a small but intensely luminous red lamp lit up on the inner panel. The fact that I had got my used sandals back was no guarantee that another service-minded person, offering to carry 230 dollars out of the room and from some mysterious location bring me a car in return, would in fact also do that. It also dawned upon me as strange that he continuously kept deflecting my suggestion to follow him to where the transaction allegedly was going to take place — he would only go so far as to 'allow' me to wait for him in the park. I in turn didn't know of any park, so I said: 'Don't you have any money yourself?' He admitted having 30 dollar on him, but he needed the rest from me. I objected that he could surely draw the remaining sum from an ATM-machine, but soon understood that his credit cards too were, of course, in the office...

Up to this point there had, for a person endowed with the capacity for wishful thinking, been something almost credible about the whole set up. From now on, however, the situation quickly deteriorated while the last act drew to its close. 'You must realise', I said, 'that I find it very hard to understand why I can't survey this transaction, especially since you have already explained to your business partner that I seem to be an altogether trustworthy gentleman. In other words, this person must already know that you're renting this car on behalf of somebody else.' Whereupon my friend, almost teary-eyed, rose from his chair, pointed to his striped jacket hanging off the back of the chair, saying: 'I can leave this here as a security'. 'That!' I retorted. 'What am I going to do with that once you're gone?' 'It's worth 400 dollars,' he exclaimed. '400 dollars!' I sighed. 'I need your watch, your wedding ring, your...' to my utter surprise he began to strip his watch from the wrist. I had to stop him. It was time for the *estocada*. 'Listen,' I said, 'I's not possible for me to give you 230 dollars in cash and then sit back here holding on to your dirty nylon jacket and a dinky toy wristwatch until it so pleases you to materialise in front of me with a Porsche Cabriolet for nine bucks a day. The deal's off. Please excuse me, I've got to go.'

I will never forget the genuinely sad eyes he cast on me while realising that his carefully concocted con act was not going to meet with success. I nearly felt sorry for him. So much ado about nothing. Truth to tell, there hadn't just been ridiculous pretension but also some very convincing lines on his part in this make-believe drama. Clearly he knew much about both law and history, and for the better part of two hours we had entertained a cultivated, almost learned conversation.

Furthermore, his conversations over the phone had seemed altogether genuine.

Still, everything, from his first to his last word, had served the unique purpose of persuading me to give him my money for nothing. It was like seeing an animal of prey yawn after having missed its carefully prepared attack. Resigned, he fished his jacket from the chair, looked at me one last time with his sad, searching eyes, and said: 'I'm truly sorry you don't trust me, but I can also understand why.' With these words he turned round, walked towards the door and disappeared into the blistering sun.

For me there was nothing left but to resume the narrow path of virtue I had so frivolously abandoned. Embarking upon it I again had to pass by the money changers with their thick swaddles ready at hand. This time they didn't offer me dollars or euros for pesos, they only wanted to know how much I had given him. 'Nothing', I said, and one of them replied, 'We really wanted to warn you, this guy walks this street every day up and down looking for tourists. He's a crook.' 'I know,' I said. 'Luckily nothing bad happened. Thanks anyway for trying to help me out: *Que les vaya bien!*'

Boca Chica

Half an hour's ride along the coast east of Santo Domingo, Capital of the Dominican Republic, there is a small resort town called Boca Chica. It has a pleasant beach inside a bay dominated, to the west, by the tall riggings of oil refineries. But these are quite far away and, seen from a local hotel, not absolutely blatant eyesores. The reason why Boca Chica enjoys local fame, however, is not only that it does have sandy beaches, otherwise conspicuously absent from Hispaniola's south-east coast — with the notable exception of tourist infested Punta Cana sitting right on its east coast. Its real claim to fame is that it arguably has one of the largest and easiest to access prostitution markets in the entire Latin American hemisphere. To go here together with your wife or fiancée would probably be a big mistake, even if you yourself were to behave in an exemplary way and pretend not to notice what's going on around you. Because even so, your wife will, and she's probably going to want to know what your opinion is in regard to this meat market. At night time the girls are simply everywhere; they are many, they are young, and at least some of them very beautiful. Sometimes it's even hard to tell what they look like since they are so extravagantly dressed and their makeup so heavy that they seem more like exotic creatures from the jungle, or even outer space, than human beings. But this they are and in fierce competition with one another at that.

Technically the Dominican girls aren't prostitutes since they can show the police a paper certifying that they are actually employees of the bars in and around which they carry out their trade. But the Haitian girls not only undercut Dominican prices, they are also illegal immigrants, so they tend to come out around midnight when the police officially withdraws from the scene. And that's when the place gets really crowded. Not necessarily with tourists though. It might be that you, as a single man, find yourself surrounded by twenty, thirty girls, all happy to offer you company to an affordable price.

During my first visit to town, and perhaps a bit paradoxically, I made the acquaintance of a Dominican woman who was neither quite young nor a prostitute. She was on the contrary doing the laundry and cleaning the kitchen in the small French-Canadian owned hotel where I stayed, and she was a very spontaneous, charming lady with a great sense of humour and a laughter that always would put me in a good mood. Part of Olga's story was that she was indebted to an eighty year old Canadian man with whom she felt obliged to stay whenever he was visiting in the Dominican Republic. As of now, he even wanted to marry her. But although that would doubtlessly give her some financial security, she wasn't too happy about the idea for several reasons, one being that she loathed having to patiently sit on the sofa and keep him company while he was watching NHL hockey games. In short, he demanded that she'd be with him all the time.

The reason, inversely, for her sense of loyalty to him was that he had paid for the best medical care money could buy to try to save the life of her teenage daughter who had been struck by a rare and life threatening disease. He was not her biological father but nevertheless assumed that kind of responsibility. The real local father had of course disappeared long before the baby was even born and left her to care for herself and the newborn as best she could. In other words, there was a sense of conflict in her relationship with this elderly gentleman. On the one hand she still felt she owed him gratitude for what he had done for her. On the other she didn't really want to spend the rest of his days together with him. As he was not in the country right now she felt free to accept my invitations.

We went out a couple of times to have drinks and/or dinner and it was on one of these occasions I made the observation that there were at least two or three guys apart from me among the thirty or so girls to be seen in our bar, in the main street and its adjacent joints. 'Oh those', Olga said, 'those are just the *chulos* (pimps) of some of the girls, so as a matter of fact you're pretty much the only potential client around right now.'

As can be expected there are quite a lot of male gringos and Europeans spending boreal winter months in this nicely temperate location, where, apart from some more typical American style resorts, there are many budget hotels where the coming and going of the girls is unimpeded by police, gate security, receptionists and corporate policies. Most of the girls actually seem to prefer to stick around a specific guy for as long as he stays there, and sometimes even moves in with him. This arrangement doesn't normally prevent the same men from occasionally taking another *chica* for the night, or just for some afternoon fun. On the whole, the easy acceptance of male sexuality being geared towards variation is quite remarkable, and whatever feminist moralists say to denigrate men dealing in prostitution, the white blokes from America or Europe are certainly not any worse than the local males who won't even pay for getting laid and in all other respects as well treat their women like dirt.

It might be unfortunate that women in this part of the world, or elsewhere, feel tempted to sell their bodies, but it's sometimes in our enlightened press made to sound a good deal uglier than it really is, the entire Latin world being full of social insecurity and poverty, making the predicament of single women left with perhaps several children to raise and take care of extremely precarious. To find a white man also willing to pay for the needs of the latter is quite a bargain. Although I can very well can understand that Olga felt reluctant to accept an invitation to marry a man twice her age just to be relieved from cleaning laundry in a hotel, there are a lot of other cases where the difference in age is not that great, and where there can even be a question of mutual attraction, physical as well as emotional.

By standard western, feminist, definition it's still prostitution for sure. To which I would reply that there are many women in our northern societies who are really nothing but *putas*, only they don't come across as such since they don't charge you an explicit fee every time you have sex with them. However, when they do cash in, they're not just happy to take your entire wallet, but also your house, your car, your boat, and everything else they could possibly come to think of and lay their hands on. Thus prostitution is just as common on northern latitudes, only it's incomparably more expensive for the buyer. For this reason I can understand the men who don't want to be stripped of everything they own a second time, and to this end have opted for an easier, financially viable and more convenient solution.

Galéras

There is a popular saying among the expats of Galéras: 'This is not the ass of the world, but you can see it from here'. The same expats — whether from Holland, Britain, Germany, Belgium, France, Canada or the United States — have one well maintained conviction in common: the place — meaning the combined effects of landscape, sea and the characteristics of its human population — is impossible to adequately describe to an outsider. For an ambitious writer and, precisely, an outsider, there can thus be nothing more challenging or tempting than to try to do so all the same.

It's almost like a sunset. I don't mean a sunset per se, but the equivalent of a sunset. I mean, there is a very good reason why distinguished artists throughout history have cautiously avoided to painting sunsets. Monet did a few, but if you look closely you'll see that he preferred to pick misty days in rainy London where the declining sun becomes a single spot of light surrounded by haze. That's a luminous effect, not a sunset. Perhaps the only really first rate artist I know of who saw nothing objectionable in turning a canvas into a pandemonium of colours, reminiscent of the sea and the atmosphere lit up by a setting sun, is J.M.W. Turner. He did it, and although it's all an inch away from pure kitsch, it never oversteps that fine line; that, I believe, is the essence of his genius. There is a profound and altogether sincere feeling invested in his artistic rendering of these oblique rays spreading their peacock feathers across the sky. I also believe it was the sincerity in his awe for perhaps the greatest of all natural wonders that saved him from falling into the abyss of aborted Western art. He was also lucky enough to live at a time in European history where the word *pathetic* still conveyed an altogether positive meaning. Other distinguished artists know, more or less instinctively, that to try to rival nature in a sunset would end up in disaster: it would be like trying to outdo the Himalayas by raising a tower or a pyramid from out of one of its valleys. Ludicrous: the tower or the pyramid are only impressive in the flat lands.

Turner was blessed with the natural eccentricity, naiveté and innocence of a child (this is also why he sometimes loved to indulge in erotic art too!) while his technique from early on was that of a fully-fledged mature artist at the height of his powers. For this reason he could do what nobody else was even dreaming of attempting. I find it significant that his last words are quoted as: 'The sun is God', and that he had stipulated in his will the setting up of a fund for 'decayed artists' — a request of course ignored by the greedy handler of his estate.

The most obvious trait of the village of Galéras, on the other hand, is that it coincides with both a land's and a road's end. The road from the town of Samaná, located on the southern shores of the eponymous peninsula, literally leads straight into the ocean. Galéras is only 26 kilometres away from Samaná, close to the north-eastern tip of the peninsula. Yet it's a world unto itself. It is perhaps the lushest part of the entire island of Hispaniola: always deeply green, even at times when other parts of the island experience seasonal drought. It is also one of the wildest and least exploited regions of the country, and has been so since time immemorial. The wide bay south, east and west of Samaná is home not only to the spectacular spawning of humpback whales, but also to an archipelago of intimate *cayos* (keys), among these the infamous Bacardi island, so-called because it was here in the 1970s that Bacardi shot a commercial which has since remained world famous.

The town of Samaná itself, in the vernacular of Baedeker's, has 'little of particular interest to offer the tourist', but its surroundings were once highly praised for their natural beauty by no less a man than Columbus. Later Napoleon had far reaching plans of turning its natural harbour into a major Caribbean hub, capable of rivalling in commercial importance both Cuban Havana and Puerto Rican San Juan. Of this came nothing except a bridge between the keys closest to town and an eagle's nest luxury hotel, a hint, no more, of what could, perhaps, have become a veritable Caribbean hotspot. Although this never happened there are still private yachts of some standing anchored off the beaches, and the big international cruise ships seldom fail to court the keys, especially during the whale season from January to April.

The town itself has critically failed to capitalise on its privileged location. Instead of moving hotels, cafes, bars and restaurants up to the waterfront and make its *malecon* one of the most spectacular boardwalks in the entire Caribbean, it has cut the town off from its waters by allowing the main road to run in between the sea and the few cafes dotting its perimetre. I don't hesitate to blame the local population for this lack of opportunism. Notwithstanding that the Dominican government has shown itself notoriously uninterested in furthering regional development, the mixture of Spanish gypsies (imported in the 19th and early 20th century from the old motherland to settle these remote areas), international swashbucklers and ancient African slaves here has created an ethnic mix that arguable belongs to the most unruly and, without doubt, to the crudest and, above all, rudest populations in this part of the world. Educated people are rare and far in between, and we're still talking about the townsfolk. Venturing into the hinterland can quickly turn into a traumatising modern day 'Heart-of-Darkness' experience, shattering conventional Western morality and prejudice like a machete splitting a coconut.

This is a country where a girl of 13 is being 'broken in' and thereby declared ready for pregnancy by her close male relatives. By the age of 18 she's already the mother of three, none of whom has a father assuming any kind of responsibility. At the age of 25 she's considered too old to be of sexual interest to any her kinsfolk and only good enough for the 'tourist trade'. Rape, murder and theft belong to the order of the day, and people regularly disappear without a trace. The police — so badly paid that bribes and financial cuts provided by criminal elements are the only effective means of making a tolerable living — sometimes pretend to combat crime. It's very doubtful in how far they actually succeed, or even want to succeed. Judging from the appalling number of unsolved cases the level of ambition can't be very high in this regard.

Even though the majority of people, even in more remote villages, do show some common decency in their daily dealings, the lack of central judicial control in this province simultaneously makes for excellent possibilities of escape, as well as of disappearance, for any individual intent on breaking the law. Galéras, to the northeast on the peninsula, is the last outpost still marked by post-colonial and neo-expat influence. It is located in the middle of a wide horseshoe bay, protected from the ceaseless pounding of the Atlantic by a myriad of submarine reefs, turning most of the water into a boiling witches' cauldron. It has a couple of sandy beaches, its *primus inter pares* being Playa Rincón in the deepest and most tranquil corner of the bay: three miles of pristine, palm lined white beach set against a backdrop of wilderness. The outer ends of the gulf are framed by two mighty petrified arms made from razor sharp volcanic rock jutting into the sea like prehistoric monsters. The vegetation at the centre of this picture is so densely green that it bestows upon the landscape a metallic sheen; the skies and their luminous hues forever shifting.

Beyond the western outskirts of Galéras there is not a single building to behold, only a gloomy ruin at a distance so hazed that it might just as well be a vision of Cerberus' doghouse before the Gates of Hades. The slopes winding down to Cabo Cabrón, at the northern land's end, apart from a few cultivated fields, are covered in an impenetrable thicket, whipped and kept close to the ground by tropical squalls. The Atlantic swell, mostly prompted by an easterly trade wind, splashes against huge distant rocks and deep caves in foamy cascades that occasionally stand fifty metres tall. The inner bay in contrast, opening and disappearing towards a more secluded west, is protected against the direct onslaught of the trade winds by the north-eastern promontory, the majestic twin-brother of the Cabo Cabrón. Beyond this point some of the most original and unspoiled beaches in the entire 'civilised' world can be visited by boat or on horseback. The zodiac, to round off the description of this eminently picturesque corner of the universe, runs diagonally across the bay, seldom or never presenting the spectacle of a sun either rising out of or setting directly into the sea. The Moon, the planets and all the stars of the galactic Orion arm visible to the naked eye follow suit, and turn the night sky into a magic cavern sprinkled with diamonds. The bay also has its own miniature key. Situated some 200 metres offshore in Galéras it puts the massive coastline in perspective, its few wind beaten palm trees conveying the image of prehistoric hieroglyphs scribbled on a mural of elemental wrath.

The human population attending to this grandiose spectacle consists of indigenous elements mixed with a colony of westerners, primarily of European and French-Canadian extraction. Americans on the other hand are not overly represented. The token representative I ran across — a profuse white beard crowned by a Santa's cap set on a heavy trunk of Irish complexion driving up and down the muddy streets of town on a beach bug — turned out to be a complacent weed-puffing ex-copper from Boston. The majority of these immigrants are of surprisingly long standing and able to recall times when there was still only a dirt road from Samaná and the town had no central supply of electricity. Internet and phone operators too only arrived some years ago, although cell phones now are as ubiquitous as everywhere else on the planet. During the day the main street, being the only road to Samaná, bustles with activity, not the least from hundreds of scooters and motorcycles. Like in any typical tourist town, the main stretch features bars, restaurants, food stores, local art and souvenir markets. And like everywhere in the Dominican Republic the locals are constantly eager to advice the tourist on what to spend his money. On the whole the co-existence of Dominicans, interspersed with Haitian guest workers, and Europeans works out smoothly. The Dominicans by themselves would not even know where to start to make their town attractive to tourists. The Europeans, on the other hand, know that very well but they in turn need the Dominicans to work for them, and so relations are both symbiotic and of mutual gain in what is today, at least superficially, a thriving, if also somewhat surreal, international community.

There is so far only one major all-inclusive resort in the area, and it's located a couple of kilometres outside town. In the village centre there are only smaller, private hotels, mostly owned by foreigners. But although the beaches surrounding Galéras are quite fascinating to walk and to look at — by some enthusiasts they have even been described as the epitome of Caribbean beauty — they are not particularly inviting for swimmers, at least not in the fall and early winter when the water, agitated by the trade winds, and regurgitated by the reefs, is muddy and the sandy ocean floor more often than not covered in seaweed, interspersed with small rocks. For this reason there is hardly any risk that Galéras will ever see a major tourist boom. It can't really change into anything else than what it already is: the adorned end of the coastal road from Samaná. Thus the tourist venturing this far away from international and heavily exploited resort areas such as Punta Cana and Puerto Plata has already opted for a different and more adventurous holiday experience. I, as it turned out, had done the same. Only of how adventurous it was going to be, I was still ignorant.

A priori there was nothing wrong in my planning. Not only had I frequented, some weeks earlier, the all-inclusive hotel complex on a weekend trip with some friends. After having finished the concerts in Santo Domingo for which I had been contracted I again returned to

Galéras, this time to stay at the remote El Cabíto, a hotel and restaurant located literally on a rock in the sea at the very far end of the last of muddy roads. Driving there on a motorcycle was an adventure in itself, especially at night. I had rented a bike directly from the gang providing motorbike taxi service in the village. I got a good price but there was of course no insurance included and before I was able to return the bike for good, I was more or less forced to pay for the replacement of the blink lights which had sustained minor injury as a consequence of my losing control of the vehicle in the dead of night on a steep uphill at zero speed. It would have been a piece of cake to glue the flexible rubber extension together that was upholding the blink lights on both sides. But the gang insisted they had to be replaced with brand new pieces. Luckily these weren't too expensive, and so I finally paid up in order to have my peace of mind.

The incident itself occurred as I was on my way home after having spent an entire evening in Little Germany. The bar-hotel-restaurant is actually owned and run by a Dominican woman, but she's currently married to Mark, a German who grew up in Argentina and never since felt quite at home in his native country. When I turned up there he was drinking beer with Wolfgang, another inveterate German expat living in Galéras for the last 17 years and eerily reminiscent, both physically and by virtue of his somewhat brusque and anarchic manners, of a Swedish friend of mine.

There is a central crossing in town where all the local motorbike taxi drivers hang out. This corner is also like a Europe in miniature where you can walk over from Germany to France and from there to Italy in a matter of seconds. Restaurant *El Tainos* on the opposite side of 'Little Germany' is a stronghold for the French enclave to Galéras. It goes without saying that their restaurant, headed by a female *cordon-bleu* chef from Paris's 1st arrondissement, is the best in town.

The owner, who used to run a brothel in Spain before he left Europe for new horizons, is originally from Toulouse. Small wonder that this is where I ended up having my dinners while in the village. Diagonally across the street from them is 'Little Italy' located, an Italian owned espresso and sandwich bar crowded with local *mafiosi*. It would be no exaggeration to say that these three places, clustered around a single road crossing, with almost uncanny accuracy represent three major European nations and their idiosyncrasies. Even though they sometimes pretend to be on friendly terms with one another, mutual animosity can be stirred up by the slightest provocation. At the end of the day the reason they just barely get along with one another seems to be that buildings can't move.

In socially hermetic environments like this, reciprocal calumny is often rampant and incriminating news spreads faster than the jungle drum can beat. This particular evening I was listening in on the gossip from the German sector, the street acting as a trench between it and the French camp. Apparently neither of the two gentlemen involved in the conversation would ever contemplate going over to the French side, not even for a drink on Christmas Eve. Perhaps they were under some kind of banishment too, because the French chef, albeit very competent in her field of expertise, is capricious and sometimes known, for what seems to be no good reason, to tell people that they are no longer welcome in her establishment. But this I didn't know as yet. For the time being I was content ordering one drink after the other while occasionally throwing some fire on the conversation.

I began asking if there was by any chance a house in the village that I could rent for a couple of months — it had crossed my mind that hanging in Galéras might be a good way to dodge another winter of discontent. Whereby Wolfgang said he had another house on his property. With hindsight I no doubt would have been better off accepting his offer. But the next day, as I inspected the house he had for rent, I felt that to live there would be like staying in a prison because of the high walls surrounding the buildings at close distance. Also the mattresses were not very inviting. He had been ready to accept my offer of $600 a month, and I guess the place was roughly worth it, not the least considering its proximity to the beach. The next day, however, as I came looking for Wolfgang, Mark intercepted me. He told me not to jump at the deal before I had at least checked out with some other people in the village what they had to offer in terms of housing. This is how I ended up meeting Jean, a Belgian real estate broker, who led me to the house I eventually came to rent.

It belongs to an American lady, he told me, and he himself was the one who had actually designed it for her. Alone its location was spectacular, even a bit spooky. The house was erected on a single block of lava that must have been a submarine reef during the latest glaciation. It had a mysterious cave too. The house, perched on top of the rock, and shaded by high trees, the roots of which crept like giant fingers over the reef, looked really big from the outside, but that was because it had to be built in so many stories to accommodate itself to the towering mountain below it. A lot of the building was in reality just supportive structure and inhabitable space.

The liveable portion of the house consisted of one very tall but not enormously large room joined to an open kitchen, annexed to the former. The salon's centre piece was a low sofa-bed; apart from that there was no other furniture except two wooden barstools next to the kitchen counter. But the room opened up through two grand doors to a spacious terrace, which was simultaneously a dining room and a deck for relaxing in the hammock during the heat of the day. The view from here included two private homes, as well as a vast, adjacent tropical garden — magic to watch when the Moon was up shedding its liquid silver on the leaves of the banana trees. Beyond it all there were other buildings nestled in colourful and luxurious vegetation. All this could be seen day and night since there were large windows, like so many grand facets, all around the living room.

Next to the terrace was an outdoor space housing the barbecue, where also the wooden recliner could be installed and padded for optimal stargazing and optional wine drinking. There were footpaths meandering around the house made from flat stones; all kinds of shells decorated the alcoves and there were one or two indigenous sculptures in the garden. The low bipartite wooden gate was at some distance from the house itself, and in order to reach the entrance door one had to negotiate another stone laid footpath while being very careful not to miss a step, since the rocks were not only deep below in the dark but razor sharp as well. Apart from the big terrace there were a number of smaller balconies, enabling the occupier to move around the building in constant pursuit of the best angle in relation to time of day and personal mood. From the living room, right behind the sofa/day-bed, a straight staircase led up to the second floor and the bedroom. It contained a queen bed under an oblique wooden ceiling, a fan and a mosquito tent, and on ground level some shelves, straw boxes and wardrobes for storage of personal items. Adjacent there was a nicely tiled bathroom. When I first came in there all of the landlady's toiletries were still there, as though she had just left the house to go for a stroll and never came back. Sure enough, Jean explained to me that she had actually left her house quite abruptly and hastily some months ago, and that this was the first time she wanted to rent it out in her absence.

Some things inside were overdone, such as the amateur wall frescoes featuring palm trees and parrots. There was an odd mixture of wannabe hippies and Martha Stewart's country lodge in the way she had decorated and set up the place in general, the crowning symbol being a framed photo of a red-dotted Indian woman in white sari on guru-like display for inner peace on the book shelf above the bed. The books laying around in various locations were invariably of the kind which only highly middle-aged women with spiritual inclinations can take an interest in, and that I can't even remember the titles of.

The kitchen was functional and though it wasn't very large, it too had a very high ceiling. The utensils turned out to be adequate, even though there was, as always, not one sharp knife in the wooden block. Plates, cutlery and glasses were nice enough as well. Still, one could feel that in spite of the serious efforts made to turn this into a personal and charming abode, there was something indelibly sombre and joyless about the place, as though abandonment had been writ large in invisible ink on the walls. I couldn't really put my finger on it. It was just a hunch. Nothing more. But one that made me hesitate for a while as to whether this really was a place to actually enjoy the coming two months. Then it was the price. Jean had said he would suggest $900 per month all charges included to her, but it turned out, when I finally got back to him over the Internet from Fort Lauderdale some weeks later, that she wanted $1000. I reasoned with myself, realising that even though a thousand was quite a bit over budget, I'd probably spend considerably more per day travelling around, taking new hotels from one day to the other. And even though I really felt that there was something occult, even sinister, about this place, I accepted the offer.

Perhaps I should have listened to that inner voice that tried to persuade me to take another route? I don't know. But the fact is that while still in Fort Lauderdale, I frequently had dreams set in a strange and bizarre jungle environment. One dream in particular struck me as ominous. I dreamed that I was attacked by a snake that leapt from the ground and stung my forehead. I ran around in an unknown town trying to convince people that I needed to be taken to a hospital immediately, otherwise I would die. But nobody seemed to have the time to listen to me. I guess it was from the sheer lack of interest showed on their part that I decided to wake up and put an end to my misery.

This dream visited me after I had returned to Southern Florida from the Dominican Republic to have my violin repaired. At that time I hadn't as yet decided if I were going to go back to Hispaniola for the winter. Neither the Dominicans nor the expats in Galéras had impressed me to the point of actually making me feel welcome there. My main reason for wanting to return was actually that haunting, dreamlike character of the place.

During my second guest visit to Galéras I had deliberately sought out and stayed in the secluded environment of El Cabíto, a bar-restaurant with only two rooms to rent on the edge of the world. The small complex, located too far away from the village to comfortably be reached by foot, is accessible with a vehicle. A regular car, though, wouldn't suffice. Portions of the road consists of hills, indeed stripped of vegetation but full of stones and meandering roots taking every chance they get to rip off the muffler. A four wheel drive would seem a minimum requirement, but with some skill it was also possible to get there on a motorbike. As mentioned above, I rented such from the bike taxi gang hanging out at the most strategic street corner of the village main street. At face value the rent was surprisingly reasonable. But then again, there was no insurance included. Considering that it required some skill to run a bike up to Cabito, especially at night, this was to take a gamble. When sober, in daylight and spared the pools created by recent heavy downpours (and it does rain in Galéras, sometimes a lot and, in particular, all year round), I found myself being on top of the situation. However, there was also the midnight road home after a generous round of cocktails and a no less generously sprinkled dinner at the Frenchies' place.

I'm sure I could — and should! — have made it on this occasion too, if only I had kept my head cool enough when the bike stopped in the middle of the worst uphill under a sky so clear that it seemed to rub its countless stars like bundles of glistening grapes in my face. Then the wilderness took over, the sounds of the dense tropical forest leaping to my throat as the mechanical noise subsided. In a matter of seconds I was thrown back to the primordial darkness whence the world was created, and into which it plunges back every night for its regeneration, more often than not hiding every trace of its victims, the majority of whom was not even known to the world when alive. Although it would be a considerable exaggeration to say that I feared for my life, I did feel the need to get that darn' thing working again (it was tricky enough to start and accelerate the 'thing' even in broad daylight, the clutch being oversensitive: letting go of it only a fraction too fast would stop the bike dead in its tracks, whereas letting go of it a fraction too slowly would result in the engine spinning more revs while releasing even more noxious fumes.)

The bike wouldn't restart no matter how hard I tried. Normally I would have understood a bit faster that the angle at which the bike was poised was too steep to allow for a new kick start. Even in these circumstances I did understand — it just took me slightly longer — this to be the case. But instead of letting the bike gently roll straight backwards, notch by notch, I tried to manoeuvre it. I think I even tried to turn it around. The consequence, of course, was that the bike fell out of my hands while I, luckily, managed to let go of it without inflicting any physical damage on myself. The bike was essentially fine too. Only the rubber arms holding the blink lights back had suffered some minor damage, and a plastic glass cover would have to be glued and put back into place. I didn't find the lost blink light glass that same evening but the day after when I passed the same spot on my way to the village. At less than half the distance I ran across one of the bike taxi guys going in the opposite direction with some load. Ever anxious to find a reason to squeeze more money out of a tourist, it took him about three seconds to detect the damage through his rear mirror, and to come after me in order to inspect the vehicle. I now knew the jungle drum was on, and that they were going to cause me grievances because of this. Sure enough, as I returned the bike after the five days' rental period was up, they presented me with two brand new parts for which they expected me to pay in full. It was clear that the rubber arm could have been glued together without even leaving a trace and the glass as well. But they wanted money, and the hunt for money in Galéras, because there is only so much to be had, is unabashed and crude to the bone.

It was a relief to me that the parts turned out to be inexpensive, so that I could finally get these guys off my back. But it did confirm my longstanding, and well founded), suspicion that renting any kind of mechanical equipment in Third World countries can be quite wonderful as long as absolutely nothing happens to them. When misfortune strikes, however, things can get really nasty, not the least because of the irrationality and overt corruption of the legal system presiding over any issue involving financial liability. So even though it's quite true that the only thing you risk by drinking and speeding in a Third World country is to kill somebody, including yourself, things might get really out of hand if you do run someone over, and even stay to assess the damage.

I remember that my friends in La Côte d'Ivoire, many years ago when I was regularly playing and partying there, used to tell me, before they lent me a car, not ever to stop my car alongside the road if I thought I had hit upon something. Although it may be a genuine accident, chances were, especially in rural areas, that the dead child found in the ditch hadn't been killed by you, but had been placed there, already a corpse, by family members as a means of extorting money by threats from tourists, unable to foresee and effectively counteract such elaborate scam. Also, once you've stopped, you're on their turf, and they might find ways to coerce you into cooperation, if nothing worse.

Speaking of so-called Third World countries (as opposed to Second and First), I have made some observations over the years that I would like to present as a list of informal, yet salient, criteria of 'Third Worldliness'. The list in itself is symbolic rather than exhaustive, and although there are a lot of charming absurdities that only apply to one or a few so-called developing countries, I have decided to stick to generalities, that is: traits that everywhere would indicate typical 'Third World' conditions. Although my selection of distinguishing features is subjective, perhaps even idiosyncratic, it's my hope that the reader who has travelled in this type of *developing* environments will recognise these definitions with a sardonic grin of satisfaction.

You are in a Third World country *if*:

- If everything in and of the state is basically and profoundly corrupt (which naturally prompts the question if there is any political state in the world that is *not* corrupt and thus Third World?).
- If nothing really works but there is always 'a way'.
- If you have to pay the authorities when entering or leaving the country. If you have to do both you're actually in a Fourth World country!
- If the price of taxis are either totally negotiable or strictly determined by government regulations — amounting to the same.
- If there's always a taxi and a willing driver to be found.
- If there are no ways of proving whether you've been drinking and/or speeding behind the wheel.
- If the government doesn't care whether you've been drinking and/or speeding.
- If road patrols routinely consist of heavily armed military.
- If general traffic rules and regulations are mainly interpreted by the public as recommendations that one does best not to follow, and the only rule that applies for real is the 'one way street', although one has

to know this beforehand since there will nowhere be a sign to warn you against driving towards oncoming traffic.

- If the paint on the bathroom walls have been allowed to stain the shower tiles as well. In this particular respect, Italy, Spain and France would easily qualify as 'Third World countries'. The Greeks and the peoples of the Balkan countries, on the other hand, don't do this. I guess they admire the Germans and have to some degree been influenced by them.
- If painting the doors also on the inside is considered an unnecessary expense.
- If rebars are still sticking up through the concrete in building constructions generally considered 'finished'.
- If electric fixtures look like a nest of vipers and in effect is just as dangerous to touch (here again Italy, Spain and France are earnest candidates).
- If you have to get up from bed to turn the light off in the room.
- If the Internet only sometimes works, or works badly, and there is absolutely no explanation as to why, let alone a possibility to have the connection re-established, the bottom line invariably being: 'Use the Internet while you can!'
- If the shower only sometimes works properly.
- If the shower has only cold *or* only hot water (this actually sometimes happen!).
- If it's very difficult to turn the shower on and/or off.
- If the trickle from the shower is feebler than your own stream.
- If the torrent of cold water from the 2 inch wide shower pipe rather makes you believe you're standing in the midst of the Niagara Falls.

- If there are frequent water cuts for no apparent reason and without previous warning (such interruptions can in fact go on for weeks).
- If the water closet gets stuck because of cotton ball thrown in it (you'd be very happy to see waste alone disappear when flushed, since it's never to be taken for granted that it will).
- If there are frequent power cuts unprovoked by natural disaster, and rather provoked by political leaders not making sure that the country's energy bills are paid on time.
- If the ATM machine doesn't accept your credit card, informing you that the problem lies with *your* bank.
- If the ATM machine credits your card without giving you the money (see account on page 72).
- If making a credit card transaction (for example buying an airline ticket) online is nearly always refused and you never will receive an explanation as to why.
- If VISA, Mastercard or American Express are not accepted as means of payment in major food and department stores (as is the case in Germany).
- If it takes the car rental company two weeks to waive the security deposit on your bank account and meanwhile sold your credit information to a third party.
- If tipping is appreciated by taxis, in hotels, restaurants and bars, but not really expected.
- If people smile and are nice to you for no reason.
- If everybody around you calls you 'my friend' ('my brother', qualifies as well).
- If inequality between human beings is taken for granted.

- If equality between human beings is taken for granted but largely remains a concept waiting for a content.
- If nobody, except a bunch of university students demonstrating in the capital, has ever heard of 'human rights' but everybody knows the word 'respect'.
- If people around you seize any pretext to produce noise (again France, Italy and Spain are given candidates).
- If there are scooters and motorbikes everywhere, at all times.
- If people attend religious services other than those associated with weddings, funerals and baptisms.
- If people dress up in traditional attire year round.
- If the bank is either closed or overfilled with people patiently — waiting.
- If the banks and companies don't even bother to invent pretexts for stealing your money.
- If you can pay yourself out of nearly every problem.
- If there are cheap and good shoe shiners.
- If the bar 'bouncers' rather try to throw you into the bar than out of it.
- If waiters are actually nice and doing their job without dragging their guests into it.
- If, as a rule, the paved roads are full of holes.
- If you hesitate to brush your teeth with tap water.
- If bureaucracy is as complicated as bribing is easy.
- If you start to grow patient with everything that doesn't work and can't be fixed.
- If there's always *another* way of doing it.

- If the idea of having a thirty years younger girlfriend starts to appear both reasonable and advisable to you.
- If prostitution *both* quickens and saddens your heart.
- If you find yourself brooding about what 'all this would have cost back home'.
- If availing yourself of a gun for self-defence at times seem like a reasonable idea (I'm here primarily addressing a non-American reader, as an American one is likely to take such need for granted).

Which brings us right back to the story. As I said, I was at the point of leaving Galéras behind once and for all. Staying at El Cabíto had given me all that I could possibly ask for: a glance into the wilderness from a platform suspended above the ocean, simultaneously providing food, drink and shelter. John, the sympathetic Dutchman and owner, whom I subsequently came to meet with, was at this time still in Europe with his wife and daughters. He had constructed this oasis by instinct, thinking little about how to eventually turn it around financially — just to build a road to get here must have been quite an undertaking. At present the hotel was run by two trusted native employees: Manuel (amiably gay and quite accomplished as a chef) and young Maritza (my guess: 25 years old) and cute enough to know next to nothing about almost everything. Surprisingly she was studying French in some of her spare time, which seemed to be just about all her time. Besides being cute she also gave me a discount, even knocked off a whole day's rent when I insisted there had been no water in the shower during daytime for three days straight, and no electricity after midnight on any given day. The absence of electric light was mostly a problem on the one dramatic occasion (mentioned above) when I returned home late, and when I had to try to find my way to the bathroom in the middle of the night via slippery stairs.

The basement of my modest bungalow was uninspiring, with moist concrete hanging off the walls and a bathroom providing no more than bare necessities. The bedroom tucked in under the roof on the second floor, although it too was a basic amenity, was a different story. It was part of the attic of the house, and only had room for a double bed with a mosquito net around it, and a chair to sit in. The gable facing the sea consisted of a wooden railing. Sitting in the chair, or even laying in the bed, I had a panoramic view of the Bahía de Galéras, quite especially of the distant and mystic looking Cabo Cabrón. I believe it was under its influence that the land and sea began to also haunt my dreams, as the hours went by and the sun set. To my relief, there were no mosquitos: gone with the wind.

El Cabíto is precisely what the name implies: a small cape and the last outpost of civilisation before one would reach, on hard to find paths, the major Cape defining the eastern limits of the bay, and the legendary Playa Fronton, located just beneath it. One of the attractions of the Cabíto is the air columns which the ocean swiftly presses up 15–20 metres through narrow shafts in the marine basalt caves. The sound of this lends association to some kind of sea monster, rapidly exhaling, and it chills the blood of the visitor at first. Another major attraction is the spray of water produced by the waves as they hit the rocks 15 metres below the wooden deck housing the bar-restaurant. Sometimes, when the winds turn and come heavily in from due north, the restaurant service becomes inoperable as the swell breaks up in rainbow coloured cascades hitting the rock on which the outdoor patio-restaurant has been poised.

Even closer to the water is a small terrace, carved out of the very living rock, with a long wooden table and a couple of chairs. To sit there and just watch the fury of the elements is a treat in itself. If the sky is clear, not only do the sun's dying rays turn the caves and the rugged coastline into a tapestry in the Mountain King's abode, but the arrival of the planets, the zodiac and the Moon is a spectacular royal procession carried out under the canopy of the Milky Way. I was lucky to own this place for five days. I was the only permanent guest, with the exception of a solo-traveling New Zealander, but he was camping out on the El Cabíto grounds, so I didn't see much of him. Other guests only came by to eat or have drinks.

As for myself, I spent most of my time watching the hours go by in the form of ever changing clouds and their hues. Sometimes I would write for hours on end while the sun hammered the thatched roof, undisturbed by a staff that seemed to have gone underground. I knew the cleaning lady was somewhere around, by all means very discreetly so. As evening approached I retired to my quarters, took a shower, poured a drink and sat in my chair, observing Day and Night change watches: eternal monotony, yet always in a new key and variation. Slowly the forest green faded, the rock turned pink, violet and finally went through all shades of grey, before it immersed itself in total darkness. Soon the land was no more than one silhouette against another — the sea — and a third, which was heaven.

I then solemnly walked the slippery path down to the restaurant surrounded by the sounds of the jungle, the leaves rustling in an inexhaustible trade wind. The idea imposed itself, that I really must have done something right in my life to witness this. I was mostly alone on the deck even at night, since the few other dinner guests would soon empty their cups and retire to the anonymity whence they had emerged. That set the stage for me. I'd bring a glass with me to the lower terrace, lean a chair against the rock and stretch my legs across the table. I'd then gaze into the immensity of my own mind slowly turning into a mirror — of the universe.

There have been moments when I asked myself if my main motivation for travelling is to get away from or finding myself? I now believe it's neither. Travelling seems to me no purpose in itself. It may be that in the end I'm trying to repeat the trick of Sisyphus, who locked up Death himself in a cellar when he came to get him, and then ran away.

Needless to add that the gods finally found out about Sisyphus' ruse. They got hold of him and condemned him in no uncertain terms. Ever since he eternally pushes a stone up a mountain each and every day, only to see it roll back down into the valley in the evening.

But we're all like Sisyphus, really, eager to confer some kind of meaning, no matter how ephemeral, on our daily activities. We don't have much choice to act differently, since a life without some kind of goal is either a total detachment from human existence as such, or a barren desert to traverse without the hope of even reaching the opposite shore. Travelling is also, for the one who tries to gain something from his experiences and encounters, a great academy of life. It makes us naturally tolerant while challenging our convictions and inherited prejudice. By this I don't necessarily mean that the prejudice is always exactly identical to what modern civilisation defines as such. The person convinced, for example, that any issue concerning race and origin is but a social construct, and that everybody in this world would reason along the same lines as 'we' do if he'd only be given a decent chance to do so, might in fact be in for a big surprise.

For instance, I remember discussing the idea that God resides within Man himself, and only there, with a Dominican musician in the country's capital. He listened attentively to what I had to say and then gave me some advice: 'When you travel our country', he said, 'try to keep a low profile, because you're thinking in ways that are alien to us; your opinions, if expressed in the wrong company, might get you into trouble.' By this I don't think he meant primarily that God would punish me for my heresy. Some other person might get quite upset though, to the point of actually wanting to physically hurt me. I understood he was right, and that my libertarian discourse in this devoutly Catholic society had all the accoutrements of blasphemy. In other words, what might have appeared an interesting neo-Gnostic concept in a largely atheist, and philosophically trained, European society, here would seem an outrage, not to say an attack on the fundamentals of life itself.

To this man, his marriage was a covenant concluded before God, with the Virgin Mary protecting his children from evil.

But the whole issue of whether man was god or god was man faded into insignificance in the light of the spectacle about to unfold. Clearly discernible by the naked eye from planet Earth on a clear night are about 4000 stars in the so-called Orion arm of our galaxy, in itself consisting of an estimated number of 200 billion individual stars. The Orion arm, thus named because it contains the major stellar constellation of Orion, is one of the branches of the spiral galaxy that is our Milky Way. The centre of the galaxy, located beyond the zodiacal constellation of Sagittarius, can only be 'seen' through radio telescopes (or other telescopes capable of registering wavelengths outside those of visible light), because it's hidden behind thick clouds of star forming gas. What we can see, unaided by lenses and mirrors, is but a fragment. But what a fragment! Above a sea in uproar, to the accompaniment of a heavily exhaling sea-monster, stars, thousands of them, covered the sky from east to west. Their background, a nebulous veil, was wrapped like a turban around the head of heaven. Awestruck I felt these stars to be my true home, the 'place' in which my soul and spirit really belongs, perhaps even the place from which I came, aeons ago, and to which, my terrestrial chores accomplished, I shall once return.

It may sound presumptuous on my part to claim celestial origin. But I intend no presumption, I only see in the stars a reflection of my innermost longing and feel, in their presence, an immense relief, as though my entire being were swinging and tuning in harmony with the immense distances separating us — from them. I know man as a physical being can't survive out there. The human spirit, however, there finds its one and true element. That's all I want and all I need to say in regard to this mystery, by all conceivable standards, the profoundest of them all.

On this lofty note I should perhaps have left Galéras, in this way keeping a rather favourable opinion of its various attractions. But I came back, just a few weeks later, to take up residency in the house I had meanwhile rented (see description above). The first days I spent most of my time stretched out on the large recliner reading. The doors to the terrace were swung open to let in the breeze from the nearby sea — from the small balcony outside the bedroom I had a pretty good view of it above the treetops.

Jean, from the rental agency, had been there to inspect the house and sent his Haitian crew over to do some repair work on the thatched roof. They had also wiped out most of the wasp nests under the beams around the house. However, some of these nests remained and there were still living wasps in them. I decided to take personal control of the situation and on the next day bought a spray can full of insect poison at the local *mercado*. With this I began my own improvised wasp holocaust. I was pretty sure I had killed them all, but one of the wasps, mighty pissed off with what I was doing, was still hiding behind a beam. As I prepared to withdraw into the safety of the bed room, believing I'd finished them off, he decided he was not going to go down without making me remembering them all forever. 'Here's for everything you've made to my friends and family!' he buzzed frantically and charged at full speed, from a distance of three metres, right onto my forehead. The sting itself was one thing. But I know, from experience, that I have but one conspicuous allergy, and that is the one against wasp venom (In Nicaragua I was once bitten thrice by a scorpion, but that didn't affect me in the least). Some hours went by, but by then half of my face was so swollen and disfigured that I could not have shown myself in public without frightening people. It was like a slimy balloon in which my eye had become completely invisible, only betraying its existence by the quantities of pus expulsed from the socket itself, trickling down my inflated cheek like the sticky juice from some overripe plum violently squeezed open.

That evening (I was stung on a Friday afternoon) and the following day I decided to stay home, licking my wounds. By Sunday evening, however, the swelling had gone down sufficiently to at least make me reasonably presentable to the public under the guise of sunglasses, so I went to the French at *Les Tainos* restaurant to have dinner. I sat at the bar and talked to several people, none of whom seemed to react to my wearing sunglasses in the middle of the night. I was now definitely over the worst part of this dreadful experience, and I decided to put a calm end to this dramatic weekend by retiring to my quarters and have a last glass of wine under the stars. Back home I lay down in the sun chair and watched the Moon as she slowly emerged from behind a cloud. It was a tranquil evening. My neighbours had gone to bed. The Moon shone on their gardens and on the never finished mansion, still in bare concrete, situated behind the wall behind my head. I had taken pains, before I rented the house, to ask Jean if the construction work next door was in any way going to be resumed in the near future. He assured me it was not. For now it was just another ghost building abandoned in mid-construction because its owner, most likely, had run out of money. I looked up towards the adjacent coral rock and cave towering in moonlight at the back of my own property. This was the only direction from which the unexpected might be expected, since at the end of the other slope of this intensely sharp rock there were no neighbouring villas, nor a wall or barbed wire preventing intruders from gaining access, just a vague terrain overgrown with thicket. On the other side of this dense greenery there were a road and some buildings, because I had previously heard the same local voices making their ways through the jungle at daytime, although I had never been able to see anybody.

But I wasn't going to be overly worried about that. I closed up my house by carefully checking all doorways while also making sure the divided iron lattice before the French terrace doors was secured by its middle with no less than two sturdy locking devices. I then went to bed. Although there was indeed a large fan above the bed, I felt that having the sea breeze bring in the scent of moonlit tropical gardens and salty mermaids would make a perfect accompaniment to my sleep. So I went over, opened the door to the miniscule balcony, situated slightly above the slanted thatched roof over the terrace, and left it ajar. The natural fan produced proved to be just perfect and I fell soundly asleep.

It might have been two hours later, I'm not exactly sure. But from what I felt to have been deep sleep, I woke up discovering two silent, human-like, silhouettes standing next to my bed on the other side of the mosquito tent. I didn't have much time to think, but it was enough for me to realise that these two figures were hardly the two mermaids I had conversed with at the French bar, nor some friends of longer standing. I don't know either what the plan behind my sudden move could have been, but I think it's an almost instinctive reaction on my part, for example, to try to get personally and physically out of a car that has been stopped for inspection at a border control.

Now this was some kind of border, and an insurmountable one at that. I just stood up, and in the very next moment I towered right before the two burglars, trying perhaps, to get past them, or even hoping that they would be sufficiently scared and leave. I might actually have scared, or at least surprised them, because out of the darkness something hard and heavy hit my head several times in rapid succession. I'm not sure how the light came on after that, but it did. At this point I just stood there, like some defenceless animal in for slaughter, with blood streaming all over me, the iron taste of it in my mouth, trying to quickly determine how badly hurt I had been so far. The only wound I was aware of at this time — since I traced its fleshy furrow with a finger — was a deep cut across my forehead. Perhaps I was surprised to still be conscious; indeed, to be alive. I had the feeling that my wounds were not actually life threatening, at least not yet. But I was bleeding profusely, and the thug who had been handling the machete now also put a knife to my throat, while still holding on to the machete with the other hand, motioning me towards the staircase leading down to the living room. I didn't put up any further resistance. As an answer, he weasel-like moved in right in front of me. He had very shiny, unpleasant looking eyes, but his speech was, if not sweet, at least short and to the dagger point. He hissed: '*Dineeeroo!*' I indeed noticed that he wasn't shouting at me, rather coarsely whispering. This was also the first time I got the feeling that he too was a bit scared. But his colleague, bigger, darker and dressed in camouflage, didn't seem to be moved by the circumstances in the least. Throughout the entire encounter this was the thing that intrigued me the most: how could he be so sure that I would be unable to inflict any damage on them? It was almost an insult, the way he calmly moved around, turning his back at me, even crawling on the floor with his big butt turned in my direction for long periods of time, looking for my money.

Still today I don't know if he did this because he knew he could kill me in the blink of an eye or if he was plainly stupid. I wish I would have had the guts to prove myself right in my suspicion, but then again, there were two of them, and as soon as I'd turn to either of them, the other would have come after me. And I was still bleeding. Heavily. They had wanted to tie me up with a rope, but I got them out of the idea by actually leading them straight to my money. It was hidden in such a special place that they must have realised immediately that this was it. I had placed my wallet in the middle of a small folding ladder.

To my astonishment the camouflaged man didn't just take the purse and then inform his colleague that the mission was completed. He used a knife or a screwdriver to try to bend open the entire plastic pocket underneath to try to find more. But there was nothing there. I knew it, but I didn't want to see the result of their disappointment. The moment had come. I wouldn't fight them, although I would have loved to give that big, fat, black ass crawling on all fours on my floor a jolly good kick. Let me be as close to honest as I possibly can: the reason I didn't do it is because, I think, I was afraid of what harm they still might be able to inflict on me. Because this is also when I had my chance — to escape. Suddenly — and for once that dreaded word inimical to all literature is entirely appropriate — *suddenly*, I discovered that by blocking my exit through the kitchen door — remember I still have a knife and a machete pointing at me — while the other guy was searching for my money, they had both left the steep staircase leading back up to the bedroom unguarded. So I just took a tiger leap (or two) up these stairs, then ran like a stampeding wildebeest through the bedroom out on the balcony. Once there I turned into a monkey and allowed myself to slide down the thatched roof, only to land, barefoot, as a human, on the sharp coral rock underneath.

In retrospect, the pain of my feet were worse than that of my head, but this leap had set me free. For the first time I unleashed the remaining power of my lungs, while my heart was beating its way up my throat: '*Ladrones! Ladrones!*' (for some reason I know I only shouted this word twice). At the same time I continued running on my mutilated feet, with my face, body, white shirt and trousers entirely covered in blood. I knew there were plenty of neighbours around, but I wasn't too sure they would respond to my distress. Once I was outside the gates of the property I knew that the burglars would not risk coming after me. I guess that at this time they were quickly packing up and preparing to disappear. Although I had probably lost quite a substantial amount of blood, I felt pretty sure I hadn't been mortally wounded since I could still walk, even run without losing consciousness. Nonetheless, I had to get all the way down to the central crossing in the village, a good 500 metres from my home, before I finally met another living soul, and that alone must have been a sight like something out of a third-rate horror movie: a ghost in white clothes drenched in blood, staggering down the dirt road in search of someone to scare.

At first I tried to get into the hotel where an Englishman of my recent acquaintance was staying. But although I was pretty sure I could find his room, I was stalled in my attempt by the bloodhound on guard on the premises. I could hear him come after me through the corridor, and I quickly retired, closing the otherwise open door of the hotel behind me. As I re-entered the street, I saw, to my relief, two young cops on a motorbike coming down the Samaná road. They saw me too but, rather surprisingly, didn't seem to take much interest in my appearance. I had to approach and describe to them where my house was located, and limped after them as they set off in its general direction on their bike. As I came closer, still limping on sore feet, I met them on their return. They claimed they couldn't find the house. I pointed it out to them, but although they now went to its gate, they never dared to enter the property, let alone the house itself. I shouted to them that the thieves only had knives and machetes (they on the other hand were equipped with handguns), but they still refused to make the effort to search the house. They were just standing there, dumbfounded as it appeared to me then. At this point people started to appear around me, notably a Belgian couple running a guesthouse across from my home.

The forces of civilisation thereafter began to mobilise. It was, I guess, around two o'clock in the morning when the female village doctor arrived. I was sitting in a patio chair, attended to by the Belgian couple, patiently awaiting her verdict. She took my blood pressure, inspected my wounds, and then determined I was in a general condition stable enough to permit an operation on the spot. She brought out her equipment and began to stitch me up. It turned out I had several more wounds than I was aware of. In the end I believe she had to make some 60 stitches to five different cuts in my head. She didn't have to shave my crane though, and she must have made an amazing job, since all the wounds are now perfectly healed, and the scar conspicuously running obliquely across the right side of my forehead is only to be detected at a certain angle, with the light coming in from the right direction. Three hours later, the operation was over and I was sent to wash off in the shower. I was given some dry clothes and a clean bed to sleep in. Before I was left to recover in the small bungalow, she again read my blood pressure, confirming that it was ever so slightly above normal, but, considering the circumstances, this was, in her opinion, perhaps not so strange. She also insisted I must keep ingesting a pretty awful tasting cocktail containing what one would normally receive intravenously. She then gave me a sedative in the butt and I dozed off, not too unhappy with the night's events. After all, I was going to survive this unfortunate encounter with people who couldn't care less if, at this point, I was dead or alive.

    The next day I was awakened by the arrival of the police who began to ask their usual questions. After having made some notes, hopefully pertaining to my answers, they left. I had decided that I was in no mood to move back home. Jean arrived, confirming that the place had literally been a bloody mess; it had taken the cleaning lady several hours to finish up after me. Strangely he was also able to confirm that neither my violin, nor my computer had been stolen. This was undoubtedly good news, and it confirmed my suspicion that if I wouldn't have escaped, and they would have instead tied me up against the iron lattice, they would undoubtedly also have taken everything of value they could possibly carry. It's possible the violin represented nothing of value to them: if only they'd known that — given the right time, customer and place — they might have got 6,000 dollars for it! Instead they almost killed me over a mere 100 bucks, a bunch of credit cards they were unable to use and a camera, which, as I discovered later, they had thrown onto the coral reef while hastily retreating from the crime scene. It wasn't even broken; as a matter of fact, until quite recently I was still using it.

    There followed a week in which I was interviewed by local police and even taken to identify an individual apprehended. He was taken out of the local arrest and paraded in manacles in front of the building. Another woman, robbed in her home too, had been asked to join me in the effort. But we both had to conclude it wasn't the one, and without further ado the guy was accompanied back to the arrest.

I stayed in the Belgian guest house for almost a week recovering from my wounds. Once my head had been stitched up it was my feet that hurt the most. The flesh had been torn off its undersides, quite especially the sensitive middle area between heel and toe. To walk was a bit like I imagine was the case for the mermaid in H.C. Andersen's tale. She had been granted the parting of her tail at the cost of feeling each step as cuts of knives through her legs. As a rule I managed to make it to the nearby bars in the evening and after a couple of drinks I would forget most of my handicap.

I had lost all of my credit cards along with the cash, but Mr. Toulouse kindly let me run a tab at his establishment until I got hold of some money. This I managed to do by transferring funds directly from my bank account into Jean's bank in Brussels. The reason again I could do that was that the thieves had not stolen the small electronic device by which I could access my Internet bank and my personal account. Once he had received the money into his account he was able, in principle, to give me the equivalent in local currency, or dollars, but he nevertheless had to drive down to Samaná to get the cash, and that didn't happen until several days later.

Meanwhile I was stuck with the Belgian couple. It was one still holding together because of the husband's consistently repeated 'Yes Dear'. He was under her thumb and I believe his greatest happiness consisted in being able to go off for a swim in the ocean every day. I guess he was *gentil* as the French say, but he was also *con*, as they might add — a devastating qualifier. That he was also Belgian wouldn't have made him any more endearing in their eyes, and I shall refrain from speculating further on his character.

She on the other hand was obnoxious. She had an ocular malfunction that made her eyes stare at a 45 degree angle apart from one another. This trait became particularly annoying when she tried to focus and scrutinise my eyes, which happened all the time. I tried to stare her in the forehead every time she addressed me to avoid being caught in the dizzying oscillation. On top of this she was bossing me around with relentless 'the Doctor said', pretending to be a nurse, or, still worse: my mother! Although they invited me to partake in their lunch every day, they proved in the last instance to be neither very generous nor understanding. I don't know if he was just too subjugated to even dare to argue against her.

Whatever the case, I from early on suspected I was eventually going to be in for another nasty surprise. I knew their guesthouse to be overpriced for clients coming over by plane from Europe. I was also rightly suspecting that she just might in the end treat me as one, and consequently ask me to pay for my stay on the same conditions. She did. Although well aware of my financial situation, especially in regard to lost credit cards and cash funds, she demanded me to pay 50 Euros a day for the near week I had spent on the premises. I told her this was too much to ask for and after some hustling managed to negotiate slightly better terms. But their pretension of being ever so helpful and caring was irreparably gone. After having laid the money on the table (I had to get an advance from Jean and an impromptu loan from a visiting Dutchman to manage it) I just turned around, thanked them for their initial help, which had been real although almost impossible not to render, and then refused to give them even the benefit of a second glance. I just walked out of there.

Even today I don't have much to add in their defence. Their behaviour was poor. They knew, since I kept telling them so, that I would of course be willing to pay for accommodation, but to ask for 50 Euros a night for a simple hotel room at the back of beyond of the rural Dominican Republic, was downright outrageous. When I told the rest of the European enclave about what had happened, it infuriated them too, and I know Jean almost got into a fist fight with the husband over the issue, which he too apparently considered an outrage. Most French (except one of them, being a friend of the Belgian couple) were appalled (or at least convincingly pretended to be so), and further confirmed in their entrenched anti-Belgian sentiments.

Notwithstanding, I have to admit, that apart from the occasional benevolent gesture, the entire village, whether represented by indigenous elements or foreigners, was ferocious in its pursuit of money. Behind whatever civilised façade there was a crude calculation for survival in terms of money. Not that the people behind bars, shops and restaurants would try to openly cheat you, but they were never quite generous either and would rarely grant you a deal if you suggested one. Even as I passed by an inch from the sword of death and everybody knew I was out of money by an understandable cause, few, except the ones mentioned, stepped in to offer me a drink or some credit. I thus felt the sting and stigma of being poor in an unforgiving world.

As soon as I had left the guesthouse the Belgian woman must have called the female doctor, whom I also owed money for the operation, and alerted her to that I might be about to leave Galéras without paying my medical expenses. How otherwise to explain that as I reached the street corner of Little France, Germany and Italy 300 metres down the road from the Guest House, the *Doctora* herself stood waiting for me there, in this way making sure I wasn't hopping on a bus or taxi without having paid her first. Explaining the situation to her I did manage to also negotiate her invoice, this time with a smile from the understanding woman who knew she might have salted the bill just a bit.

At this point I was nonetheless almost completely out of money again, and still needed to stay two more days in town before I could take a bus to the airport in Puerto Plata, from where I had booked a flight to Dusseldorf by using my German friend Simone's credit card, the details of which she had given me over the phone. Explaining my dilemma to a Frenchman who runs a hotel close to the ominous street corner where all the scooter and motorbike taxis also hang out, I was at first offered a room for free, but he soon changed the terms to 'whatever I could spare', since 'we too are struggling to stay afloat', etc. I can't remember what I finally ended up paying him, but it wasn't exorbitant.

The room was actually very nice. By now, however, my goodwill was clearly running out, and Wolfgang, the German, who was probably sour that I hadn't rented the rickety extra house on his property as my vacation abode, would typically sit at some table drinking beer while shouting to me passing by that: 'Your sunglasses are too small for your fucking big head, Lars!'. Had he backed up such compliments by also buying me a beer, I think I wouldn't have bothered. But he made it clear he wouldn't and I felt that lack of generosity to be an impediment to what might otherwise have been a budding friendship. In the end it was perhaps the German Peter—who together with his indigenous wife (she's the owner) has run the Hotel-Restaurant I refer to as Little Germany for 17 years—who summed up the general attitude of the people of Galéras most succinctly: 'I don't trust anyone and I have no friends except my wife and my dog'. I have no doubt that he meant it, literally.

As my sojourn there was coming to its precipitated end, I was inclined to feel the same way, except I had neither wife nor dog. But I did have the Dutchman Tom, owner of the El Cabíto who would sometimes come down to town in his jeep. Tom must be one of the few remaining true romantics who created his eagle's nest without even thinking about what it should be used for or what the balance sheet was going to look like. He certainly would invite me for beers every time he was in Galéras. But although he really is the nicest guy, he had somehow managed to attract the evil eye of Audrey, the cordon bleu chef of the Tainos restaurant (Little France). She made sure he knew he was no longer welcome in their bar-restaurant since, allegedly, he was 'stealing clients from them'. Tom was completely bewildered by this absurd accusation, but then again there might be another picture here which I, the newcomer, was unaware of. Be that as it may. I hope they have by now found it in their hearts to forgive one another. I quite especially remember when Tom — always fresh looking, with a neatly groomed beard and a stylish long hippie shirt — and I finished off a late evening at a very local bar off the main district. We were standing at the bar having rums and there was absolutely no way we could talk ourselves us out of the fact that a young woman wanted to have us both at the same time. Tom even offered her money to leave us alone. She might have wanted the money too but not without also being used by the two of us. 'It really is quite difficult', I remember Tom musing wistfully, 'when they are so young and beautiful'.

Indeed, human nature is inscrutable, and it was, believe it or not, with some regrets in my heart, that I had my last coffee and Internet session in the French bakery before squeezing myself into the crowded taxi taking me down to Samaná, where the bus to Puerto Plata was waiting. I guess the nostalgia I felt, and still feel, in regard to this rather indescribable place, is that the people there, with all their petty schemes, have something unabashedly real about them, as though the general indifference of this place to Western conventions of morality has rubbed off on Europeans and Canadians too and made them seem more unabashedly egotistical and brutal for sure, but also more genuine and true than many other people in the Western world hiding their naked greed behind corporate or other 'respectable' facades. One last example may serve to round off this account of human eccentricities — my own included.

One day prior to when all the financial commotion described above took place, Jean and I finally made it to town in his four-wheel drive to pick up some money. I thought it might be a good idea to combine this with a visit to the local police station in order for me to get a written report that I in turn could present to the insurance company providing travel insurance via my Visa card. Arriving and staying at the police station in Samaná was yet another quite otherworldly instance. Jean left me on its door step. Since he too had some errands to run we decided to meet an hour later at a beach café.

I was shown into the police headquarters by a policeman dressed in civilian clothes. He had no holster for his gun. Instead he had stuck it inside his pants in such manner that the gun barrel reached all the way from inside the buckle of his belt down to his crotch. Once inside the office — a naked room with huge flakes of peeled off paint and a single light bulb hanging from the ceiling — I was asked to hand over my passport to another policeman behind a computer screen. He threw it over his shoulder into a heap of paper at the far end of the table. Without even noticing where the official travel document landed, he continued typing away on the computer. I found myself a seat although I hadn't been asked to take one. I just waited for something to happen. Not much did. Except that the guy with the Beretta enhancing the relief of his jean showed up a couple of times, whereby the two men entertained loud conversations. Their Spanish was incomprehensible to me. Finally, the one with the gun left the room.

I waited a little more, still amazed by the scene. The remaining policeman resumed his typing, frequently commenting the process aloud to himself. Seeing that I hardly filled any intelligible function in this context, I asked him if there was any idea for me to hang around much longer, since obviously he had not the slightest intention to even ask me what I wanted. He looked over his computer, semi-closing his eyes as though trying in vain to focus on my person, and retorted: 'What did you say you wanted?' I replied that I hadn't so far hardly said anything because nobody had asked me. At this point my reticent interlocutor seemed to understand that the dread wouldn't go away by itself and that he might, in fact, have to do some work. I began to tell him my story which he wrote down in a surprisingly flowery Spanish, speaking of me as being savagely attacked not just when asleep but while *'disfrutando de su sueño'* (enjoying his sleep). On the other hand, the 18k gold chain with its stylised Thor's Hammer — the former bought from a Lebanese jeweller in Abidjan, the latter acquired on a visit to Reykjavik — which the perpetrators had ripped off my neck, in the report turned into some yellow adornment, discarded as an almost irrelevant loss.

The gold of course was and is replaceable, but, truth to tell, this little amulet fused two apparently irreconcilable aspects of my ancestry into one. At first glance it consisted of a cross, the anomaly of which was that it was hanging 'upside-down' when suspended from a chain. The loop was set within the jaws of some hound-like figure giving the token an animistic appearance. It was explained to me that the tripartite cross at the bottom was a Christianised version of the infamous Thor's hammer. This symbolism only appeared in the Norse world toward the end of the 10th century AD, and signifies the transition within the Viking world from the pagan pantheon of Valhalla towards that of Jesus Christ and the Holy Trinity. Considering my own character to be essentially pagan, modified by Christian vices and virtues, I always found that the amulet aptly expressed some of my inner contradictions. Sometimes I would receive criticism for it though. Many people thought it symbolised some cult of Satan. Perhaps not without reason, since a hound made into a cross really is an odd symbol for a God-fearing person to bear.

Along the same line others would say that it is impossible to faithfully serve two masters. These critics therefore discarded me as a hypocrite, if not a traitor. All the same, I was happy to wear it until one day it disappeared and was gone for many years. It turned out that my son's mother had stolen it from me and had held on to it ever since. Why she finally admitted to having it in her possession, I don't know. She claimed I had said she could have it, which I of course vigorously denied. In the end she returned it to me and I put the chain with its unusual symbol around my neck again.

Now, I was never so crazy as to deliberately travel around in Latin American countries with a piece of shining gold hanging around my neck. But the whole thing was not very big and it happened that I forgot to remove it when arriving from Europe. For example, I was very grateful when a bus driver in Santo Domingo pointed out to me, that for a gringo to walk around with solid gold around his neck in the streets simply was to be asking for trouble. I immediately realised he was right and removed it. Why I was again wearing it the ominous night when the two burglars stole into my rental house in Galéras, I can't tell, but that was the moment when that ambiguous symbol, cursed by the evil hands and eyes of my son's mother, was forever taken away, prompting me to find a new stance between Heaven and Hell.

Speaking of which: midway into his report the police officer enthusiastically saluted the arrival of a very young girl. She was about to take a seat when he ran up to her, pulling her out of the chair. When she was standing upright he started to show off her assets to me, turning her back to front and back again while appreciatively commenting on her silky hair, perky tits, protruding buttocks and slender waist. The next natural step would have been to discuss a price, although, or perhaps precisely because, she might be a cousin or even a sister of his. I admitted to be very impressed by her beauty but politely asked him to finish the report before we attended to this next matter, obviously of much more vital interest to both him and her. He grudgingly returned to the computer to complete his writing. He then handed me the signed and stamped document.

At this point I recalled that the police in Samaná, alerted to their existence by a phone call from a bus driver, had arrested two men leaving Galéras in the early morning of the very same night in which I had been attacked. They had been passengers of his bus and for undisclosed reasons aroused the driver's suspicion. These had been quite well founded though. One of these two men on apprehension turned out to be wanted for a total of 18 murders in the Dominican Republic. Suspecting that these two sweethearts just might be identical to the guys who had paid me a surprise visit, I asked if I might see a photo of them. To my astonishment the policeman showed absolutely no interest in the matter and waved me off, letting me understand that my audience was over and that I'd better not outstay my welcome.

I was temporarily taken aback, but even this only for a moment. It dawned on me that the demonstrative reluctance on the police officer's part to do his job could have something to do with the fact that his official salary was meagre. I had not offered to pay anything for him to write me an official report. This meant that once I had also turned down the offer to take on his female cousin, he would not be able to count on any extra money. In his eyes he had done everything that could be expected from him, and it's more than possible that the last thing he and his colleagues wanted was for a fair-skinned Westerner to turn up as a key witness in their 'investigation'.

The corruption of the judicial system here is so unfathomable that one can never know if, or to what extent, the local police are actually feeding off the robbing of tourists in the region by secretly receiving a percentage of the spoils. Even if the two delinquents arrested for murder were in fact non-identical to the ones that had visited me, it could also be that the two policemen who refused to go up to my house to look for signs of the perpetrators were actually in cahoots with them, yes, that they might even have seen them escape prior to coming down the road and finding me. Behind the house there is a thicket which the robbers must have crossed to reach the road on the other side. Continuing down that road towards the road leading to Samaná they must eventually have ended up being in the vicinity of the two young police guys on their bike. I don't say that they must have met. But it's not altogether improbable. After all, there must be a reason why so few crimes are ever prosecuted. To get away with murder in the Dominican Republic is the easiest thing. Try to tell these people that crime doesn't pay, when it might be the only thing that really does.

I was indeed tested by Destiny in Galéras. My response and the outcome of the action was such, that even if it really was cowardice not even trying to fight these thugs, that defensive course of action saved my life, because if I had failed to successfully impose myself on them, they probably would have killed, or at least hurt me very badly — perhaps made me an invalid for the rest of my days. On a positive note: my skull had not cracked *entirely* open from the machete hammering on it, although that was surely because the one they used had not been recently sharpened. It's also possible that the person handling it had turned the blunter edge against my head. How very considerate that would have been!

Psychologically too I'm robust enough to candidly admit my shortcomings and to be grateful for every extra day in the light of the sun. I have had no subsequent nightmares linked to this intrusion and haven't developed any new phobias. All I need to do really, to put this unfortunate event in its proper perspective, is to try to imagine what a real battlefield, or even a civilian self-defence, situation would have been like back in the days when dying or surviving was the result of man-to-man combat, not with the simple intention of finding a couple of dollars in each other's pockets, but of cutting each other to pieces for the sake of cutting each other to pieces. And let's say that you did indeed survive — by your lucky stars, physical strength, courage and general resourcefulness — how much pain and horror would you not have experienced in so doing? And perhaps all the same eventually perish from an insidious infection, festering in one of your many wounds.

Zauberberg

For reasons of discretion for the people concerned, and as a precautionary measure, I can't give you the real name of the Andean village I came to visit after my sojourn (described earlier) in Colombian Santa Fé de Antioquia. I have thus given it the fictitious name *Zauberberg* (Magic Mountain), after Thomas Mann's famous novel set in a sanatorium environment in the Swiss Alps. This is not because there are many similitudes between what happens to the protagonist in the novel and what happened to me. In fact there is really only one but salient resemblance: I suffered a mountain spell of sorts there.

A 'mountain spell' is not primarily, or even secondarily, associated with lack of oxygen, snow blindness, or something like that. It's a psychological condition, an ominous feeling of having been taken into custody by a spiritual entity residing in the mountains. In rural Scandinavia traditional folklore has often identified this condition with some kind of action exerted by the trolls, resulting in psychological obsession and aloofness in the human victim. If not counteracted in time, tragedy and disaster strike because the origins of this obsession are inhuman, demonic, the initial symptom being a growing reluctance to even think about descending from the highlands into the plains again…

As for myself I arrived to Zauberberg after a bus trip that took three hours longer than expected because a landslide had blocked off one of the mountain roads, forcing the driver to turn round and choose an alternative and more time consuming route. Though everything else at first seemed normal, it soon transpired that I had arrived in the village just one day before the annual *Fiesta de las Orquídeas*. As a consequence there was only a hotel room to be had for that night. In the morning I had to give it up and found myself reduced to the hopeless task of asking for shelter in every hotel, big or small, that I could possibly find. The same hotel managers and owners who one week earlier, or later, would have bent over backwards to accommodate me, could now hardly be made to look up from their newspapers. And though I could see entire rows of doors ajar, revealing so far unoccupied hotel rooms, the answer was unanimous: the rooms were reserved in advance and taken. In truth they weren't. But the hotel owners knew they would eventually be able to squeeze entire families into those rooms and charge them per capita. In the circumstance I was just bad business and nobody would give me a break.

So I ended up in Lucia Malóca's place, which was rather like being a visiting family member (albeit a paying one) in a family home. The room I was given, next to the street and only separated from it by two solid wooden shutters (no windows), was very spacious, furnished with two beds, a couch and a TV. The plan of the building was such that all rooms had entrances from an outside corridor facing, on the opposite side, a large uncovered space combining a living and dining room 'under the stars'. The likewise uncovered toilet and shower was to be found at the far end of this outside patio, behind a wall opposite the kitchen in the laundry area. The latter could have been a nice little courtyard as well, with a neat view of the surrounding mountains. Instead it had a high wall to protect the house from the dirt of the henhouse on the other side. Sitting down among the clothes fluttering in the wind, the only outdoor scenery I could behold from here was a patch of sky filled with birds. The shower, as far as I remember, only had cold water which is pretty much standard in Colombia for all cheaper accommodation in temperate climates. Standard is also the measly trickle it produces when actioned. But none of this really mattered as I was about to enter the twilight zone.

First of all, there was the party area extending from one corner to the other of the central plaza. The frequency of sound waves alone, pitched to storm frenzy, and caused even the incredibly loud fiestas of Santa Fe to pale in comparison. Add to this that some bars and cafes had chairs and tables placed so far towards the centre of the extensive plaza that the waiters had to 'fill the unforgiving minute with sixty second's worth of distance run' every time they took and executed an order. Yet these waiters were cheerful, never complaining, or seeing a difficulty in the situation; they weren't even expecting you to pay them a tip for their incomparable efforts. Music blasted out from just about everywhere as horsemen and, especially, horsewomen showed up in slick attire: shining boots, tight trousers, black and white hats, and colourful shirts wrapped up in a knot over the lower ribcage allowing flat stomachs and generous décolletages to be seen and duly admired. The equipages would typically ride right up, almost into one of the bars, and order a tray with shot glasses filled with aguardente. These were then taken in one go while the party remained in their saddles. The drinks consumed it was time for yet another show-off around the square. And, it goes without saying: more shots!

The typical Colombian country horse is not very big but strong all the same. It has been trained to perform a so-called *paso fino*, which is a super short trot making a very energetic sound as the horse's hooves move like drum sticks over the cobbled streets. But they can also gallop. For example, I saw — and this was at night time, mind you — a young boy, perhaps eight years of age, straddling his horse bareback, with his baby brother poised in between himself, the horse's head and the reins, as they thundered down the plaza at what seemed to me vertiginous speed. What it seemed like to the boy's parents — in particular as far as the younger, hardly more than a wet baby, was concerned — is perhaps an even more interesting question. No matter how good a rider the boy was, the undertaking was both arguably and objectively risky. As for the really little guy — poor thing! — he could only fanatically hold on to the horse's mane and thereby to his young life. Which he did with great bravery. So I guess this is simply how they break them in — I mean the kids, not the horses!

To what might be considered inspired lunacy, there is also a darker side. Some twenty years ago Zauberberg had been in the grip of malevolent forces. At present this was all but history. But. Because if one just ventured one or two blocks beyond the party plaza one would run into armed paramilitary, posing like sinister shadows on the rim of the light posts. And they weren't stationed there to calm things down in the plaza — by midnight simply ablaze with human passion — as much as to prevent unwelcome party crashers to enter town. Even the villagers themselves, invisible behind their shutters, wouldn't hesitate to open fire against serious marauders were they to show up. Nonetheless, anyone living a couple of blocks off the plaza would have to pass by, on his or her way home, these statuesque men in camouflage suits capable of unleashing imminent destruction. Then again, this is something to be considered as part of normal circumstances in Colombia and if anything, people are grateful that there actually are troops there to protect them, just in case.

From one thing to the other, in a country always full of glaring contrast. Lucia Maloca, my landlady, was the spinster among eight sisters (she also had three brothers). By external, independent, expertise she was in addition classified as a bipolar. Upon entering her house I indeed noticed she was nuts, but as the reader knows, my choices by now were sorely limited. The house she lived in was the one the father had once bequeathed to all of his children. However, the rest had founded their own homes and kept busy raising families. That left Lucia alone to take care of the family heritage. On an occasion like this she would rent out rooms to make some extra money, and that's where I came into the picture, henceforth just waiting for its frame. Since Lucia took a liking to me she had me introduced to her many sisters and brothers at a barbecue party that took place in a villa outside town. In the course of the afternoon, as I spoke to one of her sisters, I came to mention that I wouldn't mind staying in Zauberberg for some time. Whereupon she, her husband and their daughter, offered me to remain in their country cottage located above the village, since they were just about to head back to the big city after their vacations. I gladly accepted and thus only had to stay in Lucia's place for a couple of more days.

By this time, though, she, like the rest of the hotel managers in town, had begun to squeeze as many people as she could into her house, which was more and more beginning to resemble a summer camp. My nearest neighbours, for example, were a man and woman in the form of a couple. Their bedroom was only separated from mine by a curtain, and though I had no reason to complain about them, the reverse might not have been true. One night I brought little Alba with me home. It was just one of those things that happen. She wanted it and I needed it. But although — for fear of arousing Lucia's jealousy — I had admonished her to be very silent and discreet when entering the house, she started to get on the phone trying to make her teenage daughter understand why she was running unusually late this evening. It wasn't just Alba calling. Of course the daughter started to call back every five minutes. Finally, I had no choice but to ask Alba to either turn the telephone off or to leave right away. But she didn't want to leave, business unfinished. In an attempt to solve the dilemma, I resourcefully recalled that there was a small bedroom at the far end of the corridor. The main problem was that we needed to pass in front of the door to Lucia's own bedroom to get there. This we did. After which things developed in a satisfactory way and I could finally lead Alba back out of the room, down the corridor and let her out in the street before the *alba* of the day and before anyone could take notice.

Or so I thought. Whether Lucia had actually been awake, or received her information from a third party (and that could only have been my neighbours), I don't know. The truth is that she, although I took pains to immediately and silently restore the room to mint condition, found out about our nocturnal activities and began to give me glances insinuating I owed her something as well. Technically I certainly didn't, but Lucia was not one of those ladies who'd give up easily. For days, even weeks, after I had left her house and moved in at her sister's place just outside the village, she would look me up in the central plaza at night and make me company whether I liked it or not. She would even drive her scooter up the hills and otherwise unannounced pay an impromptu visit to her sister and brother in law's home, in what seemed an attempt at surveying my activities rather than making sure I was doing OK. In the absence of the former she obviously felt it was 'her' house too, and though I had paid a rent, albeit quite modest, to stay there, she would typically hang around for as long as she wanted. At least at the beginning. After a while I learned some techniques as to how to dodge her, for example, by going into hiding, or, by hearing the sound of her moped accelerate up the hill, meet her halfway feigning to be on my way to run errands in the village.

So what was so attractive about all this that it nearly gave me the mountain spell? Well, as I said initially, a mountain spell isn't a rationally explainable phenomenon, and Lucia's lunacy was but an ingredient in a cocktail, potent in many other ways too. First and foremost, I think it was the house itself. Rather its surroundings. Perfectly placed on a hill side, surrounded by a garden in which I gathered my own bananas, oranges and mandarins, and from which I produced my own fruit juices, it had a commanding view of the mountains and the intense metallic greenery of the coffee plantations. Then there were the clouds, constantly appearing in new phantasmagorical formations above my head. There was also the history of the place, but above all a feeling, once the agitated swell of the village party had abated, that time here simply ran differently than in other locations known to me. It was almost like an illustration of Einstein's famous example of a traveller who comes back to Earth after having voyaged in space at near the speed of light, only to find that his own perception of having been travelling for only minutes is contradicted by the fact that not only his parents, siblings and friends have meanwhile died, but that his own children have disappeared too. In other words, time here had come to a kind of standstill for me, although I could see it was actually moving faster and faster for some people around me. This takes a little explanation.

After Alba there was Theresa who, once I got rid of her lady friend and chaperone, proved to be very warm and stimulating company for some time. But in truth, both Alba and Theresa were eventually to be eclipsed by Asíle, who ultimately is the one for whom time actually accelerated as my own inner clock began to lag behind. She, as opposed to me, had an acute sense of urgency, at least she subsequently told me so. As for my own part, once I had incidentally met with her, as another stranger on the path of life, I was just curious to know if I were ever to meet with her again. In due course we did but I was never really anxious that it wouldn't come to pass. Perhaps I knew that it was simply destined to happen. As things began to noticeably speed up in the vortex of time mixed with strong emotion, I was suddenly forced to realise that I had begun to outstay my own welcome to myself. Had I remained just another day longer, the inevitable would have occurred already at this early stage, with only all too foreseeable possible confusions and complications. I simply had to clear out of town before it was too late. But then too late caught up with me and I was just about to lose my passport as the mailed invitation from her was renewed, for me to come back and visit with her anytime. I truthfully had to answer, that in normal circumstances I would have been happy to lose my passport in order to be forced to go back to Zauberberg, but as things stood there was going to be a potential problem with my seeing her again, and that was that I would probably not be able to prevent myself from falling in love with her. This was, again in the circumstances, a winner takes all proposal. I expected her to cautiously back out of the trap I was inadvertently setting. Instead she rushed straight into it, and that's how the story of Asíle *and* me began for real.

Capurganá

The plane took off from Medellín's centrally located Olea Herrera airport at precisely 9:50 AM. I had had a vague idea about where we were going, but was still unaware of how remote it was, considering we would allegedly still be within the bounds of the civilised world, albeit at its rim. The plane was the smallest commercial aircraft I have ever boarded. Some 20 passenger seats in all — half of them empty — reminded me more of the seats of a Guatemalan chicken bus than that of a plane. There was no hostess on board, and the captain and his co-pilot were in full sight from the passenger cabin, conversing leisurely with one another, gesticulating in the air.

While bags and provisions were loaded onto the plane, the captain waved a jovial goodbye to the ground crew and casually jammed his side window. Other orifices of the aircraft were shut in the same unceremonious way. With the cabin sealed, we were on our way. I stared hypnotised through the window at a dark discolouring in the fuselage that my heated imagination was only too keen to interpret as a crack in the structure supporting the wing. Realising there was nothing I could do about it, even if there was a crack, I confided in destiny.

Up and into the clouds. The pile of red bricks named Medellín disappeared behind us. The sight of the Valley of Caucas, surrounded by the two cordilleras making up much of central and southern department of Antioquia, offered a pleasant contrast: a symphony in various shades of green, interspersed with drier patches, cultivated fields and small villages hidden in the mountains, only to be reached by winding dirt roads subject to the constant threat of torrential rains and landslides. From the air, however, everything looked placid and picture perfect, the hills meandering like tranquil waves in an ocean.

Some 45 minutes into the flight the mountain swell receded. The last slopes merged with the coastal plains and the clouds, originating in the warm moisture of the Earth, became denser. But it was still possible to discern, here and there, the immense stretch of green canopy crowning the Darién *selva tropical*. Out of nowhere the curly surface of the Gulf of Urabá appeared on starboard while a stretch of coastal wilderness unfolded portside. A rugged coastline, huge rocks, reefs and entire islands appeared clad in trees and bushes in wild disarray. In between these unforgiving entities I spotted secluded bays with tranquil turquoise waters, and in between these miles and miles of unkempt beaches separated by capes of volcanic rock on which the waves of the Caribbean Sea hurled themselves, spurting into the air in foamy cascades. The whole thing would have made a perfect Spielbergian Jurassic Park backdrop, but it was just as well that I couldn't detect any dinosaurs raising their heads above the treetops to watch our arrival.

Notwithstanding, the landing in Capurganá was truly spectacular. After having followed the coastline while slowly descending, the captain initiated a sudden turn towards land. Through the cockpit windshield I could see ourselves heading straight for the green mountain ahead. All round us there seemed to be nowhere to go. We were completely enveloped by the jungle, and the hilltops, in all directions, stood tall above our own rapidly dwindling altitude. Then there was a sudden and unexpected clearing. A narrow passage opened up between two green crests. We headed straight for it. As soon as we came abreast with the hilltops, heading fatally for another mountain side, the plane again made a last sharp starboard turn. And there it was, straight ahead of us: the landing strip.

Final descent was forcibly brusque and steep. Hitting ground we could feel there was probably some reason behind the plane's seemingly under-pressurised tires, a fact I had noted already as we boarded. An unforeseen object or a hole in the ground could possibly flatten a fully pumped up tire more easily than a half full one, or perhaps send it off course by landing and take-off. When stepping out of the plane into the humid midday I noticed that the tires looked almost rectangular in shape while the aircraft was posed on ground. Whatever the reason for this might be, it was a fact. Another fact was that two eras in human evolution here meet face to face: the taxi to the village centre is an ass harnessed in front of a rustic wooden cart on the sides of which four red, plastic chairs have been suspended, attached by simple ropes.

Here we were, a heavily armed Colombian soldier controlling ID documents there. Beyond him the local Hannibals, Gustavos, Nelsons and Hectors eager to offer accommodation, boat trips and horseback rides. Beyond them ultimately, the 'taxi driver', with a thin wooden stick in his hand to guide the docile donkey. Our papers were cleared and we understood a donkey taxi to be unnecessary, since the plaza, coinciding with the soccer pitch, of the jungle metropolis was to be found only a stone's throw away. The flight captain once again waved — this time to us — and in the next moment his propeller craft was off, back to Medellín, returning a few scattered souls of European extraction to civilisation. The plane gone, everything on land returned to its habitual state of indolence, like water closing around a stone thrown in muddy water.

Even the dogs are lazy in Capurganá. This laconic observation has the merit of also being true. By nature and acquired habit everything, except the lancias with their oversized Yamaha outboard motors, is slow here. Slow to the point of non-existence. After some searching we found a hotel room to our liking, at the end of the balustrade on the second floor with its own adjacent deck right by the tumultuous sea, next to the pier from which all maritime traffic — the only traffic — in town is directed. But it took the hotel manager, young Joselito (quickly nick-named 'Don Tranquilo'), forever to make up his mind about accepting the proposal we made him for ten consecutive nights in the establishment he was allegedly running for a Medellín-based owner. He finally consented with a facial expression betraying he had probably been forced to conclude the worst deal of his life. Although the hotel was empty; although it would cost him personally nothing to swing a door open; although this, in the dead waters of low season, clearly was a mutual win-win situation. But money talks, sometimes slowly, but nonetheless inexorably. Asíle's rubbing of ten virginal, sweet smelling 50,000 peso bills under his nose proved too much of a temptation. He gave up and we got our room at the suggested price.

Which didn't prevent him from trying to make our life difficult in other ways, such as suddenly and unexpectedly denying us access to the kitchen (he was eventually paid off by Asíle for the continuance of this service as well) and declaring that the owner — lurking somewhere behind cloud and mountain a thousand miles to the south — was categorically opposed to the idea of letting us use the washing machine. We did try to pay ourselves out of that impasse as well, but here Don Tranquilo was adamant. Most likely, he had indeed asked the owner for permission on our behalf, but he or she probably suspected Don Tranquilo would never admit the machine was ever used by guests and keep the money for running it to himself. At the thought of which the owner had concluded it was better if the machine was used solely for bed linens and towels of the hotel. But even here frugality prevailed. After a week we both felt an exchange of towels and sheets would be welcome, but as nobody in the staff seemed to care too much about our request, Asíle went into the laundry room and availed herself of what we needed.

By and large our accommodation was quite comfortable. It had contained no less than three different beds plus a two storied bunk bed — which would certainly come in handy and generate mega bucks during high season as hotel and hostel owners in the area have the habit of charging accommodation as per head and not per room. We asked to have some of these extra beds removed. The request was granted and in exchange we got a refrigerator from another room. Still, the double bed had a mattress in typical Colombian style, made of rough fibres straight from nature tightly knit together, that is: hard as a rock. In return we enjoyed the benefit of no less than two ventilators, one suspended from the high ceiling, and the other hanging off the red brick wall, providing efficient cooling in addition to the more or less permanent sea breeze sweeping in through the man-made holes in the wall above the sliding doors. Having sliding doors enabled us to calibrate and direct the amount of breeze allowed inside, in this way saving the flicker from precious candles from constantly going out. The amount of water dispersed by the (cool) shower was acceptable too. And as I said, we had our own terrace overlooking the pier, the centre of activity in the village.

Gazing further across the sea we were rewarded with the sight of two small islands, one furiously overgrown with thorny vegetation, the other consisting of a solid piece of huge white rock thrown into its present location by a frustrated extra-terrestrial giant trying to hit two mastodons with one stone. Beyond these landmarks the sea was open and, in the present season, dominated by grey skies and a humid atmosphere, the silhouette of the opposite shore of the Gulf of Urabá remained out of sight. Behind us was a stretch of cultivable land on sea level, but the hills rose steeply and abruptly behind this patch to rather impressive heights, all of which were covered in luxuriant vegetation, home to an almost dizzying array of wildlife: birds, insects, butterflies, primates, mammals and reptiles.

On a good day electricity in the hotel would typically be up and running from 9 AM to 2 AM. In other words, the ventilators and the ice box would stop humming in the wee hours and come back on spinning to morning coffee. During this period, the electricity provided by a communal, petrol fed central power plant was shut down and only the establishments owning their own generators would be able to continue providing energy. It is, however, very possible that some of the hotels, allegedly having no electricity source of their own, do in fact have them. They simply want to save themselves the cost of running them since electricity comes at the price of a petrol that is surprisingly expensive in such proximity to the black veins of Venezuela. As a consequence, only the 'luxury' hotel of the village and some homeowners intent on saving their stock of frozen fish from decomposition run some lights and iceboxes in the dead of the night. Otherwise the place, on a moonless night, is pitch dark. Add to this that 2 AM to 9 AM are only the official hours when electricity is not provided. More often than not the lights will go out at any time of the night, sometimes leaving you with no other choice than to try to find your way home like a blind man bereft of cane and dog.

But man has not become the master of this planet for nothing. Adaptation is the prerequisite of survival and we soon found ourselves accepting this state of affairs as natural. Slightly more difficult to get used to was the surprising scarcity of food articles in this lush farmland and the rather arrogant pride that the locals took in informing their customers that this or that item was unavailable. As mentioned, there is enough farmland available in and around Capurganá to allow the village to grow its own supplies of vegetable and fruit. But the people here take no interest whatsoever in such activities. All the hotels and nearly all of the businesses are owned by the *paisas*, whereas the majority of the indigenous population seems content to just hang around, occasionally pulling themselves sufficiently together to answer: 'We don't have it'! As a consequence, and with the possible exception of fish (there are still fishermen in the village) all foodstuffs, including fruit and vegetables, are brought in once a week from Turbo — a port town set at the bottom of the Gulf — by a wooden diesel-engined ship painted in vivid Caribbean colours, but decrepit enough otherwise.

Thus, if you happen to arrive in Capurganá one or two days before the food ship is scheduled to arrive, chances you'll find even two mouldy tomatoes in the grocery store are next to nil. Although avocados are practically dangling from every second branch, they are rare to find in the stores, not to speak of bananas; two oranges with nearly no juice inside them, if per chance they exist, typically cost more than a dollar, etc.

As far as the alcohol situation is concerned the situation, somewhat surprisingly, is much better. In addition to the customary selection of Colombian beers (Aguila, Pilsen, Club Colombia), there are Chilean and Argentinian wines, Scotch whiskies, Bailey's, rum and, of course, the ubiquitous *Aguardente Antioquenia* — one restaurant even has a bottle of immobile Cointreau perched on its liquor shelf.

Asíle and I spent our first afternoon ever together resting, getting to know each other in exactly such ways as a bed, albeit hard as rock, is conducive to. For two years we had both been fantasising about each other, and there might have been, on both sides (and for sure on mine) an indistinct suspicion that in the last, critical and decisive instance, the spark, the soul, the emotion, the chemistry — call it what you like — in spite of all good will to the contrary simply wouldn't be there. I was relieved to feel all my apprehension in this regard vanish like mist before the sun.

In Cielo

Having travelled all the way to the primordial wilderness uniting Colombia with Panamá we were of course interested in witnessing first hand its attractions. One of the places we heard about was El Cielo, a waterfall in the jungle, about an hour's walk from the village. Passing by the airport, to get to the path taking us there, I noticed a sign on the latticed fence at the end of the runway. It didn't say 'Parking prohibited', or even 'Trespassing prohibited' as one would perhaps expect, but: 'Tying horses to the fence prohibited. Fine 50,000 pesos'. I imagined the local metre maid arriving, dressed in uniform, issuing a ticket containing the iron branded ID of the horse owner, pasting it to the forehead of the innocent animal. The rider would then step out of the bar finding himself the victim of the implacable judicial system and, as we all do in such a situation, trying to argue with the representative of the local Parking Enforcement.

By all means, I don't know how rigorously this prohibition is upheld; I don't even know if anybody was ever fined for actually tying his horse to the airport fence. What I do know is that all kinds of creatures — dogs, cats, humans, adults and children — walk the runway freely at any time of the day. Chances to get hit by a plane are rather slim though, especially if you avoid walking the runway around noon on Mondays and Fridays, the only two days in the week when flights are scheduled. Even so, only minutes before we witnessed one of these flights arrive some days later, a little girl, perhaps four years old, calmly strolled up the runway all alone. She did get off just in time, but she could just as well have been present on it when the aircraft at 250 km per hour slammed the tarmac. In seconds it covered the distance from touchdown to the sheds acting as the airport terminal.[8]

But this day was not a flight day. The runway seemed more akin to a scene taken straight out of the fantasy television documentary *The Earth after Humans*. This last vestige of human technology behind us, the track led past a botanical garden that could have used some more... well, gardening. Here and there some buildings could be glimpsed through dense greenery. Horses and donkeys alternated with dogs as our fellow travellers. We arrived at a river bed and continued along its course, having to cross its (luckily) feeble current on several occasions. At one point we came upon two men digging a ditch. Our assumption that they were redirecting the course of the river proved wrong. They were digging for gold, which does exist in some quantities in the river beds, in their deltas and along beaches subject to the undermining effect of the sea provoking landslides, thereby revealing grains of the precious metal in the freshly exposed black sand. The tropical forest was nonetheless hot and humid and it was relieving to finally arrive at the makeshift wooden structures serving as entrance, lodge and ticket booth to the site.

We came to Heaven with a minimum of expectation. Although experiencing it first hand was not a major deception, let me put it this way all the same: El Cielo is a pleasant piece of aquatic scenery, but it's not the Niagara. It is no more than a small depression in a hardly water-filled jungle river, dropping some 15 feet over a rocky distance of about 50 feet, at its far end producing a trickle into a natural pond — just big

---

8   Allegedly a young American woman visiting Capurganá actually was run over and killed on the spot by a landing plane. Assuming she could jog freely on the runway — just like back home along the beach of Santa Monica, with a headset distributing her favourite music — she had turned literally blind and deaf to the lethal danger approaching from behind.

enough to drown a cat in — that with a lot of good will, and at times of intense precipitation, could be defined as a cascade. But he who seeks shall find. At the top of the waterfall another basin filled with water has formed, big enough to allow a few breaststrokes in either direction. After a good walk up the river bed the water is mercifully cool, the light subdued by thick foliage, and the sounds and sights of the surrounding forest enchanting. Spending a small hour wailing in this natural tub was all we really needed to be rejuvenated, even reborn — the songs of birds and monkeys still echoing in memory. After that, drying up, getting dressed and descending towards the village was easy and we arrived there, picking flowers off the airport fence, just as the sun, setting behind the hills, announced nightfall in an hour.

At the latitudinal level of Capurganá, the predominating northeasterly trade wind at this time of the year sends squalls and waves straight from the Caribbean Sea. From this location — close to the Cabo Tiburón, Colombia's last rocky outpost before Panama, the coast of which runs in an east-western direction for miles to come — the sea is wide open all across to the distant leeward islands, to Jamaica, Cuba, Santo Domingo and Puerto Rico. Because of all the reefs dotting the coast, making the entrance to its bays hazardous, the sea is choppy and infested with treacherous currents. This also makes swimming risky. A small stretch of the beach in Capurganá does allow for it though, and this is where we went one day when it pleased the clouds to spread its curtain wide enough to let through the glorious sun.

A trip to Panamá

Some days, of what was still supposed to be regional summer, were dominated by rains and massively grey skies. We consequently seized the occasion to do outings whenever the weather appeared at its most promising. Beyond the ridge delimiting Capurganá to the northwest lays a bay with a small settlement by the name of Sapzurro. One early afternoon we set out for it, carrying enough water to survive a couple of hours in the heavy humidity, only to soon find ourselves embarking on a steep hill. Halfway into the ordeal we ran across Nelson and his co-workers, responsible for the preservation of the eco-system and even, believe it or not, for the cultivation of fruit and vegetables. There were, according to Nelson, just in the limited dominion he was administrating some 8,000 avocado trees, carrying an average of 100 avocados each. That would make a yearly yield of 800,000 avocados, but none of the villagers seemed to be interested in harvesting them, so chances were that the fruit would just hang there until falling from its branch and returning to dust. Nelson, nonetheless, was happy with his job and assured us it was a good and worthwhile thing. We agreed and paid the suggested amount of pesos for the maintenance of the site and its arduous path.

Rested and ready to take on the final challenge of mounting the summit we bravely continued and 20 minutes later found ourselves panting on top of the ridge from which the bay of Sapzurro and that of Capurganá could be overlooked simultaneously. But we weren't all alone. From practically every branch, some of which obstructed the path, a multitude of three-inch black and sinister looking spiders — of the kind you wouldn't like to go to bed with — were suspended in their webs. I took the precaution to avail myself of a stick and to beat the branches in front of us as we were advancing to make sure there were no spiders ready to slip down the most invitingly moist cleavage of my Lady. To be honest: I wouldn't have felt too happy having one of them crawling down my chest either!

As though that wasn't enough a choir of howler monkeys began to call from some trees in the valley, instantly freezing our blood to ice during the most intense heat of the day. Luckily there were also fabulously coloured flowers, fruit and butterflies to divert our interest and as we were now rapidly descending, having left Capurganá out of sight, the tranquil horseshoe bay of Sapzurro, flanked by a wilderness that hasn't changed much over the last 10,000 years, lay before our eyes. Coming there is like entering a naturally circumscribed arena, contained within and yet distinctly apart from the rest of the world. We walked the perimetre of the bay, admiring the forms and contours of the surrounding *selva*. Coming back from a refreshing swim in the innermost corner of the bay we ran across Cecilia while looking for accommodation for the night — it had been our plan all along not to return to Capurganá that same afternoon.

Cecilia is a native of Medellín, but has spent most of her ceaselessly active adult life in Sapzurro where she sells homemade ice cream to the stray tourist when not busy in her garden, or somebody else's, cooking, cleaning, or running a thousand errands motivated by her concern for everybody. She also has a small cabana to rent out on her intimate property, the houses of which are painted in Caribbean red and white and surrounded by a neat garden. Cecilia was very sweet and caring and brought us coffee, and fresh fish for dinner, as well as breakfast in the morning. She liked to communicate and was eager to share her opinions with us. Shortly before nightfall she once again passed by the terrace of our cabana to pick up the empty coffee thermos. I mentioned how impressive the selva seemed to me, and she looked up with a tranquil smile on her face, seeing it just as I did in that moment, enveloped in the last, rapidly fading hues of the day, and she pensively completed the sentence forming in my mind: '...with its mysteries and unfathomable secrets.'

Next morning we had but one thing on our minds, and that was to take Asíle on her first trip ever abroad. It might sound like a complicated manoeuver. In reality it was a piece of cake. Panama is at as convenient a distance as distances ever come in this country, meaning there will always be a hill to overcome. This one proved to be moderate and the two sheds on top of it, surrounded by their sand bags for gunfire protection, housed the local Colombian and Panamanian immigration and customs offices. The Colombian military official did go through our bag and then sent us on to his colleague on the other side of the border, seven metres away. The stocky Panamanian in charge of visits to his country just took a good look at us, me in particular I felt, and then waved us on. We were now, as though transported by a magic wand, in Panamá.

At first the only noticeable difference between the two sides was that Sapzurro is as beautiful as La Miel is ugly. But that turned out to be a superficial observation. The more artistic truth is that La Miel is as mercilessly exposed to the fury of the sea as Sapzurro is protected from it. And some houses only appear to be abandoned because they lack a roof. In reality they're full of inhabitants who don't seem to consider this too much of an inconvenience. The northeastern trade wind blows half a gale, having crossed the better part of the Caribbean Sea before landfall. Here, precisely here, we were out of the Gulf of Urabá and on our own. Surely there are some villages or even small towns further up the Panamanian coast, but from this vantage point the farthest thing the naked eye can see is unlimited expanses of green jungle and a coffee-coloured ocean. Nonetheless, this is where Adam and God meet in the sky, this is where two of the Latin American states most implicated in the drugs and arms trade of their respective continents meet and shake hands. This is where North America becomes South America, and vice versa, although the most apparent dividing line, for commercial and geographic convenience, is the one drawn by the Panamá Canal.

We were soon to see concrete evidence of how close at hand this whole business was. On the pier in the village's slightly more sheltered Playa Blanca, where smaller ships and their cargo can actually be received, four 300 HP Yamaha outboard motors, unopened, in their original packaging straight from Japan, cleared through customs in Miami, had ended their journey as possible evidence of criminal activity. The policeman who showed us around said there was an ongoing investigation and that the primary reason the Colombian person showing up in this free trade zone had been denied the right to collect the goods, was that the number of the ID he presented did not correspond with its associate name. This means the Panamanians must have asked their Colombian colleagues for assistance in establishing identity. And with good reason. The cargo was decidedly suspicious. The police lancias too have a battery of four engines mounted to their aft. But they are only 200 HP each. Four 300 HP engines, totalling 400 HP more than that of any police speedboat, would make a lancia running illegal products (provided the sea allows for it) capable of outspeeding a police boat in hot pursuit.

Strangely, and if I understood the explanation correctly, the man presenting a false Colombian ID had not been detained by authorities on either side. If this is true, I can only speculate about the reasons and your guess is as good as mine. It should be kept in mind, however, that Colombia still has something of a feudal social structure, in which not only a Pablo Escobar was able to thrive, but where a lot of other *gran señores* are still ruling their dominions as though they were also the ones responsible for the making and maintaining of public order. In other words, it would be practically impossible for an outsider — not to speak of a foreigner — to find out what kind of deals are struck on a daily basis between these rural lords and the national authorities. The four outboard motors might or might not be part of some sort of scheme. Two things remain for sure: those engines had been paid for prior to their arrival at the pier in Panamá, and the person sent to pick them up had not wanted his true identity to be known.

There were some open beach cafes in Playa Blanca primarily serving loud music. In prolongation of the pier there was also a huge new hangar-like building that hadn't as yet opened its gates to the public. Its future inauguration, however, promised to be very interesting, judging by a large sign on its front featuring, like a mirage in the desert, the two magic words of free enterprise: Duty Free. The immediate reason for this unexpected intrusion of civilised commodity in the midst of wilderness surely is that Colombian inhabitants of this road less coast benefits from a state-sanctioned free trade agreement with Panamá. In return the Colombian state feels free to disregard these communities in every other respect and provides nothing to further such services as schooling, communications and healthcare in the region.

We were told this outlet on Panamanian soil would soon be offering everything from electric appliances to hardware goods, household and food items, as well as alcohol at tax free prices. But there is a hitch. The customer will only be allowed to bring an item bought at the Panamanian duty free facility to a few other municipalities in the Colombian Darién. To bring such tax-exempted goods to for example the port of Turbo across the Gulf is illegal. This is one of the reasons why all vessels docking in Turbo — a Hispanic edition of Monrovia, New Guinea, and a new candidate among my earlier top ten contenders for the honorary title 'The world's ugliest town' — has to report its cargo to heavily armed coastal guards, the facial expressions of whom betray little to no tolerance with violators of the law. In fact, these stone-faced guys don't even make an attempt to point their machine guns away from you while interrogating the captain as to his apparent or hidden intentions.

But if one lives in Capurganá or its surroundings, this store is definitely going to be an El Dorado, not the least as far as alcohol is concerned. I managed to buy a litre of Grant's whisky for 35,000 pesos (US $20) in a small liquor store in la Miel. The same bottle (*con estampilla*) cost 60,000 in Capurganá, almost twice as expensive. To be honest, there seemed to be a little discrepancy in the price marking of the liquors in la Miel. The bottle I eagerly weighed in my hand had in fact two price tags glued to it: one indicating 35, the other 45,000 pesos. I didn't want the salesman to get confused over this, so I discreetly scratched off the superfluous tag with my fingernail, subsequently exiting the candy store as happy as a child.

A staircase in concrete meanders down from the border control (on the Colombian side there are only makeshift wooden steps to facilitate ascent-descent), to eastern Panama's first urban agglomeration. It's not very beautiful but definitely offers easier access than its equivalent on the opposite side. At the end of this stair a straight road takes one past roofless homes to a simple solitary cross stuck in the ground right in front of the foaming rocks of the roaring ocean. It rather looks like an illustration to one of Cortez' diaries: '... and there, wrecked by the sea but miraculously still alive, we planted the Santa Cruz, for us to show gratitude to our Lord Jesus, who perished on the cross to redeem us from all sins, and to celebrate the splendours of King and Country and, last but not least, to remind the wretched Indians that we would continue to disembowel their pregnant women as long as they tried to commit suicide in order to avoid having to work.' In harmony with such solemn sermon Asíle threw herself onto the cross, her arms stretched out in the manner of the crucified, and, even more interestingly, offering her naked chest up to my avid regards — there are indeed photographic evidence of the blasphemous event. This was the moment I realised that Asíle was quite my match: she obviously was nuts too! I've told her many times since that she's a *loca*, but she insists that's not something inherent in her nature, but that I make her that way. A comment which in turn struck a familiar chord of eternal and irredeemable guilt, resounding since times immemorial (or at least since that of Luther) in my Protestant soul. Remember: Adam was modelled from clay or something similar, but Eve was formed from his rib once his body existed. By female logic he forcibly therefore is responsible for her being the way she is, and even for the serpent being irresistible...

That concluded our trip to and Asíle's first visit to a country outside her own. As we mounted the staircase leading us back to Colombia, we expected having to show our passports again, possibly even to declare my merchandise (at this point in time I was still unaware of the free trade agreement). But we met with the stocky official — more like a solid cube of flesh and bone really — in the stairs. He was descending to finally enjoy his lunch, and although there was someone up there to replace him, it proved to be a guy of the same age and general temperament as his Colombian counterpart. At this time they no longer cared to uphold the idea of separate border controls and had joined forces in the Panamanian boot. As we passed in front of them they cheered, waving us on to new adventures while laughingly continuing to entertain each other.

We found Cecilia at her post in the harbour, but the day had been slow with few tourists interested in homemade ice cream. That hadn't tainted her good spirits though, and she was just as eager as ever to share news with us. Meanwhile I bought some refreshments from the local salesman and managed to forget my small plastic bag containing several hundred thousand pesos on its counter. We were just about to enter the scaringly narrow lancia headed for Capurganá, when I realised I must have lost my cash. Retracing my last steps I arrived at the shop. The owner made no attempt to conceal the truth, but I have to admit his strategy was watertight. Instead of holding onto the small transparent plastic bag to see if I would return — possibly accusing him of theft or at least for knowingly having withheld the money — he pretended he never realised it contained any money, and had thrown the bag into the garbage can below the counter. But Asíle, by Colombian instinct, quickly refreshed his memory and the plastic bag mysteriously surfaced again out of an indistinct heap of banana peels, juice containers and cardboard. All the money was in there, and although I realised the guy was only waiting for me to disappear beyond the horizon, I still gave him a bill for 'helping' me to recoup the lost money. It was a piece of theatre, but well worth it. I could have lost very much more. It's even most surprising that the man didn't categorically deny having seen the bag, which he very well may have done. But I do believe Asíle's hypnotically big eyes, scrutinising his, tipped the balance in my favour.

The lancia didn't depart as immediately as we had been led to believe. First its captain took his sweet time to refill gas at the gas station, the pump of which had to be fixed before we could get to its essence. Then he swung around the bay in the hope of picking up further passengers, allowing us to once again admire the formidable jungle adorning the mountain slopes. But then the engine rocked and we headed straight for the waves, that we, *gracias a Díos*, only had to meet head-on for the shortest time, as the boat then turned southwards, waves subsequently rolling in on the aft.

Still, I can't overemphasise the ruggedness of the rocks along the coast and the narrow straits they create. This, in combination with the fatalism of the pilots and the general unpredictability of the sea, makes any sea-bound excursion in these waters an adventure in its own right. Please don't think this is only in the timorous tourist's imagination: a thousand flotsam flip-flops dotting the coast line between Sapzurro and Capurganá bear testimony to the cargo lancia recently wrecked off the coast. And again, only a week after our trip back to Capurganá, the captain of a passenger lancia misjudged a wave and saw his boat tip over off Turbo, throwing everybody inside it into the sea. Luckily the speed must have been moderate and there were other vessels close by, but the potentially fatal event could just as well have occurred in the midst of the Gulf, giving the impartial witness little reason to assume that such calamity would, in the event, meet with an equally happy end. But all's well that ends well. On our ride from Sapzurro we were spared any such annoyance and could crown our expedition to the back of beyond by crawling out of the boat safe and sound at the choppy landing in Capurganá. Soon Papi emerged refreshed from the shower to pour himself a stiff one from a bottle of Scotch, brought within easy reach, and for his comfort, all the way from Panamá.

La Coquéra

At only half an hour's walking distance up the coast from Capurganá there is a narrow precipice in the jungle called La Coquera in honour of its many coconut palms. On three sides this small geological indentation is hemmed in by vertical mountainsides. The fourth vector opens up towards the rocks and the ocean. A priori there is nothing to suggest this would be a pleasant place to spend a life time in. But thirty years ago local boy Nelson decided otherwise and built himself a nest in this unforgiving environment. Ever since he leads a secluded existence here. True, there are tourists visiting his abode during the day, and it is quite impressive how the man has managed to turn so many natural objects and shapes into useful household items — his drinking glasses for instance are hollow coconuts placed on coconut tops sliced horizontally at the top and turned upside down, allowing the sphere of the coconut (the glass) to rest firmly on the hollow, not unlike an egg in an egg cup. Simple but ingenious. There is also a big natural bathtub, fed by trickling mountain water, which Nelson has arranged nicely for his own comfort and the benefit of the visitor, and from which the view over the sea is rather impressive. To immerse oneself there during the heat of day is simply merciful, and that's what we did.

Nelson also has electrical appliances and produces his own energy from solar panels on the roof. All genuine and in exemplary ecological style. Still, I invite the reader to imagine being there all alone, surrounded by relentless wildlife during a night charged with an electric storm, listening to the rain hammering furiously on the tin roof, waiting for the waterfall above to come down in torrents, and huff and puff your piggy away. Even if you survived that, the only way leading out of this sealed enclosure still is a forbiddingly steep path which by now has turned into a black landslide of mud, where you will just slip your way into the rocks beneath and then fall into the ocean, from which there definitely would be no return.

But then Nelson didn't look like someone who would worry about imaginary problems. His suspended model fish made from different kinds of organic spheres collected from the trees in his hollow are graceful and humorous; he has used all kinds of trees and branches to make and decorate walls and fences; even the water basin is a piece of hollowed tree trunk and its water switch a conch. In this setting he treated us to delightfully cool lemonade. After having chatted for a while we parted in good spirits, but not before having wished Nelson good luck for the coming 30 years in his Saint-Anthony style retreat.

The walk back to town once again confronted us with the natural wonders of the coast: its small pebbled beaches, its nearby small islands shooting up like reptiles from the bosom of the water, its jagged skyline and intense vegetation.

Aguacate

A good hour's walk south along the coast from Capurganá there is a settlement called El Aguacate. Initially a road leads in its general direction, passing across a (at this time of the year) dried up riverbed and the coastal plain until the latter hits upon another petrified protuberance. In order to advance further there is no other possibility at hand and foot than to take on the rocky challenge. I asked an elderly man, enjoying a meal outside his humble abode, if the path from here on would be identical to the beach itself. In a voice resounding of myth and saga he informed me that this was not the case. No, 'the sea is at one side and the path is on the other'. This proved to be true in so far as the path never completely merged with the water. However, it came indeed as close as a few feet from it. Still, there was the path and there was the sea. By all means the walk culminated in a 500 foot coastal climb (at least that's what it felt like, although it's actually just another very steep walk) which made arriving at the top feel like something akin to breaking the surface of water after having ascended through crushing masses of it.

From the narrow ridge at the top Capurganá, to the north, and the windward side of Aguacate are visible simultaneously. But that's the last thing you see of the former. Once we began descending we noticed, apart from even denser vegetation, an agglomeration of houses exposed to waves unperturbed by an opposite coastline whenever the trade wind dominates. Believing these scattered buildings to be all there was to Aguacate, we at first felt slightly disappointed. But the path continues, and after we had passed over a last hill of modest height, the following descent took us into the heart of the small bay that makes up downtown Aguacate. This is also where the pier and landing for the boats are located. The village and its well-kept properties bear witness to the interest which eccentric Europeans and laid back Antioquians, long since retired from the hustle and bustle of their native Medellíns, take in the place, and the overall impression is that of a tranquil garden set against the ever impressive background of the selva. We took a well-deserved break and then continued the path further down the coast where views went from spectacular to breath-taking.

La Moira, a mile to the south, is not even a village but just a locality with a few plantations and some corralled domestic animals. But from its shores the magnitude of the Darién wilderness appears unimpeded, allowing imagination to run amuck, with vistas reminiscent of Kublai Khan's *Xanadu* (as rendered by Coleridge), of landscapes transforming into architectural visions impervious to measure and reason. From here, days of hiking could be imagined before there would again be any signs of civilisation. After having nibbled at that piece of *terra incognita*, we felt, without even telling ourselves so, that our visit to Capurganá and its surroundings had come to its natural conclusion. We could have changed our plan to take the boat next morning further down the coast, and instead have moved over to Aguacate to hang out there for another week or so. But the feeling was that we had done what we had to do. The return to base thus came to be shrouded in a peaceful melancholy of farewell, so appropriate to the strange, yet profound attraction, of this enigmatic landscape. We met one single person as we were going back. I immediately assumed it must have been the German I had heard about, because, as opposed to locals, he didn't bother to say hello. In fact he didn't even bother to look up as he passed by us. Must have been the German.

We came back to Capurganá just as time was getting ripe for a shower and a sunset cocktail. I bought ice for our drinks just as afternoon turned into evening. An hour later the world was embedded in darkness over which Orion and his faithful *corredor* (*canis major*) stood watch.

Triganá

Our ten days in Capurganá were up. The previous evening Asíle had bought tickets for the morning lancia and I believe she was all ready to go as I was only beginning to wake up. Luckily our quarters were only about 20 steps away from the pier and after a cup of coffee I packed my few belongings — Asíle would unerringly take care of everything else. On our way out we did spot Don Tranquilo at a distance, barely managing to produce a wafting of the hand for goodbye — relieved probably that there would be no more complaints from obnoxious guests about his tendency to turn his stereo system on full blast after midnight for the benefit of some locals seeking amusement in the hotel's waterfront 'restaurant'. The morning departure was attended by a strong military presence and a boat crew indifferent to the welfare of the passengers and their luggage. Asíle had wrapped our bags in the plastic garbage bags available on the landing, but since everyone used the same convenience, while the bags themselves were moved around by careless hands, there was after a while no telling which ones belonged to us — a difficulty which only presented itself in clear relief as we eventually disembarked at the boat's first port of call.

Before that there was a two hour boat ride ahead of us. I mentioned earlier that the only things that move fast in the area are the lancias with their over-dimensioned outboard engines, allowing maximum speed at the cost of minimum comfort to the passengers. It was only now that it began to sink into my mind how lucky we had been to opt for a flight straight to Capurganá from Medellín, instead of spending an entire day on a bus in order to then embark on a three hour boat trip against the choppy, unpredictable swell of the Caribbean in the Gulf of Urabá. In truth, just going with the waves is an ordeal. The lack of general security is one thing. But that really is 'no thing'. I had taken the precaution to strap money and passport in watertight plastic containers onto my body, vainly hoping that if worse came to worse we would still be able to swim. I soon realised we wouldn't stand a chance were the lancia to capsize. Alone the speed of the boat would have been enough to jolt us against the concrete hard sea surface and instantly kill, or so incapacitate, us that we'd only be good for the sharks afterwards. So there was really only one hope: that we'd make it the ordinary way. But even the ordinary way meant some degree of discomfort.

Sitting up front, as we did, being among the very last to embark, it involved getting constantly hissed seven feet up into the air and then brusquely deposited on the backside of every single wave. It suffices to have the slightest spinal problem to be maimed for months to come, unless, of course, you do as I did, and that is to raise slightly from the seat every time the prow of the vessels descended in free fall towards the sea. This is how I passed the next two hours, keeping close to Asíle, holding her hand while finding her very brave. She in turn sported an irresistible smile on her beautifully curved lips throughout the voyage. It was only afterwards I understood that she too had been terrified. At least that's what she led me to believe, because I never knew — although she kept reassuring me, here as well as in many other instances, that she was in dead earnest — if that's what she really felt, or if she only wanted me to feel better about my own misgivings, blended as they were with a strong dose of enthusiastic fatalism. Standing up and sitting down alternatively for the better part of two hours, throwing weary glances at a distant coastline shrouded in mists, I thus acquiesced.

At the end of the second hour we approached a series of small islands, or should I say deadly dangerous looking rocks, jutting out of the frothing sea. We passed between them at full speed and in the next instance the boat rounded a cape. We were protected from both wind and waves, and in particular from the mercilessness of Captain Ahab apparently having mistaken me for *Moby-Dick* or some other object of his intense hatred. Getting up and out of the boat proved to be our last ordeal in connection with the transport, since no one would lend us a helping hand to reach the wobbly, wooden, makeshift pier, at this time of the day standing under 20 inches of water. In addition, and as I mentioned, all luggage stored in the prow of the boat had been put in black plastic bags and sealed off with strong tape to prevent water damage. Problem was they had also been tossed there randomly by someone who couldn't have cared less whether the passengers knew where to find them. Since the rest of these were destined for Turbo, the last stop on the run, the remaining passengers would find the time to sort things out once arrived. We on the other hand were the only ones to disembark in Triganá and we had to help ourselves to find our luggage as best we could. Here Asíle once again showed a wonderful presence of mind and after some trial and error selected the correct black wrappings out of the bundle while I, standing on the pier up to my knees in water, hoisted them up as quickly as I could, trying not to drop them back into the sea. Loaded like a camel destined for the unforgiving desert I then managed to reach the shore; Asíle followed right behind me carrying the handbags.

Meanwhile, additional cargo was thrown into the lancia by the port crew; there was an exchange of excited remarks as the pier readied itself to sink to its grave under the weight of the five people loading stuff from it. Then the familiar roar of the outboard engines, a strident turn and the lancia again gained the open sea. Around us the stillness of a tropical morning moving towards noon closed in. It was like a sudden vacuum from which we only emerged gradually, little by little perceiving the density of the jungle around us, the sounds of its animals and birds, the humid smell of its porous sandy banks. It all seemed beautiful and desolate at the same time — another one of those 'end-of-the-Earth' kind of places where notions of beauty, placidity, simplicity, melancholy and despair no longer seem to contradict one another, but rather enter the mind as indistinguishable representations of one and the same thing.

Knowing the day to be early and the housing market ours — the total absence of tourists was salient evidence of this — we took our time to first have a general look around, then inspect a couple of bungalows, all a bit depressing and, more importantly still, thoroughly overpriced. The narrow beach, principally composed of fine, black sand, was only partly navigable by foot, here and there intersected by huge tree roots and rocks intersected by trails, making pedestrian progress with luggage along the beach slow and painstaking. But there wasn't really any other principal road and we noticed that many of the locals had the habit of taking to it on horseback. In order to avoid being bogged down and left to wither like two dead branches in the incoming tide, we left our luggage at the tienda serving as cafe, shop, restaurant and landing dock in one. A cold beer was necessary before we set out to seek shelter, which we ended up finding in a private home owned by another motherly lady recently returned from her native Manizales to start taking care of all the things that had deteriorated during her absence.

It was past noon and Asíle felt we should have something to eat. Though I could certainly have done with a bite, the local cuisine on offer in the village seemed so far from inspiring that I'd rather just have another beer. However, as we returned to pick up our luggage we opted for lunch at the tienda and ended up receiving a bony fish unceremoniously reduced to a brown amorphous chunk by rancid oil. I simply couldn't finish it and Asíle, though habitually braver than I, wasn't too happy about hers either. Although it would be unfair to say the dish was expensive by Champs-Élysées or Beverly Hills standards, it still wasn't for free which instantly made me start dreaming about an accommodation where once again we could cook our own meals.

Happy to get out of this deadlock where the proprietor family was now also having lunch — unperturbed by the fact that the oil in their deep frying device had remained unchanged over the past two months — we found shelter in a room on the second floor of Rita's spacious house with its second floor terrace offering what, (abstraction made for a couple of trees blocking the view), could have been a panoramic vista of the bay from a tangle of hammocks swinging in the breeze. The room itself, at the back of the second floor terrace, wasn't too bad. It had an adjacent toilet where the flush seemed to work and a trickle of water from the wall even made an almost plausible impression of a shower. To take one was another matter because there was no floor console to prevent water from the shower to flood the entire bathroom. But the real novelty was that all the walls, including that of the bathroom, just went half way up to the ceiling, rendering privacy, in connection with any intimate activity of your imagination, well-nigh impossible.

There was also a young woman living in the house with an even younger child, susceptible, as kids are, to crying whenever the crudity of life pitilessly revealed itself. Borrowing from the kitchen, asking for a tomato as though it had been a piece of gold, or a garlic clove as though it had been a truffle of the same size, as well as searching for utensils, felt like an intrusion on my part in spite of the inhabitants' cheerful reassurances to the contrary, and I soon grew tired of having to guess where cutlery and plates were hiding instead of being shown to their storage places right away. We did spend the night in the house, and although the rooms did have window frames these had no glass windows. Now that really wasn't necessary either considering temperatures there are always reliably tropical. Ideally though there should have been mosquito nets. Their absence made the one and only net covering the bed all the more important, but it was too small to properly fit around the mattress, with the consequence that swarms of mosquito bastards found sneaky ways to my veins feasting on blood of Englishman all night long (Asíle, being next to native, was better off in this respect). But we survived and next morning the kind and talkative landlady presented us with an alternative, feigning the sudden arrival of guests of her own during the weekend as an excuse to get rid of us and simultaneously cater to our comfort.

This is how we ended up on Juan-Guillermo's property, a very friendly, most capable and efficient Antioquian in his early 40s who had grown tired of city life and sought refuge on a patch of land he had turned into a Garden of Eden of his own. Notwithstanding some minor inconveniences — which I shall soon describe more in detail — being received on his turf turned out to be a stroke of pure good luck. A lush enclosure no more than 70 yards from the beach, with its own little pond inhabited by a young cayman, a wealth of plants carrying sweet, delectable fruit, flowers big as trees, the trees in turn housing an entire family of fierce and dragon-like but in reality peaceful iguanas, sculptural art work, a kind of tropical loggia with a second floor acting as a platform for beds and hammocks, shower and toilet on ground level decorated with mosaics and a well equipped kitchen just waiting for my eager hands.

If only I could find the ingredients to occupy them. Here too all the local stores were eerily empty of produce one or two days before the arrival of the cargo boat carrying weekly fresh supplies to the coastal communities. At this time there weren't even potatoes, let alone tomatoes, to be had for money, and this in a country where all you need to do to make a stick grow is to plant it in the ground. But this is where ever-resourceful Juan-Guillermo himself came into the picture. Not only did he have some left over vegetables in stock; on my request he also put an order together for ground meat, chicken, wine and a bottle of whisky to be brought by the next day's afternoon run from Turbo, where he'd be sending a local boy with the morning lancia anyway to run errands.

Meanwhile he got us installed in the treehouse in the corner next to the entrance. It was actually a bungalow of sorts built on stilts and accessible from beneath only by a ladder. One could close the hole in the floor with a kind of sliding hatch, otherwise folded up against the wall, but it was a business that required both timing and precision as the planks constituting it were heavy and the bipartite platform, divided by hinges, always had a tendency to come crushing down by force of gravity threatening to crush a few violinist fingers en passant. The abode with its high ceiling and ample natural light was charming and had a nice double bed covered by a mosquito net of suitable dimension. A toilet decorated with mosaics and a circular outdoor shower room filled with plants and round pebbles directly under sun, moon and stars completed the picture. Once again we were facing a situation where the house had indeed large window openings but nothing in them, not even mosquito nets.

But we had our own arsenal of insect repellents, the application of which was quite necessary after nightfall provided we didn't want to take refuge under the mosquito tent of the bed right away. But while insect repellents are there to fight off smaller marauders, they can't prevent one inch black bugs, enticed by the electric light, from infesting an open space such as this. Asíle had an amazing hand with them and would simply collect them off the ceiling lamp shade, designed and stitched together from palm leaves (she's an excellent seamstress) and amass them in jar where they would roll in wine for a while only to eventually perish happily by an overdose of alcohol. The frogs, on the other hand, were too big to be put in jars and killed off by a cheap round of drinks.

Readers of Gabriel Marcia Marques, widely regarded as one of Latin America's finest representatives of a narrative style sometimes subsumed under the heading 'magical realism', may recall mind boggling episodes from his books where pink frogs start to rain from heaven. The reader may admire, accept or dismiss this image as a product of suggestive creative fancy, poetic license, call it what you will, but he will not normally believe it can actually happen. But whereas it's true that cats and dogs don't actually rain on you, in spite of the rhetorical figure insinuating it, the raining of frogs, I assure you, is not uncommon in Colombia, where what is sometimes also referred to as 'surrealism' makes up an integral part of the everyday. Thus, I repeat, frogs do fall from heaven in Colombia. It all starts with a regular rain, always conducive to open wide the sluices of heaven during the monsoon season.

At ten o'clock, every evening all year round, the local power grid in Triganá shuts down to save precious gasoline, since that what it runs on to produce electricity. It can also seize the opportunity to shut down for two weeks or more, but that is a slightly more exceptional although not too infrequent occurrence. Whatever the situation, the light at your disposal is now either a torch, a candle or a fluorescent insect. The rest, the entire universe around you, including the impenetrable jungle, is black as pitch. It is in this situation — at first rather cosy since the roof actually does prevent the water from inundating your bed — that you're brought back to reality by a sudden thumping sound indicating a big UFO has just landed in the dark a couple of feet away from you. This dull, wet, subdued sound is followed by a squeak so loud that at first it freezes the blood in your veins to ice. Seconds later, as you realise that it's 'just a frog', there is a second landing followed by the same squeak, then a third... And now they begin to converse for real at your expense. Your house has turned into the most perfect shelter for their chit-chat and flirting during a squall. But mind you, the rain can go on for several hours and their conversation correspondingly.

Facing the challenge with incomparable presence of mind, Asíle again proved to me why I must infinitely admire and love her. These frogs are no small and cuddly creatures that you can allow paternally to crawl around in your open palm; they are moist-eyed, light green, slimy toads, four to six inches long and half as wide, legs and feet not counted. At the mere sound of them Asíle would jump out of bed with her flashlight and, although they clearly inspired horror in her too, grasp them with a plastic bag to protect her precious skin and hurl them out of the windows. You would perhaps imagine this to be a vain effort, but frogs are intelligent creatures and after a while seemed to realise they were party crashers, and so would either stay outside or gather around the *oeil de boeuf* under the gable roof where Asíle couldn't reach them. Over there they were sufficiently distant not to overly bother our night sleep. As for the rest we could only pray to Rainman that our mosquito net would be strong enough to resist the impact of a frog landing on its roof, so as to prevent him, or her, from competing with *El gran Capitan Papi Camaro*n navigating the twin peaks of Mount Bora Bora from beneath the cotton sails.

Speaking of shrimp, it was Juan-Guillermo, again, who managed to find us two pounds of large shrimp fished straight out of the Caribbean. By the Capurganians we had been told shrimp had to be bought and brought from Medellín, which seemed quite a detour for them to arrive at our table. Of course it wasn't true. More likely the Capurganians are just too lazy to fish for them and therefore prefer to pretend that they don't exist. But Juan-Guillermo knew his fisherman. At this time the grocery and wine shipment from Turbo had arrived, so there was olive oil, garlic and lime to marinate the lot. Peeling and marinating them, I couldn't help coming to think of two comparable moments I had once enjoyed.

One was on the island Ko-Chang in the south-eastern archipelago of Thailand, part of the Trat region bordering Cambodia. There is a fishing village there famous for being constructed on wooden piers. As it is a tourist attraction it has certainly changed character over time, nowadays featuring several hotels and restaurants on the water, or rather, just above it. I was drawn into one of the latter by a small pond in its centre filled with unusually large tiger shrimp. Ordering them on my plate involved selecting the ones I wanted with a net on a rod from the school, with the subsequent result that I was served eight of these bastards straight from the grill together with an old bottle of Chablis that I miraculously found waiting for me inside a transparent cooler in the middle of the restaurant. It was reasonably priced too and, in spite of the vicissitudes it must have traversed in order to end up in this exotic show case, still delicious, leaving behind iridescent curtains inside the glass when moved around. Sitting down at an outdoor table by the rim of the lagoon into which the moon placidly poured her liquid honey, savouring my charcoal grilled gambas with lime and a perfectly cool white Bourgogne of exceptional quality, was an experience that almost certainly must have made me shed tears from sheer bliss.

Which leads me to the other unforgettable experience attended by members of the shrimp family. This time in Nicaragua. A couple of years ago I rented for two months, straddling Christmas and New-Years, a cottage in San Juan del Sur on the country's southern Pacific coast. It's quite a picturesque town, attracting a fair number of tourists from both hemispheres, although the northern winter is its main season. It also has its expat community comprising Americans and Europeans alike, many of whom run bars and restaurants. It also, alas, attracts surfers — a single-minded crowd I'm only all too familiar with from my one year sojourn in Puerto Rican Rincón, one of the world's top ten hotspots for this brain killing activity — or maybe it's the other way round: because you're stupid you find nothing better to do in life than to surf the waves!

The main attraction of San Juan, Nicaragua, on the other hand, is not the height of its waves but its natural harbour: a true horseshoe bay with a beach of fine black sand. Still, the sand covers no more than two miles' worth of coastline. Inversely it's very wide, especially in ebb-tide. It's framed by rocks rising to the size of mountains at both ends, protecting the town against sea and wind from this direction. But this natural barrier — as I came to experience during several days with almost scarily blue skies, when it was almost impossible to walk upright outside and certainly very dangerous because of all things flying through the air — doesn't prevent turbulence originating in the Caribbean, given free reins over Lago Cocibolca and funnelled through a corridor of conical volcanoes, from hitting San Juan with gale force winds. Low lying hills, partly cultivated, partly clad in greenery, characterise the surrounding coastal plain and there is only a forty-five minute car ride to the shores of Cocibolca from which the island Ometepe, with its volcanic twin towers, raises majestically out of the lake.

My visit to that island preceded my arriving in San Juan and was remarkable for several reasons. First it was the spectacular boat trip from Granada to get there. There are only two runs per week, but if scarcity of time is of no immediate concern, one of these departures is definitely worth waiting for. Sitting directly on the deck, pinned up against the wall with my mochila acting as a cushion and the rumble of the engines as a musical accompaniment, I enjoyed a fabulous afternoon and sunset over the volcano Mombacho as the ship steered clear of the islets off Granada, ploughing a furrow through the lake's turbid waters.

When we arrived to the island it was dark and I can only vaguely remember what the hotel in the town of Altagracia, where I came to stay overnight, looked like. Next day was vowed for exploration, but first of all I needed to get out of Altagracia which, in spite of its lofty name, was a bit depressing (Nicaragua in general has its share of poverty and although the Ometepe island certainly has a developed infrastructure capable of accommodating tourists, there are some gloomy places one happily avoids.)

So from Altagracia I took a taxi to the beach community Santo Domingo where I found myself an acceptable fifteen-dollar room. The rest of the day I walked the alternately sandy/rocky beach and hung out in the hotel cafeteria, getting to know what to do and where to go. However, as dinner time approached I decided to try the restaurant of a nearby and slightly more upscale hotel. This is where I ran into Ricardo and his two female friends Sarah and Tonia. They were all three Nicaraguans, but Ricardo had once crossed the Rio Grande like another Rubicon, and after some adventures as an illegal immigrant managed to become a naturalised subject under Uncle Sam's watchful eye. This of course didn't happen just like that. Ricardo had been fortunate to arrive in the United States right before his native country was taken over by a government considered communist by the US presidential administration. Practically overnight he became a political refugee and allowed to apply for citizenship, which he was granted. Ever since he's been a stout pillar of American society; since several years a civil servant in a managerial position.

Tonia is his cousin and what I didn't know then was that the lively two mature girls were actually lovers — I guess I hadn't really met with lesbians that friendly towards me before! In fact, they were absolutely charming and so was Ricardo, whom I didn't think of at the time as being gay either. We had a most inspiring and amusing dinner conversation, after they had asked me to join their table, at the end of which it was decided that we should explore one of the island's major attractions together next day: the waterfall midway up the Volcano Madéras on the southern sphere of the island.

I deliberately say sphere instead of hemisphere, because it seems like a more appropriate description. The island of Ometepe, seen from above, has the shape of an hourglass with a flat narrow isthmus as its waist. Each of the two spheres is the result of volcanic activity that over time has created two heaven-raging cones. The northern volcano, slightly higher than its southern twin, is still active, whereas the latter, apparently extinct, has a water filled crater. Perhaps this crater to some extent feeds the water fall of San Ramón. Whatever the case, in

December the water was still abundant in the fall and the trip to get there a perfect adventure.

The waterfall of San Ramón can be reached from the *Finca Mystica*, located above Punta el Congo on the coast. From there it's roughly a two hour walk to the cascade, on a trail that gradually merges into a riverbed, turning the final ascent into something of a challenge. The landscape this day was immensely scenic under a brilliant sun, the trees full of monkeys and parrots. We had such great fun getting up there since Tonia had some problems walking the entire distance and, feigning complete exhaustion, theatrically fell into Ricardo's arms, or vice versa. But our problems were all dealt with in excellent spirits and no one sustained physical injury. Sarah, the older of the two girls, and perhaps suspecting what lay ahead, had wisely refrained from joining us. Instead she was comfortably installed on the Finca's terrace enjoying the views from there together with some coffee. Meanwhile Ricardo and I joined in with the crowd swimming in the lagoon and we were crying out like children from the sheer joy of taking a cool shower in one of the powerful trickles branching off from the cascade.

But as though that swim had only wet our appetites, we found ourselves next day at the famous *Ojo de agua*, which is a natural pool, hidden in an oasis, only a few kilometres from where our hotels were located. It is indeed a natural pool but it has been enhanced in various ways, with a full service restaurant and deck chair service of drinks and snacks. The entrance fee is modest, the turquoise water fabulous, clear and temperate. To sit in the shade of some broad-leaved tree and watch the sunrays play in and out of the foliage and through the living water, is a truly poetic experience, making at least one visit to the springs of Ojo de Agua mandatory for anyone visiting Ometepe.

Before our ways parted Ricardo, driving his cousin and her friend onwards to San Juan del Sur, told me that if I ever came to Miami and didn't have anywhere to stay, I could always call him up. This subsequently happened and it was on this occasion that Ricardo straightforwardly told me that: 'Of course you can stay in my home, but I want you to know that I'm gay.' I remember answering that his being gay wasn't a problem as far as I was concerned, hoping in turn he wouldn't mind if I wasn't. Seeing and confirming a relieving sense of humour in each other, this made for a solid beginning of our friendship. But even though Ricardo loves a good laugh and mostly sees the general craziness of life through the benevolent spectacles of comedy, he has, as can be expected in a person with his emotional disposition, some feminine traits that sometimes play tricks on him. For example, at one point he got very upset with me because I had told him ('out of the blue' as his version has it) that I thought it was ridiculous of him to even pretend being a woman (he does like to dress up and act like one on special occasions!) when for physical reasons alone it's impossible. What I really meant by this he never considered relevant. He was just hurt and, exactly like a woman pretending to be offended, would hardly talk to me for a couple of days. I finally had to ask him the compulsory: 'What is it with you, Darling?' only to receive the suffering-female-standard-riposte: 'Nothing...'

Of course it didn't help trying to explain the reason for my comment was that I had once, when he was dressed up, put my arm around his shoulders to see what it would look like, only to realise that whereas my arms are normally long enough to not only reach around a woman's shoulders (even if she's quite athletic), but also to play with her tits, I could hardly even reach around his shoulder with my fingertips, let alone play with his tits. 'With such a broad back there's simply isn't much hope for you to ever become a woman', I concluded in a matter-of-fact tone of voice. But this obvious observation — necessarily if also perhaps tragically true — didn't please him all that much, though I think he finally forgave me and even began to laughingly tell his friends about the terrible insult he had had to endure from me. As for myself, I was quite relieved to see that he had apparently gotten over his resentment.

Over time I not only became close friends with his sofa bed in the living room but with his dog (may he rest in peace!) as well, entrusted as I was with the responsibility of taking him out during the day. I was also happy to cook for Ricardo and myself, meaning we from time to time ended up almost having a little bachelor household together. But then again Ricardo, as I soon realised, longed to be in a stable relationship, and not just have casual sex (nothing seems to come easier to these guys than to call each other up and unabashedly ask for sex, in this way simply spelling out what a man only dares to think when asking a woman he desires out for a drink, or even dinner.) As of late he's been blessed with such a prospective life partner, and so has grown a little distant towards me. But I don't consider this chill as a prelude to any major ice age, and besides I'm sure *Ricarda* will be very proud of having cut such a blazing heroine in Lorenzo el Magnifico's latest book!

By and large it's interesting to note how widespread homosexuality and, in particular, transgender behaviour is in various parts of Latin America, otherwise perhaps better known for their pronounced macho cultures. There is the phenomenon of the so-called *muxes* among the Zapotec Indians in the Oaxaca region of Mexico. These are not necessarily homosexual men, but are definitely effeminate such and very fond of dressing up and behaving as women on festive occasions, which in this party prone region means every other day. Paradoxically they form no subculture but are integral parts of the artisan community, known for their skills in dress making and the decorative arts.

Recently I witnessed the New Year's celebrations in the Andean town Baños de Agua Santa in Ecuador. Apart from displaying enormously intense and enduring fireworks, this fiesta coincides with hundreds of young men dressing up as women, gathering in groups and performing in improvised street theatre plays. Once again one would perhaps think that the Indians, with their traditional modes of life, would feel estranged by these transgender shows. On the contrary: they are absolutely fascinated by them and cluster day and night around them, laughing, giggling, applauding and endorsing them in every way possible. Even here it's hard to tell the men who are actually homosexuals fond of cross-dressing from the ones who just enjoy dressing up in this way and act as women on this particular occasion.

Apart from these and similar events elsewhere, there are also a steady percentage and, so far as I can tell, pretty even distribution of 'regular' homosexuality throughout Latin America. Typically gay communities and lifestyles are of course most noticeable in the larger cities, but very frequently more intimate tourist hotspots, such as Nicaraguan Granada, in addition to the 'regular' *putas* also offers '*putos*', as well as male children prostituting themselves. The latter is of course another sad side effect of cynicism taking advantage of poverty and destitution, but though some foreign tourists certainly are to blame for these abominable practices, some of the worst scenarios, even involving the death of street children, are actually domestic affairs.

For example, there is the case of Luis Garavito, a Colombian psychopath branded by the press as the 'worst' serial killer in recorded history. In 1999 he was finally apprehended by the police. In the subsequent trial he confessed to having raped, tortured and murdered 147 boys between the ages eight and sixteen. However, the total number of his victims may be as high as 300, many cases still pending investigation. Though his accumulated sentence amounted to 1,853 years in prison, the Colombian legal code at the time only admitted a maximum prison sentence of 30 years. One would assume that Garavito at least got that much. But as he showed himself helpful in the police search for the bodies of his victims, and because of his many candid confessions, his sentence was, somewhat surprisingly, reduced to 22 years in prison, with the possibility of an even earlier release for good behaviour.

Garavito himself has certainly picked up on that last suggestion and in a 2006 TV interview assured that he had been possessed by the devil at the time of his unspeakable crimes, but that he had now become a religious man, even the priest of his own church, and upon his release would start a political career destined to help and raise public awareness of the predicament of abused children in Colombia. It is thus possible that the man responsible for the rape, torture and cold blooded murder of 300 children is soon going to walk the streets again as a free man, if this has not already happened. Whatever the case, I would at least think twice, as a parent, before sending my children to his 'reformed' church for catechism…

Now, this all happens within a legal system where members of the terrorist organisation FARC, responsible for thousands of lethal attacks on civilians, sit comfortably at Fidel Castro's invitation and expense in Havana, forcing the president of Colombia to go over there to negotiate deals involving complete amnesty for these mass murderers, and where a peasant (this is an actual case) is sentenced to nine years in prison for simply being in the possession of a handgun for his own and his family's protection. His crime? He didn't have a license. Here one could really argue that the poor in the end don't stand a chance to see justice done. Meanwhile a corrupt government unimpededly seeks to strike deals with its even more criminal rivals. In reality the latter, no matter how vigorously the government would like to deny it, make up an integral part of the political and economic system of the country, providing countless people with jobs and money that the official authorities would otherwise have to add to their list of impoverished, though otherwise capable, citizens ignored by the state.

San Juan del Sur and a return to the pleasure of crustaceans

While we were still in Nicaragua Ricardo, Tonia and Sarah expressed a wish to meet with me again in San Juan del Sur, where, as I said, they were heading next. However, when I got there some days later they had apparently travelled on towards the mountainous region of the north. At the last hotel I visited on Ometepe I had been the only guest on a beach primarily frequented by a cow herd on its way to or from its grazing grounds. The water on this southward side was less wind driven and consequently calmer, but it wasn't really any pleasure to take a bath in the turbid water; instead I regularly went back to the absolutely delightful Ojo de Agua for my swims.

What I did enjoy on the other hand was the serene silence of the place and the splendid sunsets over the mainland. Thus it was not until reaching San Juan that the tables turned, the ocean being as inviting as the noise in the streets grew unbearable: Nicaraguan youths have a habit of celebrating *la Fiesta de la Virgen Immaculata* by detonating veritable bombs in her honour, and this goes on, day and night, but preferably at night, where hitting the bull's eye is to send a bomb fifty metres up into the air and detonate it there at four o'clock in the morning. Ricardo, having once been a cheese selling street boy himself, tried to explain this as 'their culture', to which I immediately delivered the heart-felt reply: 'No, it's their lack of culture!' That said, let us rather turn back to the ocean and the peaceful contemplation of the same.

The swell of the Pacific entering the bay of San Juan has an average amplitude of eighteen seconds — I ignore what distance that would make between the wave crests, but I have personally, standing in the water, counted the seconds passing in between the breaking of these waves. So that's just about its frequency: eighteen seconds of silence between the roars every time a wave that might have travelled several times the circumference of the Earth makes a landfall. The phenomenon instilled in me a sensation of unfathomable vastness second only to that produced by the thought of the universe itself and *its* wave lengths. The Pacific, in this sense, is a well chosen name for this elemental entity. To my imagination it seems too grandiose to even allow for the existence of gods or goddesses, at least such of 'only' superhuman European stature. Even Allah and Jehovah seem like petty tribal idols in comparison. It would take something like the rough monolithic Easter Island statues to give this immensity 'a human face', and even so it remains impersonal, enigmatic, and indifferent to man and his destiny in the highest degree.

So, in order to protect themselves from this mass of divine indifference, the local community has raised a huge statue of Christ in genuine fiberglass on top of the northern rock. It is like a more modest version of the Christo of Rio de Janeiro, but it's still very impressive, if not designed in the very best of taste. It's also lit up in the night and from my terrace up on the hill, at the opposite end of the beach, I had a crystal clear view of our Lord and Saviour any time of the day. It so happened that one of these coincided with New Years' Eve, the early part of which I had decided to spend in splendid isolation. An oil barrel cut in half served as a barbecue on the terrace and the guardian of the compound — oh yes, this time I happened to live in a gated community located above the commercial harbour area. To access it one had to pass through the poorer part of town where the streets at night are as dimly lit as they're conspicuously empty.

On a hillside dominating this part of town Italian Roberto — originally from Lago di Bolsena in the heart of ancient Etruscan country — first had a house built for himself and then married a young Nicaraguan woman (or if it was the other way round). Then he invested in a series of bungalows which he rents out to strangers like me. The only access to the complex is by way of an extremely steep asphalt road. It is abruptly barred by a huge iron gate which doesn't have any smaller door in it. There is of course also a heavy chain to keep the gate together and a padlock that has to be opened and closed even after a dozen Flor de Caña. If that operation fails, there is in the last instance always the armed guardian in his cabin opposite Roberto's house. Before he would descend it was in my best interest to make him understand that I was not one of the louche local elements so as to prevent him from pointing his gun at me. But the good man was well aware of the intricacies of that gate and this is where I come back to where I was: it was precisely he who helped me collect some dry wood to light up my barbecue for my own, very special New Year's Eve Party.

I mentioned that the compound was situated above the commercial port. One of the advantages with this is that the local fish dealers are all close by and their catch cheap to come by. I believe three pounds of fresh lobster tail — some smaller some bigger — cost me something like 12 dollars. These I had cracked open with the aid of a hammer and a knife and marinated in olive oil, garlic, black pepper, fresh coriander, red hot pepper, salt and lime. Evening come they had been soaking in a refrigerator environment since the day before. The ice box also contained two bottles of Argentinian white wine and after sunset I began to prepare my feast by opening the first of them while waiting for the moon to cast her silvery net into the bay. Christ with his outstretched arms was lit up on the mountain and so was I down in the valley.

I assume the reader is familiar with the fragrant scent of for example hickory. What I had in stock was a whole range of such fragrances released from the embers of tropical wood. Once I had obtained a Luciferian glow, I put my lobster tails to work on the grill—all of them. I left them sizzling on either sides for a while and then carefully poised them on my plate while filling up another glass. There was bread on the table and I poured a *noisette* of home made mayonnaise on a separate plate—lime goes without saying. Then I went on the attack and believe me: since there were no human witnesses to my debauchery, I didn't bother too much about my table manners. I simply stuffed myself with one chunk of juicy, fumigated lobster tail after the other. It was an enjoyment so intense that I have no idea whether minutes or hours elapsed before I had satiated myself and emptied the second bottle of ice cold white wine—I like it that way, especially in the tropics! After having contemplated Christ in moonlight through the rosy curtain of inebriation and carnal self-indulgence, I brought myself together, emptied the glass and descended to hit the celebrating town, passing on the remaining pound or so of grilled lobster tail to the night guardian, who was happy to receive such a treat during his lonely night shift.

From the rest of the evening I have vague memories. I recall negotiating my way past the hotel guard at the lower entrance of the town's luxury hotel. From its terrace, poolside, I finished off the last night of the year with gin and tonics that had turned kaleidoscopic from all the fireworks, in an ambience of chatting tourists and an American gentleman of a certain age flying high on champagne and Viagra, ready to take on not just one, but two or three of the stunning escort girls making up his suite, thus, perhaps, ever so slightly overrating his stamina. As for myself I eventually found my way home, sober enough to watch my steps all the way to the iron gate. Once there I was at my wits' end and I called the guardian to open it for me, feeling that this would in some sense make us even. Speaking of even, I might even have had a final nightcap, or two, on my own terrace to top things off—but that I can't clearly remember. The day after I was simply too tired to do anything, which by the way is not so easy to do as some people might imagine, since doing and nothingness really constitute a contradiction in terms. The only real way to do nothing is to be nothing, which simply is another contradiction in terms, leading nowhere.

That said, let's finally return to the Darién, Bay of Urubá, Colombia. Here I was, again in the possession of shrimp. With a freezer/refrigerator (I never quite understood what it was originally designed to be) that was only up and running for six hours a day, there was little time to lose even though its insulation was so effective that the interior of the box would actually withstand 18 hours of daily exposure to the hot outside air without turning meat, fish and poultry inedible. But I figured it was not a good idea to tempt the devil and proceeded to quickly marinate the shrimp. Then it was just to wait. Evening come, these creatures too turned out to be absolutely lovely. I tossed them in with spaghetti in a sauce I had reduced from their shells together with whatever vegetables available and white wine from which I extracted my stock. I was happy with the result and the aphrodisiac effect of all these *al dente* cooked shrimp was not lost on Asíle either, who henceforth would begin spinning a whole yarn around the one and only 'Gran Papi Camarón' and his prowess.

Admittedly, 'shrimp' is not exactly a term of endearment by which most men would like to have their family jewel referenced. Luckily there's shrimp and there's shrimp. Some are even called Jumbo! After having savoured several of these particularly succulent and fleshy animals I thus felt inclined to interpret Asíle's insistence on calling El Capitán by such a family name, as a compliment, and decided to adopt her suggestion as a relevant designation. From this very moment and onwards *El Gran Papi Capitán Camarón* was to be an integral part of our intimacy, not only offering a perfect pseudonym, but quite literally turning him into a personality of legendary stature, later to be confounded (at my enthusiastic behest) with Captain Morgan, who alone in the tiny isolated Caribbean island of San Andres is said to have had 52 wives and sired 53 children with the same — I have the story, rendered in an inimitable Creole twang, straight from the mouth of the female guide at the San Andres Island House Museum: 'Whodattfo?' (For whom is that?): 'Dattfome!' (That's for me!). Yah Man!

As time went by I did indeed make some attempts to aggrandise El Gran Papi Capitan Camaron even further by promoting him to *El Coronel Cola de Langosta*, but for some reason that superlative never quite gained the same notoriety as Capitan Cameron, and so, 'willy-nilly', I had to acquiesce to that particular title, notwithstanding that the Coronel was sometimes respectfully mentioned in this context as well.

But ours wasn't just an empire of the senses under the auspices of raining frogs. For me, and I suppose for Asíle too, the sojourn in Triganá was also a propitious time for peaceful recuperation. Since there was less to see and to do in the immediate surroundings, we soon found ourselves in rather meditative moods — I would typically spend most of the day laying in the hammock in our bungalow, listening to the birds, watching the hours go by and the sun come round, while reading Octavia Paz' critical essays on artistic modernism and the crepuscule of the western avant-garde. I had found the volume in Rita's home and realised I must bring it with me without further ado. Theft? No, since I was the one really needing to read that book at this moment and it wouldn't be missed, its absence not even noticed, the book having been put on the shelf by an unknown hand in the first place. Meanwhile, Asíle had turned the extra bed into a day sofa on which she was reading too — a younger Spanish writer the name of whom I have forgotten — occasionally interrupted by me asking her to help me explain the meaning of a Spanish word or the intricacies of an idiomatic phrase.

Paz writes a very clear and intelligible prose though, and his essays on modernism in art and poetry are to my knowledge some of the very best works in the genre. It was simply delightful to have his voice as a spiritual *cicerone* in the jungle. His voice reached me all the way from Mexico and I have always envied Latin American writers their prerogative of being able to mix more or less radical political agendas with both deep emotions and aesthetic concerns without becoming *too* pathetic. The reason for this, I believe, is that emotion is at the core of Latin literature. This certainly doesn't prevent Paz from also being an important art critic and thinker, which is where so many poetic natures have found a kind of spiritual home when the initial élan of youth and folly has abandoned them. I'm not in the position to judge his poetry with any authority, but then there is only one writer in the entire world whose poetry, taken as a whole, I can truly say I enjoy to read, and that is Baudelaire's. But he too was an astute art critic and I have always relished his essays on various subjects just as much as his poems. Which goes to say that poets invariably make the best literary critics — not to say the only ones!

We entertained a silence shared. Often I found myself content to just notice her move about, take a shower, comb her hair, put something together, take something apart, all of which she did with innate feminine grace and discretion. I can't remember what we talked about, although I know I would ramble for an hour and then listen to what she had to say for another. But it was all in tune with the surroundings, conducive to let any thought and feeling sink into oblivion as soon as it had been uttered. It really was one of those places, remote one could say, even though cell phone calls would always come through impeccably, reminding us that we were actually still within civilisation's ambit. As for us, we had entered a different mode in our communications. It was as if we had always known each other and yet also knew that we would always remain strangers. Strangers simply in the way man and woman must remain strangers to one another. To me Asíle is deeply enigmatic. Even her occasional female banalities, such as pretending to be offended by a straying word, just struck me as eternally feminine. Whenever she chose to have a mood, I simply refused to give in, knowing that whatever I had said was neither meant to be hurtful, nor, and more importantly, could it with any reasonable justification be interpreted as such. And sure enough, her moods would come and go like tropical squalls. What she really felt and thought about what I had said I never knew, and I also found it best that way, knowing that to ask a woman for her 'reasons' is an indecency.

To put things in proper perspective: we did have moments filled with intense action too. The most noteworthy was doubtless the day when we were supposed to pick up our grocery and wine delivery from Turbo. We had been told that the boat carrying our items would, for some reason, not arrive in Triganá but in the next settlement down the coast. To walk there along the shore should take us about 45 minutes. Not too cumbersome one would imagine. But it's one thing to walk over there empty-handed and another thing to carry a box with ten wine bottles back from it. The village itself is even smaller than Triganá and there isn't much else to do there than to watch the iguanas as they in turn patiently wait for the hens to leave their eggs unattended. As a matter of fact, we once made the experiment of putting an egg on one of the lower branches of a tree where our largest iguana habitually spent his indolent afternoons. Neither Asíle nor I ever actually saw him snatch it, although our eyes were glued to the tree, specifically to the portion of it where the egg had been lodged. As he descended he must have seized it with lightning speed, because gone it was. Which goes to prove that the hour long immobility and inertia of reptiles stands in direct inverse ratio to the sudden swiftness of their attack.

In a sense, our expedition to San Francisco was quite similar to such an attack. In a state of more or less zero activity we had to remind ourselves that the boat expected for landing on the other side of the bay in 45 minutes wasn't going to wait for us. So we jumped to our feet and strode down the beach, parts of which had further disintegrated from the morning rain and the ocean swell. A group of boys sat on a porch tacitly assessing the damage done: half of what only yesterday had been a sizeable portion of terrain between the house and the sea had vanished, making the present location of the house precarious to say the least. The only notable measure taken, however, had been to move the barbed wire closer to the shacks so that people could still pass outside the fence while having a minimum of ground under their feet.

We arrived in a San Francisco that was basking in the sun and so relaxed during siesta that not even the harbour kiosk was open. The concrete pier — by necessity sturdier than the one in Triganá which only had to withstand the soft tides of the bay, as opposed to the open sea shaping San Francisco's shoreline — lay abandoned. There was nothing to betray the imminent arrival of a fully charged passenger boat, but appearances were soon to change. After half an hour — as boredom began to infiltrate stillness — a speck appeared on the horizon. It moved quickly and eventually revealed itself as the boat we were waiting for. While the speedboat approached, the surroundings too sprang to sudden life. By its arrival some curious bystanders had gathered. Neither they nor the boat's crew would help disembarking passengers. The procedure of deposing an elderly woman and her daughter on the pier took a quarter of an hour and several times threatened to end in a catastrophe, the prospect of which failed to impress the crew. Finally, I managed to get a grip on her arm and with the aid of her daughter pull the bruised and exhausted woman out of the vessel.

We didn't have time to further cater to her comfort, though, since the boat was about to leave without its crew showing much interest in delivering our cargo either, which we had a hard time describing since we hadn't boxed it ourselves. It was eventually found and thrown onto the pier. The boxes turned out to contain all we had ordered except a bottle of whisky — that rather surprisingly was actually delivered two days later. The most immediate concern was how to get all merchandise to our village. I happened to remark to a bystander that it was a bit strange that the boat wouldn't stop in Triganá considering it being so close by. 'But of course it does', he happily answered while the roar of the engines excluded all verbal communication with the boat's captain, now steering his ship towards the very shores we had just left behind. This made me irritated and I unjustly blamed Asíle for not knowing that the boat was actually stopping at our village too, as though she somehow had an obligation to be better informed than I. There was nothing else for us to do than to charge ourselves like two mules and return whence we had come. Realising I had been unfair to my fair lady by letting my bad temper get the better of me, I insisted on carrying as much of the load as possible. But Asíle, though not very talkative, held fiercely on to her heavy charge. Even though she hardly responded to my efforts to put the irritation behind us, she carried on bravely. Upon entering the village we were very thirsty. We drank water, rested up a bit in the shade and finally reached our abode, where the rest of the afternoon, after cool showers, was spent in tranquillity. In the end harmony was restored and as the sting of the emotional skirmish began to wear off it, too, turned into a potent spice of love.

Turbo

In this and similar manner we stayed put for a week. Then we felt the need to break the spell. To do this we again had to risk our lives on the high seas. The two little dogs that had watched faithfully over us accompanied us to the pier and could be seen running along the beach wagging their tails while the speed boat headed for the open sea and the vegetation vanished into the glistening morning mist. The skipper was no exception to the ones we previously had encountered, and I might easily have injured my back this time too, had I not been mentally prepared for the ordeal ahead. Once again we were forced to take seats close to the prow, which, it must be emphasised, is the worst location for a passenger. Luckily the sea didn't get heavier but smoother as we went deeper into the Gulf. The proximity to Rio Atrato announced itself by muddy waters effectively concealing massive logs or tree branches that the captain, steadily maintaining maximum speed, would have no chance of seeing, let alone avoiding, before it was too late. All the same we safely made it across to Turbo, the regional hub on the eastern shores of the bay.

Here the Colombian army, from having been quiet and discreet in their presence in the Darién, gave everybody reason to believe that no one was safe. Every boat had to report to a group of stone-faced young soldiers, who didn't even bother to turn the points of their machine guns away from the passengers while questioning the captains. We were let through and came to behold something seemingly taken straight out of Africa. Even though I have never been to Freetown, Liberia, or Conakry, Sierra-Leone, this is exactly what I imagine them to be like, judged on personal experience of similar African ports. The only tangible difference was that this African port was primarily Spanish speaking. Otherwise the setting was a perfect backdrop to the opening scenes of *Heart of Darkness.*

Asíle was visibly depressed by the lacklustre appearance of the run-down ships anchored in the estuary and ramshackle edifices lining the piers. Some people were hanging off ship ladders, some swimming in the oily waters. There were fires. One of them must have been fed rubber or some other noxious substance since thick, black smoke billowed out from it. It was a hot, unforgiving monsoon afternoon waiting for its first lightning to crack the heavens open. But though the clouds looked menacing there was so far no sign of rain. We reached our destination without a single drop falling on our heads. On the other hand: like wasps attracted to syrup local helping hands were all over us. I got a firm hold of our luggage and blazed a trail through the mass of arms offering to help us carry it the twenty-five steps to the taxis outside. I don't know if Asíle even realised how quickly I managed to get us out of the docks, past the crowds, into a taxi and from there into a minibus taking us straight to our next port of call.

Necoclí

From our comparatively comfortable position inside the bus I jestingly suggested to Asíle several interesting venues for sightseeing, all of which she vehemently rejected. I further suggested we should move in to one the harbour area hotels to get to know the locals a bit better. Judged by their appearance these accommodations were indeed abject, but it was fun to taunt her since she would close her eyes, shake her head and present such a cute facial expression of utter horror. Had I been alone on this trip it's possible that I would have stayed a bit longer in this town just to check it out its exoticism: a mirror held up by South America to Africa!

But now we were under way to an even smaller township located an hour's ride to the north. The landscape on this side of the Gulf is hilly, but less mountainous than the one in the Darién. It is also to a large extent cultivated and has large pastures with grazing live-stock. There are cows and horses — and real Indians! Midway between Turbo and Necoclí is an Indian reserve. It announced itself by women carrying heavily charged baskets on their heads. Other women were sitting by the road side with small children playing around them as the bus, at full speed, brushed past them within inches. I involuntarily closed my eyes but when I reopened them neither the Indians by the road side, nor the driver, seemed to think anything out of the ordinary had happened. As for myself, I once again had to accommodate myself to the apparent fatalism of people living under a tropical sun. Even though the situation was indeed fraught with danger, no menace or even disrespect seemed to have been intended on the driver's part. But, having the entire road to himself, why did he have to pass so close to this little family group? And how could the woman allow her kids to play so dangerously close to the traffic? The answer my friend, the answer my friend, the answer is blowing in the wind…

On our way we also passed a restaurant named Don Tranquilo, a name that immediately struck us as the most perfect title for our hotel manager in Capurganá, who wouldn't make the slightest effort to have the overfilled, stinking trashcan emptied even as myriads of worms and insects were crawling inside it. Instead he was glued to his computer, looking for girls on Facebook. He was your Don Tranquilo all right, unperturbed in his sweet daydreams even in the face of the most abject reality.

Once having arrived in the small town of Necoclí — an Eden by comparison to Turbo — we proceeded to have lunch and then squeezed ourselves and our luggage into a moto taxi that took us out of town and some miles up the coastal road to a small seaside hotel named Tiki Lounge. Elena, the female owner, was a friend of our hosts in Triganá and that's how Asíle, charging herself with the mission of finding us accommodation, had ended up making a reservation over the telephone. Although our room had no more than basic amenities — a door to close, a ceiling fan, and a mosquito net in the window frame to keep insects at bay — it seemed a grand, almost unheard-of luxury. Not having to hermetically seal off a mosquito tent from the inside before going to bed was in itself a great relief. And not having to expect giant frogs at bedside every time there was a drop of rain an even greater one. There was also a kitchen at our disposal. It's large, rectangular air holes on the contrary neither had windows nor mosquito nets, with the consequence that all sorts of not so delicious looking black bugs, attracted by the intense glare of the electric bulb, fell head long into the food under preparation. But we got used to that as well and patiently fished out dead insects simmering in boiling water or even in the occasionally uncovered pasta sauce.

The sandy beach, at the time of our arrival filled with flotsam and jetsam, wasn't very attractive in a conventional tourist perspective and hardly invited to walks. The water had the colour of bad coffee and although Elena enthusiastically went for her daily swim there an hour before sunset, neither I nor Asíle felt tempted to follow her example. We were even more astonished to learn that the water at this time of the year was at its very clearest and the debris at a minimum. It consisted mainly of driftwood but it took several days before anyone began arranging the logs and palm branches in pyramids destined for bonfires — I believe some of my own palpable efforts to initiate this process eventually rubbed off on the staff. Some days later the beach was cleared and one night — the sparks competing with the stars for attention — we lit up a beautiful fire, raging sky high in celebration of Guitche Manito, the Indian Master of Life (more about him later on).

That same day a special guest had arrived. It was the owner of a boat sitting on the sand next to the main building, and he had come in order to bring it over to the other side of the gulf. It turned out he had his own house in the same Aguacate we had visited some ten days earlier. But his house was not located on the tranquil side of the village. Instead it sat right on the coast facing head-on the strong trade winds. I think this was all part of his plan. He wanted things to stay a bit on the rough side. It was therapy to him. I do insist on that term since he was a former Colombian psychoanalyst who had lived in Paris for twenty years and studied with Jacques Lacan. He had also been the secretary and translator of Jean-François Lyotard for many years and still admired the man. In other words, he had been a part of the post-Freudian Paris school of post-modernism and deconstruction (Jacques Derrida and Gilles Deleuze are two of its prominent representatives) that so dominated the intellectual Left by the last quarter of the 20th century, and perhaps continues to do so to this day.

I don't know if he himself is Jewish, but I doubt it. More likely he's one of many rather typical South American intellectuals engaged in the still ongoing debate on how to best free this vast continent from its colonial ballast and minimize its nations' submission to Uncle Sam. In so doing they tend to overlook the more monstrous aspects of communist heroes such as Che Guevara and Fidel Castro — in much the same way as Sartre in the 1940s and 50s had made himself deaf and blind to the crimes of Josip Stalin. However, as the steam, by the 1990s, was about to run out of existing communist societies in the world, and the horrors perpetrated in their names began to seep through the cracks of their crumbling edifices, the French Left, true to its *goût du néant*[9], took refuge in 'post-modern', dialectical abstractions (heritage of Karl Marx) amounting to a complete negation of the validity of any attempt to create meaning or even a simulacrum of cohesion in science, politics, art, music and letters.

According to Lyotard, we must question not only the official story, or the latest mediatised story in vogue, but any story (narration) pretending to universality, or even general intelligibility. One could go so far as to say Lyotard holds that the very criterion of a false pretence is that it aims at being generally accepted and/or understood, at least as long as it is advanced by state power, or some other societal authority that can be linked to capitalism, usurpation and colonialism.

Lyotard's militant Marxist stance was formed by his direct experience of French troops trying to ensure French supremacy over Algeria in the 1950s. Although in the 1960s he became a renegade, his philosophy remained an ardent advocacy of the underdog, allegedly muted into virtual non-existence by the arrogant prejudice and repressive social mechanisms of ruling elites. As a consequence of his defence of, and identification with, emotionality and instinct as valid categories

---

9 This phrase is actually a loan from Baudelaire who entitled one of his sonnets in *Les fleurs du mal* (The Flowers of Evil) 'Le goût du néant' — Taste for the void, alternatively nothingness, or in the figurative sense here hinted at: for nihilism.

of argument even within the judicial system[10], his own prose turned quite fanciful in its refusal to conform to logical conventions. He also remained very French in his paradoxical way of arguing for emotionality — while denouncing all pretensions to generally acceptable standards of reason and logic as a set of arbitrary language games — by inventing and stockpiling new verbal and philosophical abstractions, ultimately a habit derived from abstruse phenomenologists such as Edmund Husserl and Martin Heidegger.

In other words, knowing that the man seated in a chair next to me, thoughtfully sipping on his marijuana joint, blowing the thin smoke into the bonfire, at one time in his life must have been heavily influenced by Lacanism, post-modernism, post-structuralism — or whatever one would like to call these contemporary efforts to philosophically underpin the doctrine of pluralism and anti-hierarchism as an indisputable cultural value — I also realised that his life since must have taken a 180 degree turn. He wasn't just hanging out from time to time in Aguacate; he lived there permanently for several years. This man certainly was very dissimilar from the usual intellectuals of this kind, urban flowers as they are, unable to see any meaning whatsoever in exploring horizons beyond the Hudson River or the Left Bank of the Seine.

Together with an Indian guide Alain had crossed the Darién from the Atlantic to the Pacific; a five day trek in each direction. Even though he commented very casually on the experience, I can only imagine the interior of the Darién, by many standards, to potentially be a quite dangerous, unmapped territory. The wilderness in itself is of course a challenge of the first degree — needless to add that I would most prob-

---

10 In Lyotard's view, a just society should have several different accepted justice systems and their corresponding criteria — a revolutionary proposal which in these days of vociferous Muslim demands to have Sharia legislature and Islamic courts accepted by European governments as national institutions formally endowed with judicial as well as executive powers, take on a rather sinister aspect.

ably find it impossible to sleep during the night in the midst of a jungle and thus be exhausted in the day when I needed the strength to walk many miles through rough and steep terrain. That is one thing. But there is also the possibility of drug traders and other criminal elements hiding out there. Or military men 'mistaking' you for one of the bad guys... Add insects and mosquitoes... Each one of these circumstances would have been enough for me to refuse such a strenuous hike, even in younger days. But as I voiced these fears, he shrugged and smilingly assured me it was very peaceful out there and nothing to fear.

Apart from that, living in Aquacate on a permanent basis must in all respects be the very antipode of living in Paris. True, there is both a community of Antioquians in self-imposed cultural exile and some expats from foreign countries (apparently even a young Swedish couple from Gothenburg), but on the flip side of the natural spectacle, there is the remoteness of civilised commodities — such as viable electricity, a school, a grocery store with tomatoes, a hospital — and, inversely, the laid back, at times even backward attitude, of the local population. But of course, if one doesn't mind leading a rustic life in that famous harmony with nature (not always so harmonious herself), Aquacate surely is a refuge to count on and the properties there are as rule nicely maintained, helping by their mere appearance to infuse wilderness with a degree of civility. This said, I happened to know where Alain's house must be located and can only conclude that for me to live exposed to the vigorous winds there would drive me nuts.

Together with Elena — the rather hippie-like owner of Tiki Lounge — we spent a beautiful night together under the stars. Asíle, sadly, had not taken part in our conversation since she pretended to have been offended over the dinner table as I respectfully told her that she didn't have to thank me a hundred times for my modest efforts to keep her happy (e.g. cooking), quite especially considering how regally she always took care of me. I guess she felt I was being harsh and tried to mute her sincere feelings, but it really wasn't anything of the sort. After having in vain tried to get her to join us outside, I left her to weather out her frustration alone. I didn't feel that her reaction was appropriate. Sure enough, in the morning she excused herself for having been so touchy, which I thought was fair, even though I still thought it was a pity she had missed the encounter with Alain and the beauty of the polymorphous fire stretching its eager fingers into unfathomable darkness. At the time Asíle served me breakfast Alain had already managed to launch his boat into the sea and steer off towards the western horizon.

Asíle and I stayed on for a couple of more days. We did indeed try to find interesting destinations for excursions but came in for a veritable anti-climax after having been led to believe that the region boasted its own nature reserve with a volcano and a water cascade. One afternoon we arrived in a taxi to a nearby indigenous village equipped with an eco-tourist office. The latter, however, couldn't provide us with anything more useful than an approximate finger-pointed direction to the alleged attraction. We set off into the pasture land meeting two young girls riding a donkey who encouraged us to continue the trail to find 'the volcano'.

If it indeed exists (and satellite images do show clouds rising from the Earth over this location) it's got to be the smallest volcano in the world, since not even from the highest mound around was anything remotely resembling a volcano to be seen and we just returned to the village without having encountered much else than a herd of staring cows. Eager to quickly overcome our initial setback we accepted an offer to be guided to the waterfall — at least we knew that in the company of two local teenage girls we wouldn't miss the target. We went steeply into the hills and had 45 minutes worth of stiff walking before we arrived at this marvel of nature, where we expected to take a well-deserved shower and swim.

There it was, a fall of ten metres alright, but nothing that would fall in it except a trickle of water comparable to that coming out of a half-open kitchen sink faucet. It sprinkled a pile of decomposing leaves below. That was it. No pond, no water gushing forth, no rainbow, no bananas, no mango: No Nothing. We began to laugh and asked the girls if this really was the famous *cascada*. They assured us it was. Overcome by a sensation of absurdity we thankfully drank our sodas (since bottled drinking water had been unobtainable in the village) and began to head back to base. But this time we took the high road and were rewarded with a spectacular vista over the Gulf of Urabá and the hills. Both Asíle and I were a bit puffed up and red-cheeked from the ascent while the giggling local girls — the names of whom I have unfortunately forgotten — seemed completely unaffected by the effort.

From the top of the hill the multi-dimensional mountain range of the Darién at the opposite end of the bay was discernible as a ragged, hazy-bluish ribbon set against the lighter, clearer blue of the sky, in turn reflected by the expanse of the sea, darker still than the distant land but covered in golden scales. Black vultures hovered over some carcass in the valley while pelicans in formation pierced stacks of cumulus clouds travelling the maritime sky. This sight finally made our trip seem worthwhile after all. The girls had not expected any remuneration for their tour but we gave them some anyway, drank more soft drinks, said hello to the playing kids and their toddler siblings, and then walked the dirt road back for at least an hour to the asphalted coastal road linking Turbo with Necoclí. Once we hit upon the main road we turned north and finally managed to get picked up by a taxi taking us back to town. As we arrived at our residence enveloped in dusk, the fata morgana of the distant Darién in dazzling sunlight soon was but a memory engulfed by the night.

A memory soon engulfed by the night — isn't that what our entire lives are? You may choose to look backward or project forward, or you may try to remain in the present. Regardless, the invisible fluid of change runs through our bodies and forces them to in the end yield their individuality to indistinct matter. If you were someone considered of importance, someone profoundly loved or hated, someone in power, a grand creator, someone famous or someone who knew something others didn't, an original innovator even, you may stay longer in human memory than others, but even so the living image of you is destined to fade and merge with the crumbling leaves of summers passed. Your own personal memory of the things that happened to you in the course of a lifespan — the thoughts, feelings, desires and fleeting dreams to which only you had access — dissolve too and become one with the impersonal system permeating atoms and galaxies.

Yet, for all the certainty of oblivion, you hang on to the idea of being someone during your lifetime, setting goals for yourself, chasing after experiences and movements as though these in themselves were of importance. The traveller, prone to the prejudice that he moves on the crest of time, leaves others behind to languish in their stationary prisons. He might think he accomplishes two journeys in one; the first being life itself, the second all the places he takes this life to. It has more than once happened to me, passing through a village or a small town in the dead of the night, that I remind myself of that there are people who are born and die in these locations without having seen much else of the world. It might be that some of them could never afford to travel, but I specifically think of those who are simply content to remain where they are, to whom it doesn't even occur to want to go somewhere else. Seconds later the vehicle transporting me has taken me beyond their village border and soon beyond their ambit all together, whereby the inhabitants, brought to life by my imagination, recede into the woodwork, merging with the sombre row of sleeping houses along the town's dusty main road. In the morning this place, like so many others, will come to life again and go about its business as usual, and no one will ever know that my eye was there.

The night — and on this point all cosmologies are unanimous — precedes the day and is always associated with the idea of primordial chaos existing prior to time, as the eye that sees through darkness is associated with that of God. The traveller is perhaps not only travelling twice, but by force of a written account thrice. In this way he hopes to seal into in crystallised form his memory of what happened to him, and to him alone. So that when he's gone, there is a story. Perhaps one reminiscent of Sisyphus, who, according to legend, cheated Death himself by locking him up in a cupboard as he came to bring Sisyphus with him. Then he threw the key and ran away, hoping that he could stay away from the vengeance of the gods. Of course, we know that it eventually caught up with him and his subsequent punishment was to be emblematic of human creation as such. Apparently there was only eternal condemnation in store for him, but what if he too left a legacy of words scribbled on a papyrus, imbued with the hope of one day being brought back to life, or at least to a simile of such, a vicarious existence in an alien intellect at some junction in time trying to decipher the letter code left behind by a mysterious writer?

Since time is allied with the spectre of eternity we can never hope to wage and win any battle against it. It's an inescapable human condition that it takes no skill whatsoever to either be born or to die — it just happens to us. And though the process of dying may be degrading and even horrible to watch — both for ourselves and for others — the actual passage from this world to the next is an immensely thin razor blade severing the last of the threads that tie us to our earthly existence. And when we go, no matter how selfish we have been in life, there is nothing that we can bring along. The ones who were in possession of earthly riches have always hoped for the opposite and made sure their graves were stuffed with the same so that they may travel in style and comfort through the 12 regions of the underworld. But if there is not some mysterious alchemical operation by which these objects are transmuted into their spiritual counterpart, and so actually, somehow, come to exist also in the beyond, the fact remains that the burial chamber of Tutankhamun, undiscovered over centuries and therefore unmolested by grave robbers, was intact and that the many precious objects found in it had visibly been in the same place for over 3000 years.

Against the juggernaut of time man occasionally insists on holding up a cup full of bliss and happiness. But this elixir would never be so sweet and delectable if it didn't simultaneously contain the sensation of fugacity as its secret hemlock. This is why happiness is so often associated with intoxication. Not necessarily of a grossly material kind, but in so far as the essence of joy contains within it the poisonous seed of death. We are all selected as winners by being born, and we all leave life as losers, forever unable to revoke the sun from its latest point of setting. That is, if you chose to regard life from the point of view of the individual sperm. Seen in the light or darkness of eternity, life might just as well be conceived of as a punishment. Some of the ancients were of this belief, and a stark Greek proverb teaches us that the best for man is never to have been born and the second best to die young.

The loss of a beloved friend or a relative is the intrusion of the forever unknowable into our earthly existence, accompanied by the feeling that something unique on Earth, a person, an individuality, has left us and will never return again. On the contrary, as we are standing by the coffin, we take leave of a memory that will slowly fade into the void, like a shiny coin sinking through the sea; like a black and white photography, singed and yellowed by time, disappearing into an album of remembrance.

The capacity to be happy in the face of death is intimately linked with our conscious realisation of the limit set to our time together and our attempt to convey to the persons we love what they really mean to us while they are still here — this may sound like a worn cliché, in the end, facing the ultimate loss, it's nothing but and the thing you never made clear, and you really needed to make clear, will hauntingly remain suspended in mid-air for the rest of your life.

True, the child is often the purest image of instantaneous happiness, but the child can burst into tears of unmitigated despair in the very next moment and for no apparent reason. It is often at night that feelings of impending loss and grief beset us with demoniacal force. And if there was a way to learn how to face darkness — interior and exterior — in the same unflinching way as we face the challenges of a new day, I would very much like to be instructed, not the least so that I can give of myself while there is still time, and to receive from those who try to do the same for me. Meanwhile, I continue to travel.

*

As Asíle's and my first journey together was drawing to its close, I felt happy that we had been able to stand one another for a whole month without conflict. The few moments of irritations that did occur were minor and I believe Asíle too must have regarded them as trifles — she told me that she herself didn't understand why occasionally she had reacted in such or such way. To this day I don't know if she said this only to avoid having to explain herself, or if it's really true that she was simply overcome by some kind of speech impairing emotion. By all means, she's indeed a sensible, sensitive and deeply feeling woman and I can respect that. I also tolerate all kinds of seemingly irrational moods as long as they don't turn into a morose regard charged with chronic resentment. And this, luckily, has so far not been the case. In all fairness, I too had to honestly excuse myself for a couple of mishaps along the road. But what is that if not just normal in a relationship between two people? The reason for my even bringing it up is that I have indeed experienced women who dedicate their entire lives to playing the role of victims. Asíle is nothing of the sort.

I was also content to have been able to contain my natural need of solitude and independence. Though I was now certainly a bit eager to get back to my old ways — incidentally those of an inveterate bachelor — Asíle was visibly saddened having to part with me. It was her birthday and as we arrived in the busy town of Apartadó (whence we were scheduled to take a flight back to Medellín in the morning),

I ventured out in the streets to find her a gift. It wasn't all that easy to find her something that would make a suitable birthday present, but I finally opted for a handmade shoulder bag with a flowery pattern. I also found a restaurant close to our hotel proudly advertising its steaks. Since we hadn't had any decent red meat for a month I felt opportunity knocking. Asíle agreed.

The interior of the restaurant was absolutely ghastly with aluminium furniture bathing in light green neon light bestowing upon every plate of food an eerie, otherworldly glow. But there were some tables outside too and that's where we sat down. Perusing the menu, I was surprised to note that a glass of red wine only cost about one and a half dollars. Knowing even table wines to be quite expensive in this part of the world I had to check this offer out and ordered a glass. It arrived with an amount of liquid comparable to what you'd expect to find in a glass of brandy. This explained two things. One: why it was so cheap. Second: the unfamiliarity of many Colombians with this kind of beverage. To many of them wine is a kind of liquor and they don't make any effort to keep it away from warm or even hot environments. Since an opened bottle of whisky is still good to drink after sitting on a shelf for two months, they believe the same applies to wine. Just put the cork back in. After having explained to him that this simply wasn't an acceptable way of serving wine by the glass, I offered the manager to buy an entire bottle from the stock. He went away and returned with one not only opened but also one quarter short of its full content. I had to insist he'd knock off the price for an entire bottle as advertised on the menu. After he finally had consented to do this, I felt I had to also ask him for how long the bottle had been open prior to being brought to my table. With a broad smile, visibly betraying his satisfaction with this state of affairs, he proudly announced: 'Three weeks'.

Like so many other Colombian nights, this was one in the seemingly endless series of public fiestas: incredibly loud music spurting out of myriads of bars and restaurants, yes, even from the tiniest fast food joints. And once again this had to be taken into the bargain, because without this annoying din there wouldn't have been nearly as many beautiful girls parading the streets arm-in-arm or driving by in their scooters. There were of course a corresponding number of males out in the streets but for some reason I don't remember them so well. Asíle and I nevertheless found a less noisy establishment where we topped off our last evening together with a couple of gin and tonics and then hit the hay. Morning come, the hotel staff proved to be exceptionally amiable and helped us carry our luggage to the taxi, in this way ensuring that we were safely brought to the airport. It was an half hour ride and it took us through vast banana and plantain plantations over which single engine planes manoeuvred death defyingly while spreading clouds of chemicals to protect the crops from insects and disease. Little by little the sun managed to pierce through the grey atmosphere but the day remained on the cloudy side, even as we got up in the air and the small jet plane was thrown around like a hapless rag doll by capricious turbulence. But the engines kept doing what they're supposed to do and soon had us landed in the midst of Medellín's urban sprawl at the Olaya Herrera airport. Once outside the airport building, our farewell was imminent and not overly drawn out. Still, leaving Asíle alone on that bench, knowing her big moist eyes would be following me until I had vanished in the crowd, was heart wrenching, notwithstanding a vague feeling of relief, which was not so much a sign of inner indifference as simply my way of anticipating the inevitable return of my own solitary self.

Bahía Soláno

However, it didn't take too long before Asíle and I were again reunited and travelling together. This time to the Pacific.

Young Xavier had a very different idea from ours of what an hour's hike on the jungle trail to Playa Mecana was all about. After having stayed put for two rainy days in our comfortably air-conditioned room at Paolo Escobar's former Pacific hideout, today better known as the Bahía's Hotel Balboa Plaza, we felt time had come for us to spring into action. Little did we suspect that we were soon to receive considerably more of that than we had bargained for. It had all seemed straightforward enough. Supposedly there was a path through the dense forest, and, again supposedly, we just had to keep following it until we reached the beach. So much for theory.

We set out an hour before noon with swimming trunks, cameras and water bottles in our bag. Taking leave of the muddy beach avenue by its northern end, we entered an uncharted suburb where general poverty is only one step short of misery. Ramshackle sheds on stilts hover precariously over sun baked stagnant cesspools left behind by rains and some unusually high tide. Flies, mosquitoes and other insects fill the air and the children are mostly naked, in this way perfectly camouflaged against the background of the black volcanic sand and the motorcycle tires they run with sticks over rickety plank constructions servings as bridges over the foetid water ways replacing streets. The beach itself, on the opposite side of this marshland, at ebb-tide consists of a wide parallel pattern of dark furrows of sand alternating with long shallow pools. The whole thing stretches half way towards the horizon, ending with a glistening edge licked by the ocean. This monotonous scenery is framed by high walls of impenetrable greenery.

 The only signs of modest affluence here and there in this impoverished neighbourhood were the huge loud speakers and state of the art HI-FI chains adorning porches of otherwise more than humble homes, which once again highlights the overwhelming importance even the poorest of poor of Colombia attach to their music — they can go without food for some time but not without merengue, vallenato and reggaeton. We were just about to leave this rather sad picture behind when the haggard woman who had been showing us the way so far told us that we would hardly be able to get to the beach by our own since the right path, to someone who had never trodden it, was quite difficult both to find and to follow. At first I suspected she just wanted to make some money by hooking us up with a local guide. But when it turned out that the guide she had in mind was her own son of sixteen and that all she asked for on his behalf was little more than a symbolic sum, we understood this to be a different kind of arrangement than the ones proposed by the more officially established tour organisers.

 Indeed it was. Before setting off, the youngster strangely asked us if we had some other shoes. Seeing that we would have to cross a couple of small brooks before reaching the trail I didn't consider his question all too strange. I consequently removed my shoes hoping in this way to be able to eventually put them back on and keep them more or less dry all the way to the *Playa Mecana*. Having reached the northern end of the local Bahía beach we began to climb the hillside on a very narrow path where the chances of getting lost were actually quite real. At first we were quite grateful to have such an experienced guide — despite his young age — leading the way. Surprisingly soon we reached a water edge and it turned out that what Xavier had in mind was, from now on, for us to proceed by meandering along the coast. That too might have been good — in theory. In reality we were at maximum high tide. Most of the shoreline was under water and wherever there was still some room to move, the breaking of the waves, low-hanging branches and a wealth of irregular rocks and pebbles made progress slow and painstaking. By now I clearly realised that we would be wet all over and that our primary challenge was no longer to reach the legendary beach, but to survive. I voiced my concern to Xavier, telling him it would be better to turn back. I also asked him if there was a way to reach the Playa Mecana by continuing the mountain path. He said one could, but that the distance would be much greater and that by all means we were now closing on to our goal. So we continued, but not before I had urged Asíle to put on her shoes. I don't think she had as yet realised what we were in for, since she was still struggling to negotiate slippery roots, rocks and branches barefoot — a very brave but above all incredibly risky undertaking.

Soon it became almost meaningless to turn back, although that is exactly what reason and prudence kept prompting us to do. But our progress was only definitely halted by a huge cliff blocking the way. Xavier finally managed to climb it with difficulty. I in turn managed to hand him the bag filled with electronics pertaining to civilisation, only to find myself left standing up to my chest in water facing the crazy challenge of walking around the cliff and reach safety some thirty metres farther down the coast, with the swell of the Pacific pounding at me. Losing my fourth pair of Ray-Ban Wayfarer II — this one a 1980s vintage edition that I had acquired by outbidding others on E-bay — to the sea by the first wave that hit me was perhaps not as much of a calamity as just another blessing in disguise. Although I did indulge in a desperate search for this cherished item on the sandy ocean floor, the waves constantly sent me off course and threatened to pull me off the rock — so far the only thing to hold on to — and into the sea. After diving five, six times for it I gave up and was thrust back to the shore by yet another wave, just barely able to save myself from crashing into the rocks. Asíle too had been hurled back by the same wave and now sat on a stone praying, perhaps, for my safe return.

By now a local fisherman and his family in a nearby vessel had become alarmed by our vain efforts to circumvent the rock and came to our rescue. We all managed to get into the boat and were transported the remaining distance to a sandy stretch of the shore, from which again a path led uphill. From here it was just a short walk down to the other and hitherto hidden coast. There it was: Playa Mecana. Initially I was in no mood to appreciate its beauty, and to be honest, even in retrospect I don't consider it any of the more impressive beaches I have seen. Nor is it very long. The high tide had narrowed it down to practically a single sandy bank full of debris and its one and only true asset in these circumstances was its location. The view encompassed a good stretch of pristine Pacific coastline set against the high hills of the *selva*. The rest was just sun, sky and ocean, inter-punctuated by frigate birds and pelicans.

We took refuge from the scorching sun under a shelter visibly forming part of a few houses on the beach and soon were visited by its curious inhabitants. A soft spoken middle-aged man of fair complexion presented himself as the father of the accompanying two young girls (of darker skin). Though originally from Medellín, he had been living in this remote place for the last seven years, and before that for just as long in the Bahía. Judging by the apparent age of the girls they would have been little more than toddlers as their father reduced their circle of possible friendships to those offered by the jungle itself. We saw some adult women in the background but they did not come forth to introduce themselves. The youngest girl, Isabela by name, was a bit timid and hid her face under her father's arm as we tried to engage her in conversation. The elder one, Dulce Maria, was a different story. She unabashedly stared back at me with eyes full of a dark passion that seemed oddly out of tune with the mentality of a ten year old.

It was like staring a fully grown, sensuously and sexually awakened exotic woman in her eyes. Even though she had not reached physical maturity, her eyes seemed to scrutinize mine for concessions, like a panther trying to figure out whether or not she will be fast enough to successfully take her victim by surprise. But it was still just a reflection of a speechless will and desire. A fixed regard suspended way beyond the limits of her age, in a future yet to happen, and by this token even more fascinating to a mature man who has had his fair share of encounters with ferocious female beasts, and in this very moment was standing about as close to his death as she to her birth. Thus a chasm of time also separated us from one another. Apart from that, there was no question as to what nature in her really wanted... I saw it in her eyes, and I know that look, regardless of how awkward it might be to extend this observation beyond the limits set by the protective mores of civilised society. This girl seemed to me to be untouched by such prejudice, a sort of female counterpart to Kaspar Hauser, the sister of Romulus and Remus, a wild woman in the true sense of the word. Though it has indeed happened once or twice before in my life that a young girl has given me that kind of look, this one was possibly the most pitiless and uncompromising of them all.

The denouement of our entanglement was comparatively undramatic. I had anticipated that we would be forced to return to the Bahía by way of the mountain path, which neither Asíle nor I was particularly looking forward to. But after having taken a swim in the river mouthing into the sea at the northern end of the beach, we succeeded in hailing down a passing lancia manned by Indians and were taken by boat right back to the soldier check point at the and of the beach avenue where our adventure had begun. The circle was closed. We paid off Xavier rather handsomely — and in spite of that his sound judgement in regard to tourists hadn't proved to be on par with his audacity — and returned to the hotel just as the afternoon reached its half time hiatus. Little more than three hours had been the objective timespan of our excursion, but a lifetime's worth of experience had been compressed into those hours, making them stand out as mile posts on an unpaved road to infinity.

*

Bahía Soláno is a small seaside community nestled in the humid tropical forests covering a huge area of Colombia's Pacific coast in the region of Chocó. Even though its location inside a protected bay facing due north is somewhat privileged, it's not exactly a tourist hotspot. In fact it's just a hot spot. Its wide black beach remains uninviting regardless of tidal conditions and the village itself consists of a quadratic grid of unpaved streets and houses. These streets happen to be situated within the second-most-rainy region in the world — supposedly there is only in some obscure part of equatorial Africa that rain is more prevalent. Consequently, streets, roads and footpaths are muddy and slippery most of the time, and the sky predominantly shifting colour from grey to less of grey. Add to this that there are no roads whatsoever connecting the Bahía to for example Medellín or Quibdó, two of the more 'nearby' urban centres. The only two ways to get in or out of there is either by boat — and please keep in mind that the cargo ship transporting groceries and beverages from Buenaventura in the south needs up to 24 hours to reach its destination — or by plane.

The airport is in complete harmony with its surroundings and has a landing strip that wouldn't meet even the most lax local safety requirements in for example Europe or the United States. To give you an idea: although it's in fact paved with some kind of coarse, asphalted gravel, it's not fenced except by the same barbed wire that keeps the flaccid cattle out of harms' way at landing and take-off. To say that landing on the runway inevitably is bumpy is a mild understatement.[11]

---

11 As of May 2014 the pilots of the aerial companies servicing the Bahía Soláno Airport reputedly went on strike protesting against appalling landing conditions. And there we were, bumping along the runway, a couple of weeks earlier...

Strangely, considering the rustic aspect of the airport facility, there is a strong military presence in town. Next to the airport is a whole military complex housing the 23d Battalion of the Colombian Marines. There is also police and a harbour *Capitania*, regulating maritime traffic and goods transported by sea. All these factors taken together combine to paradoxically make Bahía Soláno one of the safest places in all of Colombia. Anyone planning for example on stealing something — let's say a tourist purse — would have to contend with that he can only leave by boat or by plane and that military and police are alerted to suspicious activity by the slightest hints. Trying to escape the vengeance of the authorities by taking refuge in the immense jungle would probably just amount to suicide, and I doubt that any burglar in his right mind would ever contemplate such desperate action.

There is of course also the so-called *pesca blanca*. Asked the natural question what the inhabitants of Bahía Soláno actually live from — the tourist trade could only possibly keep a tiny minority busy — our taxi driver taking us along the only existing regular road from Bahía to the the twin community of El Valle, south of Bahía along the coast, candidly responded that they were all fishermen. Hmm... During our three days in town, with a perfect overview of all activities in the bay from our third story, almost waterfront hotel room, the amount of boats visibly transporting fish or even fishing gear had been minimal. There is no way the entire population could have this as its livelihood. Only if the lucrative business of the above mentioned 'pesca blanca' could be taken into account, things would start to fall into place. Pesca blanca, being a synonym for the cultivation, harvesting and perhaps even in situ refinement of the coca-plant, is in fact a just as secretive as well established trade in the hinterland of the Bahía, enjoying the tacit support and protection of army and police. The only way to explain that such on-paper illegal activity can still be carried out with the silent consent of the authorities of the state, is that all parties financially benefit from it.

The golden days of Paolo Escobar may be gone and slowly fading in memory as well, but his legacy is still alive. As is his hotel, incidentally the one we stayed in. That it had belonged to Escobar we never knew while still there. But soon upon arrival we noticed that the spacious, walled in building with its garden, though planned and executed in colonial style, could hardly be more than 30–40 years old. Certain traits, both in the interior decoration and the outline of various facilities, also suggested that there must once have been some unusually deep pockets around.

Nowadays the large pool area is a desolate, all but abandoned, place not offering the simplest of recliners for the benefit of the guests — there is not even a regular plastic chair to sit in around the pool, although its water seemed clean enough for me to take a swim in it. But there is no doubt that it was once meant to be a place allowing a lot of cute bikinis to swing back and forth between potted palm trees and piña coladas served by a staff dressed in black and white.[12]

Significantly, it was to one of his recreational parties — replete with snowdrifts of cocaine, *putas* and *putos* — that Escobar once invited the legendary Father Rafael Garcia Herreros. How the deal was struck nobody knows for sure, but the result was that Father Herreros managed to convince Escobar that he needed to share some of his riches with a saintly person such as himself. He consequently offered to administer forgiveness of all of Paolo Escobar's sins and bestow upon him divine absolution in return for a stately ranch with a whole gamut of *ganado* (cows, bulls, buffalos and horses). Father Garcia promised that through him, and the sacraments of the church, Escobar would thus be spared the annoyance of forever burning in Hell.

Whether Escobar did in reality escape this fate, I feel incompetent to say, but it's indubitable that Father García, at least as far as Escobar

---

12 After writing this I have learned that my suspicion was entirely well founded. Escobar had people flown in private planes for parties lasting weeks on end filled with all kinds of entertainment.

was concerned, got his share of the deal. However, as the general public, informed by the press, got wind of the transaction, critics were keen to point out that Father García, by even offering to pardon Escobar in the name of the Catholic Church, had proved himself to be an even more wicked criminal than said Escobar himself. Over time the affair assumed such dimensions that Father García's earthly fate had to be decided by no less an authority than the Vatican Curia.

Hence, one dark night secret agents of *Opus Dei* showed up on the doorstep of Father García's ranch and only gave him the time to get dressed, whereafter he was discreetly taken away, flown across the country in a helicopter and dumped at a local parish far away from the scene of the crime. There he apparently still serves as a priest, unable to voice any claim whatsoever to the property once bequeathed to him by the man who used to say about himself: 'Sometimes I believe I am God, because if I say that a man must die, he dies that same day.'

But that the story of Padre Garcia is not quite over yet, is proved by the fact that from his present parish disturbing reports still come of his habit to force the female members of his congregation to hand over to him personally the jewellery they're wearing before entering the church for Mass. Father Garcia motivates his actions by saying that it is a sin before God to wear such decorations. Be that as it may. The real problem, apparently, is that he never returns the gold, silver and precious stones he's collected from the women of his congregation in this manner. These items simply disappear.

Today (as Escobar himself has long since been forced to answer for himself in front of his maker) the plaster façade facing the pool of his once private residence (presently Hotel Plaza Balboa) is peeling off in the salty humidity and the wooden railings of the guest rooms are rotting. There is a large empty bar in the reception hall close to the pool area but visibly no drinks to be served, though glasses still hang upside down from the overhead racks. Likewise, the roof terrace of the building, along with its adjacent rooms, are in a state of advanced disrepair and only used by the staff for hanging clothes. Peeping inside its former kitchen we noticed that it was still equipped with professional stoves and other appliances, at present collecting mould and dust. On other levels of the hotel there had inversely been more upkeeping, making our air-conditioned corner room with its private balcony quite pleasant.

There are other anomalies to Bahía Soláno, but decidedly of a more benevolent kind. Whereas in other parts of the world children usually play in daylight while adults tend to do so at night, in Bahía Soláno the children take to the streets by dusk and stay there playing late into the evening. As a matter of fact, the later it gets the younger the kids — I even heard that by midnight toddlers from all over town gather in the state sponsored playground to trade dairy products with one another. This testifies to the level of safety the inhabitants enjoy and their corresponding sense of security as far as their young are concerned — and there is simply no end to these. From our balcony alone I constantly noticed new kids in the street and they had great fun playing with one another in the darkness — one very cherished game being to throw pebbles at one another.

Our time in the Bahía was up. We set off in a taxi headed for the only other community in this otherwise untouched part of Colombia — El Valle. At first the road was pretty bad. Surprisingly, it got better as we began to leave the town behind. Notwithstanding, the project of constructing a cement road between the villages 'for some strange reason' had ground to a halt just as the bridge, destined to straddle the water, had stopped short of its goal just one metre from either bank of the river. The bridge was almost entirely there, but the money to complete it was gone — and that was it. Still, people needed to be able to move back and forth between the two municipalities so, while waiting for new money to fall from heaven and reanimate the building project, a makeshift wooden bridge had been constructed some 30 metres downstream. Our taxi driver didn't consider it safe enough though for his car loaded with four people and had us walking across it while he waited on the other side. How on Earth it nonetheless supported truckloads of timber and gravel, I don't know, but the sight of the official bridge stopping right before the concrete bridgeheads on both sides was perfectly absurd.[13]

If Bahía Soláno may be considered of slight interest to the average tourist, this is even more true about El Valle, which has the doubtful distinction of being poorer than its twin community to the northeast. By land it's little more than a half hour's drive away, whereas it would probably take more than an hour to go there by lancia as it would first have to head almost due north to pass around the hornlike peninsula providing shelter to the Bahía before it could turn south. The village centre, in spite of a lively commerce, is rather depressing, and its suburbs even sadder to behold. But although El Valle to the north of its village definitely has a more interesting beach than the Bahía, local hoteliers do surprisingly little to enhance its attraction. By low tide the beach looks like a polished tinted mirror inviting you to set a footprint on it by walking the virgin sand. At high tide though tons of mostly wooden debris, but also plastic junk, carried there by rivers and sea alike pile up over its entire length, and the strong tides leave behind cesspools impeding beach access. To walk the beach at this time is more like negotiating a military training ground and perhaps interesting on that account. You might also pick up pieces of wood sculpted by the elements. Which goes to say that the place is wild and rugged alright, framed by rocks and a jungle of truly epic stature. Here too the sand is of volcanic origin and the sea only restrained by some hidden reefs as it breaks in majestic waves onto the mile long beach.

---

13 Local rumour has it that some spoiled brat from Medellín, speeding up the road, failed to even notice the gap separating the road from the bridge (there is no warning sign!) and died on the spot when his car slammed head on straight into the bridgehead.

The weather was still so-so, with many a cloudy hour pierced by unexpected sun flashes that were quick to vanish again. By now all this had begun to seem just normal to me — as said, there's supposedly only a place in Congo with greater annual precipitation. We were lucky to strike a deal with what turned out to be our local garden gnome running on inexhaustible Duracell batteries: in reality a man, but size-wise on par with Santa's helpers, his head constantly covered by an exotic looking hood and he himself driven by such indomitable energy that he seemed to incarnate superhuman endurance in the body of an elf. And whether he would have liked it or not, this is what we spontaneously began to call him: *nuestro gnomo*. A title that became completely inseparable from him after he had shown us the guest bathroom in the newly constructed restaurant. It had double installations of WCs and hand basins within the same enclosed space, one of normal size, the one right next to it for small children. Or so he claimed, explaining that the child sized toilet equipment had been specially ordered from Italy and, sparing no costs, brought to this remote location. Why he had found this necessary — young children being bizarre things for a tourist to bring in proximity to such a dangerous sea — he wouldn't really explain in a manner that made full sense to us. All he had to offer in the way of an argument was that he — himself childless — had always felt it was a pity that father and son/daughter could not normally go to the bathroom and do their thing at the same time, whereas here utopia had become reality, allowing precisely that to happen. But we knew better: the small toilet seat was not primarily destined for children, but for himself once that bathroom door had been thoroughly locked behind him!

It was the same local gnome who led us to a hut on his hotel property situated on a small promontory jutting out from the mountainside well above beach level, with a terrace on high stilts offering a panoramic view over the Pacific and an adjacent natural pool, constantly replenished with wonderfully temperate water from a waterfall in the forest. It truly was an Eden where taking freshwater showers was as easy as it was delicious. From our balcony-terrace we had an unperturbed view of the beach, the ocean and the surrounding rainforest. There were of course some mosquitos and other biting things to remind us of mortality but considering the heat and the humidity — quite oppressive in combination and almost forcing one to take it very easy in the afternoons — it wasn't so bad. The proof of this is that after a while we even stopped suspending the mosquito net over our bed at night time.

The house itself had some peculiarities, the most conspicuous of which was a slanting floor that would bring you much faster to the toilet than back from it — getting back up to where the bed stood almost involved some amount of climbing! It really was an *Alice in Wonderland* kind of sensation to run up and down the house. Over time, however, the speedway to the water closet turned out to be yet another one of those blessings in disguise, since there was yet another thing to remind us of our mortality. It's a kind of indigestion which in many parts of the world is simply known as the *tourista*, an indisposition only attacking tourists and making itself felt in sharp stomach cramps necessitating frequent visits to the bathroom. Asíle got over her discomfort quicker than I and for some days I wasn't really up for much action. But it seemed that the indisposition went well in hand with the weather, still undecided if it should go really bad or just remain morose. It chose the latter and some days later we were in a speeding lancia heading south along the Pacific coast, where long stretches of unspoiled beach alternate with volcanic rock formations girdled in meerschaum.

Our goal was the nature reserve of Útria which covers a vast area of the department of Chocó. Its visitor's centre is conveniently located deep inside a narrow, fjord-like bay offering complete protection from the vicissitudes of the Pacific. It's a partly US-sponsored facility. Entrance fees finance an infrastructure comprising a museum, public toilets, a restaurant and a mile long wooden deck allowing easy access to a part of the local mangrove area, incidentally one of the most fertile ecological habitats that exist on the planet and therefore also one of the oldest, possibly going so far back in time as to the birth of the first amphibians. On display in the museum were samples of the local fauna preserved in jars topped off with alcohol, or perhaps formaldehyde, among them some impressive snakes and spiders. There was also a skeleton of a whale and the obligatory wide open jaw of a giant shark.

Apart from these zoological tidbits it was the geographical location and aspect of the bay itself which made the day. A few houses had been constructed on the opposite shore inviting the non-too-easily-scared tourist to spend a weekend on the edge of Paradise. The excursion was rounded off with a visit to one of the small islands around the inlet of the bay, famous not only for having the only beach with white sand in the entire region, but also its own freshwater supply. The rock formation on this and the other small islands in its vicinity again made me think of primordial Earth and a creation long before man was even a twitch in the eye of the Creator. Blissfully it was also here that the bowels of my own interior had its culminating explosion, allowing an intensely yellow intestinal cocktail to mix with a pre-existing local bacterial pool, perchance in this way spawning yet another biological era.

I don't know how this could be, but I have found Coca-Cola to have medicinal effects on some stomach ailments relating to tropical climates, foods and hygiene. After landing on the sandy bank back on the outskirts of the village El Valle, from where we had set out in the morning, I headed straight for the grocery store where I got hold of this ubiquitous refreshment, the drinking of which enabled me to stand my ground all the way to our cabin and even take pictures of all the coquettish pre-teen girls who more than willingly posed for us. I also ingested some pills I had picked up at the local pharmacy. After that there was a decisive turn for the better and I soon regained full appetite at our meals. These — prepared by a sweet local lady, who called us *'mis amores'*, but otherwise looked like she could crush garlics in her bare palm — normally consisted of either tuna fish or chicken fried in slices, rice, cabbage and deep fried plantain. We bought some wine (suitably overpriced for sure) from our next door neighbour that happened to be the most upscale cabin hotel on the strip to make our meals a bit more festive. One evening I even ventured into the kitchen region and, after having asked permission to do so, single-handedly cooked us a chicken stew.

The passing of the remaining few days coincided with a gracious *dolce far niente*, a non-activity mostly carried out from the sublime vantage point of our hammock. In other words, we were getting ready to hit the road. Picked up one morning by a taxi, it took some time before the driver had pumped up the notoriously flat tire and stuffed the rest of his family into the car. Eventually we arrived in Bahía Soláno where Asíle went to have breakfast while I expedited some belated e-mails. The internet café was located next to the local elementary school where the children themselves had carried out a big mural painting showing them resourcefully escaping to the top of the mountain to escape the devastating effects of a tsunami, while all the houses of the villages seemed to happily float around in the chaotic waters beneath. 'Internet café' — that's what the sign actually said. I made a point of it and although the woman in charge said they didn't have it, she nonetheless managed to come up with a cup of coffee, for which I was very grateful. Besides I don't think I have ever paid so little to go on the Web for an hour in an Internet establishment.

That said, I'm not sure either Bahía Soláno or El Valle are places I'm likely to revisit, although I'm also very grateful to have made the acquaintance of these villages on the fringes of civilisation. If opportunity knocked, offering me a chance to go on whale watching in the region as the humpback whales migrate through its waters, I wouldn't hesitate to accept the invitation. The remoteness and ruggedness alone make this place a spectacular destination. But although the presence of the Pacific certainly prevents it from being a backwater, literally speaking, it is so in all other ways and its nature, as soon as you leave any trodden path behind, becomes a potentially deadly threat. Just trying to imagine the immense distances of wild uninhabited coast making up most of Colombia's western frontier is in itself awe-inspiring. I'm ever so fortunate to have glimpsed some of this immensity with my own eyes. The images thus engraved are deep and haunting. It is nature in solemn indifference to man and his intentions in a heat often made oppressive as it reaches near maximum humidity — it literally takes days to dry wet clothes on a rack even if it doesn't rain. Thus, still today, ever inventive, inquisitive and enterprising man doesn't really know what to do with this immense wilderness. For the time being, just letting it be the way it is — as is the case with the even vaster forests and waterways of the Colombian part of the Amazonas — probably is the safest bet for everyone.

The door to the cockpit as always remains open even after the Captain has turned round to wish us welcome aboard. There are several long cracks in the joints connecting the interior lining of the plane with its fuselage, but since they're apparently not critical to the craft's airworthiness, they have been left that way. I sit at the back of the plane with seats for a total of twenty passengers. At take-off I realise we're at the very end of the runway. Looking ahead through the cockpit window, as the plane climbs steeply, I expect to see the sky, but all I can make out is a giant green wall moving towards us at alarming speed. Then there is just fog in shreds all around us and, finally, after what seems an unduly prolonged sojourn in Limbo — the Sun!

Caracól, Tikál, Calakmúl

Some of my own most memorable experiences in Central America stem from visits to pre-Colombian ruins. Apart from the more famous and easily accessible ones — such as the Toltec Teotihuacán in the Mexico Valley; the Zapotec ceremonial centre at Monte Alban outside Oaxaca in the eponymous state; Mayan Tulum; Chichen Itzá; Uxmal; Labna; Sayil in Quintana Roo; Palenque and Tonalá in Chiapas; Tikál in northern Guatemala; Copán in western Honduras; and the Olmec archaeological park in Villahermosa in the Mexican state of Tabasco — I have also on some occasions ventured beyond the beaten track and visited Caracól in Belize and Calakmúl, sitting in the midst of a protected biosphere covering a vast portion of the lands from south-east Campeche in the lower Yucatán to northern Guatemala. Let's begin with the trip to Caracól, once an important city in the Mayan civilisation but today primarily known to a limited number of dedicated archaeologists and unerring tourists, such as myself.

I had spent almost a week in northern Guatemala, on the miniscule Island of Flores on the western shores of Lago Petén Itzá. Although, or perhaps because, the place is so small, its circular waterfront is lined with hotels suiting a wide range of budgets and conveniently connected to the mainland by a causeway. I was working on some manuscript after my second visit to Tikál (to which I was first introduced a couple of years earlier), an hour's bus ride to the north-east of Flores. For the moment I was taking it easy, writing a word here and there, and attempting an occasional watercolour while now and then taking a sip from the magic pipe. In the evenings I would go to my favourite waterfront steakhouse restaurant to have dinner. My accommodation was inexpensive but for some reason — which I have now forgot — I had begun to have some annoyances with the staff. Though rudimentary, the hotel room, with a shared balcony overlooking the water, and right below a covered roof terrace with a set of hammocks swinging in the breeze, had nonetheless been all I wanted. Now, however, it seemed 'a good time to act' as the Chinese oracle *I Ching* sometimes has it.

As I'm again pondering that, I really can't go on without giving you a brief description of my third visit to Tikál. The reason I know for sure that it the third is that I know I paid the entrance fee on my first visit and proceeded like a regular tourist to the official entrance. The second time I did indeed find a perfect way to sneak into the park, but once I hit upon the inner perimetre road connecting the monuments I was careless enough to turn to the right running straight into one of the guards at the entrance booth who asked me for my ticket. Confessing I didn't have one he simply sent me back to the reception kiosk to buy one and I then again entered this Mayan site as a regular tourist. The third time I got it right — I mean left!

There is a pond behind the vast tourist complex housing a spacious covered outdoor restaurant and stores selling traditional merchandise. Access to the pond is by no means restricted but somewhat ominously sports a sign saying: 'Beware of Crocodile'. Supposedly there actually is a crocodile in the pond but I didn't see him. I dared to follow the footpath leading to the left around the pond until I hit upon an ancient drainage system, indeed a Mayan aqueduct. Having a level floor and low slanting walls it's easy to walk. All I needed to do was to follow its course for 150 metres until I hit upon the interior dirt road beyond the check point where tickets are controlled. This time I wisely took the precaution to discreetly peep through the trees before venturing onto the road. Once there I was observed by God alone and I knew that in order for things to stay that way, I'd have to keep walking to the left.

I also knew from previous visits that this road would take me to a smaller complex of temples. Though interesting in themselves I was eager to reach the Plaza Mayor and was unexpectedly offered access to the same by a footpath through the woods, marked out as a 30 minute walk. This had the advantage of making my entry to the main attractions even more discreet, as I knew I would now be able to inconspicuously slip into the very heart of Tikál. Which I did, emerging from the chatting jungle like *Chak Tok Ich'aak* (Great Jaguar Paw) himself for a surprise attack on his enemies.

One of the species crowding the tree tops of Tikál is the spider monkey. To me its representatives look like elegant waiters in black, cautiously ambulating the canopy high above the ground. It's a fascinating ballet. I was so imbued with their intricate movements while exiting the jungle that I more or less danced my way to the plaza — a slow and much convoluted dance for sure. We were at this point well into the afternoon and instead of running around like a madman, trying to again make all of Tikál in three hours, I decided to concentrate my efforts to the Plaza Mayor and its vicinities. It turned out to be a fabulous decision. I did climb its two main pyramids but then retreated to the long side of the square, seeking shade under Mayan vaults in the intense heat while drinking water profusely. I also attempted (I believe the designation to be quite correct) a couple of water colours with the result that the afternoon moved speedily. Meanwhile cumulous clouds kept painting their fantasy architecture above the horizon as the atmosphere began to smell of thunder. Being the last visitor to leave these gradients I realised it was probably best moving a bit faster towards the exit. But when I finally got on my legs it had become too late to make it safely there and I was forced to take cover under a shed selling refreshments, right next to the Plaza Mayor. What then happened almost defies, if not imagination, at least its counterpart in words.

But here's my verbal bid on it: without further ado the sky grew so dark that one would think it was already night, while the thunder storm rolled in, unleashing torrential rain paralysed by tree shaped lightning. It was a near constant barrage, like some battleship pounding on an invisible enemy, or simply man eating Tlaloc releasing his spears and arrows on the poor devils below. One aerial projectile hit a pyramid so vehemently that it tore away a huge stone from the edifice and sent it in a parabola to the ground. The immediately following soundwave was so powerful that it in turn threw me to the ground. It was a terrific blast, very close to hit home.

But the storm was as short as it was intense and gave way to a sunset in Eden. Over the pyramid, just deprived of a supporting stone, stood a rainbow against a sky as black as coal.[14] A herd of tiny, absolutely innocent looking, red brocket deer moved out of hiding into the plaza. Simultaneously appeared on the grass — a deep emerald green after the rain — a pair of snow white cranes and two peacocks, spreading their feathers like Sevillan *abanicos*, waving a thousand-eyed turquoise, blue and violet farewell to the sun, in its turn taking a spectacular leave of the radiant rainbow arch suspended above the eastern horizon. Being there, still alive, I felt as though I was witnessing an artistic miracle.

In terrestrial terms the entire drama may have lasted for an hour but I still couldn't move. Only the patting on my shoulder by the vendor about to close his stand brought me out of the spell. In a waking dream I brushed past darkening trees and through obscure vegetal tunnels eventually reached the check point where the ticket controller had long since called it a day. I didn't even see an armed guard, only

---

14 Your inner ear may at this point have begun to suggest themes from Beethoven's *Pastoral Symphony*, but if so, please abstain from going so far as to actually try to visualise the Disney-Stokowski version of the same: the flying white unicorns are not strictly necessary to complete the picture.

at some distance ahead the second to last visitor merge merged with the embers of sunset. Dusk soon brought oblivion to Paradise. But its treasures and secrets are safe with me, since I was there and then as it pleased the Creator to strike a ray of eternity in my mortal eye!

*

San Ignacio, quite pleasant, really is an inland Caribbean town with a wealth of bars, restaurants and guest houses in bright colours. But wherever you go and wherever you pay, the bill is always sprinkled with a mixture of unforeseen and unforeseeable fees and taxes — symptomatically the Belize dollar is worth exactly half of a US one, and you often find yourself in a shady financial borderland where prices are either in half or seemingly doubled.

I got my room though and it was good for the purpose, namely to serve as a platform for my visit to Caracól. Once installed I began to ask around for tours but soon found out they only might happen if there were enough people signing up for them. In theory they were running every day, but only in theory. Since participation in a tour in my view was also overpriced, I quickly made up my mind about trying to rent a four-wheel drive for a day trip. It took some time but I finally had my man. It was a rental company, duly wanting to overcharge me but agreeing to let me have the four-wheel drive that had windows that couldn't be closed, and this for a price that seemed exaggerated in Belize dollars but OK in American.

Now I had the tour vehicle and courteously offered some Canadian girls to come along for free, but they didn't seem to have much confidence in the Viking edition of Indiana Jones and declared their preference for the monkey bus. So far it was only me signing up for Lorenzo Tour's Flight 707 to Caracól. But I did as professional tour guides have also learned to do: pick up people around the hotels just before departure. I was up around seven next day and had already had my breakfast as I drove by a potential candidate. British Sebastian, studying Political

Science at the University of Manchester (if I remember correctly), said that he actually had made some other plans but I quickly talked him out of them, pointing out the bleeding obvious: the rest can wait, this is opportunity knocking! Since he was both young and intelligent he quickly found his bearings. I gave him an hour to get ready and we then met by the car.

In the beginning the road through the Mountain Pine Ridge Reserve, eventually leading to Caracól, is paved with good intentions but after passing the last major settlement that quickly changes, and a ride over a dirt road in various stages of oblivion begins. Having driven a fair stretch into the woods, we reached the forest patrol station where we were asked to wait for another hour for the convoy to form. I knew in advance the answer to my question. And no, it was not dangerous *per se* to drive alone, but all the same better and preferable to stay close together on the trail. While waiting for the monkey bus and other private entrepreneurs to show up, I and Sebastian, not wanting to waste a minute, took off in the car to visit a nearby cave in a forest setting that would make a perfect backdrop to an epic panorama in *Lord of the Rings* style.

Well, I almost lost my able assistant right there. The cave is so enormous and its ceiling so remote that these imponderables invariably turn your face upward. Which is quite dangerous since you don't realise that you're actually treading on the roof of another level in the cave. That probably wouldn't be so bad if it weren't for the fact that these roofs have big holes in them. Luckily not always big enough to swallow an entire university student, but suddenly one leg of his just went straight through such an opening and the young man found himself dangling ten feet above the floor of the cave below. And yes, there are also huge bats hanging in clusters in the Gothic darkness, abnormally long-legged spiders and a veritable subterranean lake, fed by a river running through the bottom of the enormous arches marking up the entrance to and exit from the cave. In these prehistoric waters, reminiscent of one of the three legendary rivers in Hades (Lethe, Styx and Acheron) there must of course also be blind, white lizards and fish that has not been known to exist since the Cambrian period, a mere 500 million years ago.

Once Sebastian was out of the hole we were both relieved to conclude that he had sustained no serious injury in the fall and that we could continue our expedition unimpeded, albeit henceforth with considerable caution as to where we placed our feet. The fascination the place exerted also kept us oblivious of time and ultimately caused us to run a bit late for the convoy that had just left the forest guard station. But since we promised to catch up with them we were allowed to continue. However, there were far too many natural wonders to see for us to feel any need to step on the pedal solely in order to trail behind the diesel engine monkey bus for another hour and a half, engulfed in a permanent cloud of dust and exhaust fumes. It was such a beautiful day and we leisurely navigated ourselves around the bigger holes in the road, here and there stopping altogether to admire clear rivers and waterfalls embedded in reddish rocks and greenery. We decided to stop a bit longer at these on our way back, seeing that there were other people frolicking in the natural pools created by the cascades.

We arrived in Caracól before noon. As the car engine came to a halt we exchanged the challenges of the road for a foliage interspersed with sunrays to the lively accompaniment of chirping birds. The sun was reaching for its zenith, the whole place exuding serenity and peace. It was easy to foresee that we were not actually going to step on each other's toes while exploring the monuments. Judging from the number of cars parked in front of the entrance, coinciding with this day's total number of vehicles, we were perhaps in all 20 people to populate an area of 200 km2 — well, not that there are paths to walk so far and wide, but that supposedly is the total area of the ancient city of Uxwitza (bigger than present day Belize City), and christened Caracól (meaning shell or spiral in Spanish) by British archaeologists in the 1930s, a name allegedly inspired by the many twists and turns in the one and only road leading there.

Since the mid 1980s the site has continuously been excavated by teams of archaeologists who spent months at a time living on the premises in wooden cabins especially built to house them. Patient researchers have thus managed to free a great number of monuments from tenacious overgrowth, reconstructed their architecture and, quite especially, restored a wealth of mural reliefs and stelae to almost their former glory—notwithstanding that many of the latter were carried away by early archaeologists to become part of the collection of antiquities in the University of Pennsylvania Museum.

Whereas a site such as Tikál is actually quite poor in remaining reliefs, stelae and inscriptions, the reverse is true of Caracól, offering the visitor a unique perspective on everyday and ceremonial life in this once thriving Mayan metropolis. Today its enigmatic formal and plastic language, its glyphs, murals and ruins, are shrouded in a beauty and solemnity that has prevailed for more than a millennium, because, like so many other Maya centres, it was abandoned some time during the 10th century CE, while its heyday occurred within the three preceding centuries.

The central plaza, being the main attraction, is home to one of the largest known pyramids in all of Central America. The view from its summit is that of a green ocean agitated by a gentle swell. Sebastian was leaping all over the place and I caught up as best I could. I had no camera with me, but he did and with this device he documented everything while I tried to capture some of the frieze work in rough sketches. He later sent me a series of excellent photos to refresh my memory.

In the siesta hour even the birds and the monkeys seemed to take a break. After having mounted enough pyramid stairs, I descended and found myself a stone bench shaded by a Flamboyant-Tree at the far end of the plaza and remained there, stretched out, for another hour, in splendid isolation, letting thoughts, feelings and associations freely run their course. In a very thoughtful mood I eventually rose and motioned towards the entrance complex, assuming my traveling companion would be there. The assumption proved correct. The park closes quite early in order for tourists to be able to reach contemporary civilisation before nightfall. By the time we had brought ourselves together we were among the very last visitors to leave. I can only imagine that as the sound of our vehicle died out in what was still only early afternoon, the Caracól known to tourist cameras and the Internet prepared to once again transform itself to ancient Uxwitza: a mysterious place in the midst of nowhere, resounding of ominous murmurs and whispers from an extinct civilisation receding deeper and deeper into inscrutable time...

On our way back there was no way we could pass the cascading river we had seen in the morning without taking a swim in some of its many natural pools. Indeed we did. It was all delicious save for the minor annoyance of almost microscopic leeches that would sometimes end up sticking to one's skin. Otherwise the water temperature was just perfect and the sun glorious in its slow descent, casting long shadows behind massive reddish boulders, turning the water into liquid copper. We spent an hour at least basking around in this aquatic paradise and only reluctantly took to the wheel again. The end of the day proved just as perfect as the rest of it and we happily made it back to San Ignacio. Sebastian and I made an appointment for some evening drinks to round off the adventure, but he got stuck somewhere, subsequently leaving a message at my hotel, which I didn't get until the next day. So the parting from the same spot as where we had met, that is by the car, was my last glimpse of him. But I know he will always cherish in his memory the golden hours we spent on the trail to Dreamland, and where he almost went down to Hades before his time.

*

My trip to Calakmúl, on the other hand, was a solitary expedition from beginning to end. I had spent some days on the miniscule but charming Isla de las Mujeres, directly opposite Cancún, snorkelling its waters and enjoying its sights, including some odd submarine concrete sculptures, featuring human figures in dramatic postures, that some local artists had had the foresight to sink into the waters between the island and the mainland. After having satiated my visual imagination with sculptures — there is also a modernist park of installations around the lighthouse on the southern tip of the island which in my opinion would have fared better without such additions — I went from Cancún to the southern end of the state of Quintana Roo, where lies the city of Chetumál. Although strategically placed in a crocodile infested bay in the Caribbean Sea, the average tourist will tend to regard it as a transit town with connections to Villahermosa and Palenque in the west, to Tulum, Chichén Itzá and Cancún in north, or to Belize and its coral reefs in the south. For me Chetumál was the indispensable stepping stone for a trip to Calakmúl.

The six hour bus ride from Cancún had taken me through a sizeable portion of the semi-arid forests and plantations of eastern Yucatán. In my memory the view through the bus window was monotonous, turning the trip into a great meditative experience interrupted only by our stops at urban bus terminals. From the bus station in Chetumál at the end of the line, I took a taxi to the central market area. I found myself a decent hotel and the following morning turned to the car rental in the lobby of a nearby Holiday Inn. Although I was there at its official opening hour, another half-hour elapsed before any employee showed up. Since the driver's seat of the car suggested to me was a bit wobbly, I managed to negotiate the price — renting a car in Mexico is neither cheap nor easy in the first place.

At nine o'clock I found myself behind the wheel of some sort of Volkswagen, which, although it was fairly new seemed to have seen better days. I initially had two hours ahead of me on the Mexican highway, the hazards of which involve a significant number of large road craters. But that's only half the danger. The other half consists of all the heavy trucks. To avoid the holes, they simply swirl across the dividing line of the road, if you're lucky enough to have one, and come at you at full speed without the slightest warning. Here too the surrounding nature scenery is quite monotonous and it doesn't seem obvious that this kind of landscape was once home to a rich civilisation, politically, if not culturally, comparable with the ancient Greek city-states and their colonies in constant commerce and dispute with one another.

As mentioned above, the exact cause of the depopulation and in the end total abandonment of these Mayan cities in the 10th century CE is not known. Even though there is no lack of plausible explanations no single factor — war, social upheaval, persistent drought and famine — is in itself sufficient to explain the drama, not to say tragedy, which enfolded in a region that today falls within the borders of four different countries: Mexico, Belize, Guatemala and Honduras. This leaves a lot of room for imaginative speculation. The Yucatán is an ancient cultivated landscape, much of which has lain fallow for more than a thousand years. With the aid of local governments and conservation agencies its southern extreme has today been preserved as a habitat for all feline species of the Americas — the jaguar, the puma, the lynx, the mountain lion — and their prey.

This I was directly made aware of as the sign indicating the turnoff to Calakmúl turned up along the Carretera Federal 186. Here I was prompted to pay a first symbolic toll. A few miles further into the woods it was time to also remunerate the Forest Rangers. But from their station, the ultimate outpost, there are still 40 miles of dense jungle to cover along a road so narrow that two cars can barely pass each other. Surprisingly it is paved throughout.

This single umbilical cord, twined by human hand, is the only reminder of the modern world: in all other directions the thicket remains impenetrable. I meet no vehicles whatsoever on my way and as I finally arrive at the ancient site — it too turned into a sublime ruin park by the patient and knowledgeable hands of archaeologists — Nature stands tall around me. But it takes several hours before I become aware of just how vast and omnipotent it is. By taking the longest indicated path to visit the park one initially passes by a number of smaller structures embedded in greenery, that to the fastidious Maya amateur seem rather ordinary. Then, after a couple hours of hiking, the great pyramids suddenly appear. I must of course get to the top of these. It's hot, it's sweaty, it's an effort to ascend the steep stairs and ledges, but as I stand there, on the platform of the sacrificial altar, with the wind gently cooling my bloated face, gazing over expanses of wilderness punctuated by alien-looking edifices, enigmatically abandoned a thousand years ago, then, if not before, it becomes clear to me what man's struggle with and against nature really means. Luckily, I tell myself, an invisible path leads back out of this natural womb, where the great stillness rules in couple with the great indifference, and wherein man is nothing but an intruder on his own risk. From the top of the pyramids nothing, not even a distant radio mast or a military defence tower, not even a condensation trail in the sky after a plane, remind me of the contemporary human world. Around me there is a 360 degree panorama solely inhabited by the sun, the planets and the galaxy's other remote celestial actors. To the farthest north I discern the silhouette of some low lying hills; to the south the landscape is almost flat. The tall temples — peeking out and dominating the jungle in the same manner as lighthouses dominate the sea — are aligned with geometrical precision along the abstract north-south and east-west meridians.

I try to imagine what human life could have been like in the city once in the shadow of the great pyramids, with villages and corn fields dotting the surrounding landscape. Beaten tracks, perhaps even paved roads, connect one village with another and eventually peter out to discreet paths into jaguar country, through enemy territory, towards proud conquests and bitter defeats. But as I try to visualise all this I overstrain my sensory capacity. My gaze loses focus and begins to aimlessly wander the indistinct immensity of Heaven and Earth. Even though I'm probably no more than 60 metres into the air, it feels as though I was standing on the surface of a transparent orb, relentlessly encompassing the entire physical universe, and I lose my sense of orientation. Laying down on what remains of the sacrificial altar I fall heedlessly into heaven.

I eventually managed to crawl back out of there, only to find that during my absence from planet Earth, the Demiurge had decided to play me one of his little tricks. There was originally in this script, from exactly this point onwards, an additional 25 pages (unfortunately not based on a handwritten script which otherwise is usually the case) that I have reason to believe were quite decent, detailing my adventures in Oaxaca, Antígua and Lake Atitlán. But as I was preparing to extend my story the other day, I was forced to realise that, inadvertently, I must have put the current instead of an old and discarded version of my script in the electronic bin and then pressed the button for elimination. Whether or not this too was the by now infamous blessing in disguise remains to be seen. By all means it took me three weeks in a stupor to emotionally overcome the loss and decide to undertake the rather arduous task of copying from memory the gist of the matter, still in the hope, of course, that it might be worthwhile both for myself and the reader.

A season in Puerto Rico

So from here I believe the script — now irretrievably lost in cyberspace — continued with an account of the longest of my sojourns in Guatemala's former capital Antígua. With hindsight I'd rather skip over the introduction to this part which would have brought us to the by all means lovely island Corfu off the Greek mainland in the Adriatic Sea. There was a reason for this brief stop-over though, since although Corfu isn't located in Latin America, my second visit to this island immediately preceded my return to Antígua, this time to study Spanish at one of their many Spanish schools for foreigners. The main purpose of bringing the reader the roundabout way over Corfu was to mention some of the circumstances surrounding the writing of my historical novel on the fall of Constantinople entitled *The Owls of Afrasiab*. I might have hoped to be able in this way to inconspicuously promote the story to at least one reader beyond the chosen one.

I had begun working on the script some years prior to this event, but it was in 2007 when I came to Puerto Rico and stayed for almost a year in 'Gringo's Paradise' — a section of the town of Rincón offering spectacular sea and land views — that the bulk of it was brought to completion. Except for me, and the late Bill Cady, to whom the novel was subsequently dedicated, Rincón isn't much frequented by poets and artists. Inversely this privileged corner of the island is a magnet for surfers, primarily from the North American continent — according to the aficionados Rincón counts among the ten best surfing locations on the planet. I can understand why. Just off the northwestern cape of the island (the Punta Higuero and its picturesque light house) the vigorous tradewinds over the Atlantic create an impressive swell tempting these daredevils to constantly mount the frothing horses of Neptune. Although I do admire their courage and indifference to the prospect of hungry sharks and razor-sharp rocks lurking beneath the surface, I find surfers out of their element to be a rather trivial party crowd. I wouldn't say that they're all devoid of talents besides that of being able to balance a board on the crest of a wave, but it's reasonably fair to state that they're seldom intellectually inclined. Since they're also youngsters their conversation more often than not follows the general pattern of 'I was like, I don't know, awesome, and she went: What? And I said, that's just so cool.'

Neither the imported girls, nor the local ones, hanging out in the bars of Rincón are very pretty or interesting in any other ways (whatever that would amount to!) Since Puerto Rico, without ever having acquired the status of being a state within the federation, has undergone a rather intense 'gringofication', after the United States had wrung it out of the hands of the Spanish by the end of the 19th century, prostitution proper is concentrated to the capital San Juan, and almost non-existent in Rincón. Even though the area comprises a number of resorts there is simply no comparison whatsoever, as far as easy access to female companionship is concerned, with nearby island Hispaniola, home to both the Dominican Republic and Haiti. This alone makes Puerto Rico a conspicuous exception to the rule among the larger Caribbean islands. I mention all this to underline the rather curious fact that it was surprisingly difficult to find decent female company in the vicinity of Rincón. The gringa women who weren't part of the surf crowd stuck together as thick as thieves, spending all their pent-up affections and tenderness on horses, justifiably belittling men as best they could. So there I was, on a lovely Caribbean island but with little else to do than to transform my procreational instincts into fertile literature. True, there were some rather mature ladies looking for fun; in particular, I had a married local woman after me in hot pursuit, which was not all that agreeable considering that she was careless enough to turn up in high heels and mini-skirt at my doorstep in the daytime, in plain sight from all the highly religious neighbours, all knowing each other and presumably her husband too...

At this time my Spanish was still rudimentary and it certainly didn't help that the dialect spoken in Puerto Rico is among the most guttural in the entire region, whereby one should keep in mind that nearly all Caribbean dialects of Spanish are particularly hard to grasp for foreigners. Specifically, the Puerto Ricans make almost a virtue of stripping every word of as many consonants and vowels as possible. Preferably, the beginning, the end and sometimes even the middle of the word is simply left out, or only hinted at in pronunciation, making the learning of Spanish in this environment a quite difficult task. My progress in conversational Spanish was further slowed down by the fact that every other indigenous person would answer me in English even if I had succeeded to address them in reasonably correct Spanish. For example, I remember asking in the Dollar Store: '*Por favor, en donde se encuentran los utensilios de cocina?*' (Could you please tell me where I may find the kitchen utensils?) only to see the visibly terrified female employee scurry across the room to get hold of the manager. He came over and politely asked me what I was looking for, and I said I had already explained that to the girl. 'Oh, I'm sorry', the manager replied, 'but she doesn't understand English'.

The linguistic situation was so desolate that not a single person I met could even recommend me a Spanish teacher. Most of the locals were so unfamiliar with formal grammar that they could not explain any of their verbal usages by other means than translating them into English. No wonder that I, with the novel just about finished and tons of commercial translation work done for a living, felt that I and Puerto Rico henceforth better go separate ways. I had arrived in the island in the month of October, at the end of a hurricane season that literally sent delicious avocados, the size of babies' heads, into my lap. I left it by late July. As I came back to briefly visit the place about eight months later, I learned that my friend Bill Cady had sadly passed on.

Bill's character was an odd mixture of apparent incongruities. He was rather short and stocky, a bit thin-haired and had a very pale, Irish looking complexion: snow-white skin, freckles, etc. I believe he was in his mid-sixties. On the one hand he seemed very proud of his family's military traditions and his own time in the US Marines, or Navy — I can't remember which one it was. On the other hand, he loved to sketch women in crayons and paint them in watercolours; in general he was crazy about women, but the surprisingly young ones he introduced me to (and this time perhaps not too surprisingly), seemed less interested in having sex with him than he with them. With not so subtle references to his precarious health, fragilised by a massive open heart surgery a couple of years earlier, he explicitly entertained the hopes of dying in the arms of a woman. I don't think he was granted that sweet favour by capricious Fate.

While living in Rincón I had no idea that he was so close to his demise. I particularly remember his vivacious and ironic twists in conversation, his rather hysterical sounding laughter that contrasted so strongly with the completely dead grey of his gaze, betraying a man that had already once crossed into the land of Death and mysteriously returned, albeit, as it turned out, not for very long. He lived in a villa sitting on the border between the communes of Rincón and Aguada, surrounded by portions of junk that he always promised he was about to take care of but never did. He taught me basic watercolour techniques and we had spirited conversations whenever we met, which was usually in one and the same place: Bunger's Hotel and Bar down by the sea. One would hear him arrive from afar. As opposed to the locals he didn't play reggaeton on his car stereo through open windows, but preferably something like *Siegfried's Journey on the Rhine* or *Ride of the*

Valkyries by Wagner. I think he was the only person in the neighbourhood, apart from myself, who ever listened to classical music.

Bill took some interest in my historical script (at least I'd like to believe so) and as it progressed always wanted to know how many times, and in what ways, the hero had by now made it with the heroine. He even started to sketch her and show me the invariably humorous results. I appreciated hanging out with him since most of my other acquaintances, in addition to the alcohol we pretty much all indulged in, were more into poker, weed and cocaine than I was. My best moments in Rincón were thus either associated with the rather slow but steady progress of my Byzantine story, or with long walks, even jogging, along the sandy shores connecting Rincón with Aguada and, still farther away, Aguadilla. Along this stretch the beaches, as mentioned, have treacherous waves and are dotted with reefs. To find the beaches good for swimming on one has to turn to the westward coast of Rincón (the word itself signifying 'corner' in Spanish, which is actually what Rincón is: the western corner of Puerto Rico, jutting out from a peninsula rather in the manner of a baboon's nose — look at the map and you'll see what I mean). Here the sand is white and fine and the heavy swell from the Atlantic considerably less menacing, allowing for all sorts of peaceful aquatic activities. This is consequently where the majority of the sea resorts are located.

One may ask how I managed to pass nearly ten months under such circumstances. The truth is that I, besides continuing my script and occasionally engaging my eternal love and enemy, the violin, always had a supply of commercial, thus very tedious but also quite well paid, translations to work on. I also travelled back and forth to Miami several times during that period to perform, and in January took a trip to Peru only to return to a Puerto Rico in the pristine season of tropical winter blessed with a glorious sun, immaculate blue skies and the distant vision of humpback whales migrating through the Strait of Mona (thus called after the Island of Mona strategically located midway between Puerto Rico and Hispaniola). The whales would regularly come to surface to breathe and show off their gigantic tails while ejecting enormous jets straight out of their backs. One or two evenings were so cool that one could actually use a light sweater or jacket to keep warm. It really was the best of seasons.

October and November by contrast had been unsettled with frequent thunderstorms and torrential rains causing power cuts and, perhaps even more annoyingly, interruptions in the water supply system. This was the time when I was made intimately familiar with the 'one-gallon-shower', which is exactly what it sounds like. The trick is to use precious little water while working the soap, and this only in the most critical places, in order to have enough for the rinse. But the real masterpiece is to simultaneously, and successfully, wash one's hair. I learned to do that as well, since the communal water supply could sometimes be off for a week or more. I therefore told my landlord, who happened to be running for mayor in town, that it would be better to promise the citizens reliable water supplies and the final completion of the regional roadworks that had seen no less than seven contractors come and go, than to envisage the renovation of the local skateboard facility, but then he just looked at me as though I had been suggesting a trip to Mars, and I realised that, after all, we weren't on the same planet.

Speaking of beaches, one of the more spectacular ones in Puerto Rico is the so called *Playa Salvaje* (Wilderness Beach). Paradoxically it's jammed in between the US military base in Aguadilla, the golf course and the airport. One wouldn't imagine this to be an ideal location for the promotion of wildlife and vistas of nature's wonders, but it is. Due to the military presence the area is restricted in so far that no new buildings can be added to the few existing ruins nestled in the low vegetation, of which the most fascinating is the old lighthouse built by Spanish conquistadors in the early 16th century. But although the military base is located nearby there is free access to every part of the Wilderness beach.

Like so many other places in the Caribbean, Aguadilla claims the honour of being the ground of Columbus' first landfall and there is a group of statues (some incorrigible snobs would say they testify above all to bad taste) in one of the city's traffic roundabouts, visualising his allegedly first encounter with the local Taino population. Whether that really was his first encounter with human beings in what he took to be the East Indies I don't know, but the lighthouse, of which only one wall is still reasonably intact, surely is from the epoch and, even though of rather modest elevation, offers a wide view of the sandy bay to the north, ending in steep cliffs clad in dense vegetation, privileged nesting grounds for sea fowl. There is also an array of rocks spread out over the sand, partly in and partly above the shifting waterline. In good weather it's a wonderful place to take a swim at and the sunsets here are truly mythological. It really is a wilderness beach to the point that it's advisable to be a little bit curious of who else is on that long stretch of sand before you venture on to it. I personally never encountered any problems there whatsoever and recommend the spot to anyone who would like to verify first-hand what a Caribbean beach might have looked like when the first conquistadors arrived.

Speaking not only of beaches, but also of lighthouses, there is another spectacular, and easy to visit one, right on the southwestern cape of the island. It's called Los Morillos and from its high cliffs I have spotted schools of dolphins and flocks of pelicans moving back and forth between the Atlantic and the Caribbean Seas. Mysteriously, the area around Cabo Rojo (at the end of which the lighthouse sits), and particularly its wildlife refuge, has an unusually high number of reported UFO sightings, so much so that several TV documentaries have been made on the theme trying to explain what the possible causes of these phenomena might be. Among these there is at least one attributable to natural cause: at certain times of the year huge swarms of fluorescent plankton light up the shallow waters of the wildlife sanctuary at night creating something like a submarine aurora borealis. The beach adjacent to the light house is also nice to take a swim in as it offers protection from all winds except the ones from southeast. However, on occurrence these are rare and mostly feeble.

Culturally speaking Puerto Rico unites the best, alternatively the worst, of two worlds. One person might argue that the intrusion of American Judeo-Protestant capitalism into the island's predominantly Hispanic Catholic traditions and institutions has resulted in a successful synthesis. True, without the massive American government spending (read: taxpayer's money) on Puerto Rico, and without its strategic importance as a military outpost in the Caribbean, the island would most certainly offer general living conditions comparable to those of other impoverished islands in the region. As it is there are very few apparent slums although the lower strata of society tend to be just as illiterate, soda drinking, chips eating and chewing gumming as on the North American mainland. To me one emblematic image of contemporary Puerto Rican life is a woman taking her family SUV down the left line of the pan-insular highway at 20 miles per hour while typing an SMS with her three inch brightly coloured, spiral shaped nails, enhancing her makeup and — all simultaneously — cranking up the volume of her reggaeton: talk about a female talent for multi-tasking!

In and around the capital there is the usual urban setup where and whenever money meets the tropics: the well-known fast food chains, the Sheraton, Hilton, Regency, drugstores like Walgreens and CVS, corporate skyscrapers, bank palaces, large casinos and resorts to which loads of Americans with too much money on their pockets are flown in from all over the snow covered Midwest for a weekend behind the *sloth* machine.

The historical centre of San Juan has been carefully preserved and the Castillo San Felipe del Morro guarding the entrance to the lagoon housing the Rich Port City (Puerto Rico) is restored and open to visitors. One of the more unfortunate consequences of such maintenance, however, is that much of the genuine life and atmosphere of the historical centre has been subdued in favour of commerce on par with North American spending habits. Whereas in historical Santo Domingo, capital of the Dominican Republic, you may still find a decent hotel for 25 dollars a night, you'd be hard pressed to find one that only costs a 100 in old San Juan, and if you want to visit a steakhouse you'd be seated by a hostess (Hello, my name is Sandra!) just like in the US. Notwithstanding, I once managed to reserve a whole suite for just a bit over that price at the famous Hotel El Convento for myself and a beautiful woman of Latin descent with whom I have had the privilege from time to time to share a bed. I remember there was a complimentary happy hour during which we managed to carry off a whole bottle and bring it up to the roof terrace and its jacuzzi. Once there we enjoyed complete privacy and a handsome number of gin and tonics before it was time to hit the sumptuous restaurant offering oysters and champagne.

The best or worst of two worlds? To the Puerto Ricans themselves, the fact that they are all entitled to carry US passports is of course an enormous advantage as it enables them to come and go between their island and the North American continent whenever. They don't have to apply for any kind of VISA and can settle down and work freely in any state, even in Alaska and Hawaii. This may sound self-evident, but it isn't really considering that Puerto Rico is not formally a state within the union but technically its own commonwealth. At least on paper it's a semi-independent state with its own legislative and executive bodies — a Senate and a House of Representatives. But even though Puerto Ricans do run local elections to appoint their own Governor, US legislature dominates nearly every aspect of its civic life. Inversely, there are no Puerto Rican US senators and I believe only one token (non-voting) representative in the Congress. Furthermore, Puerto Ricans, although in all other respects fully acknowledged as US citizens, are not allowed to vote in presidential elections. But this, with hindsight, might be a rather small price to pay for generous kickbacks from Uncle Sam in return, constantly preventing the country from socially and economically falling in line with neighbouring island states such as the Dominican Republic, Cuba, Haiti and Jamaica. There is a small political party advocating independence but so far the majority of the population has been smart enough to avoid listening to closely to that siren call — according to a 2012 poll a majority of the islanders are in favour of achieving full statehood within the US.

With so many relatives and friends in all the major US cities, and with Puerto Ricans spread all over the world — they are even to be found in Jerusalem — there is very little reason to rock the boat, especially since the island is one of the most densely populated in the world. So even though unemployment is rampant and the US Coast Guard is constantly busy scooping up poor Dominicans dumped on the deserted *Isla de Mona*, or the even closer *Isla Desecheo*, by unscrupulous traffickers, a steady flow of subsidies compensates for a feeble industrial output and ensures an average living standard well above the Caribbean median. Another effect of the US pumping money into a system that would otherwise crumble, is a near complete lack of agriculture. Although practically anything could be made to grow on the island it's really only coffee and, to some extent sugar cane, that is locally produced whereas tomatoes, salads and cucumbers are imported from abroad. The supermarkets sell exactly the same items as in the US but prices are not conspicuously higher than on the mainland. And, true, they do have their own avocados, but these don't have to be cultivated as they come straight off the trees everywhere on the island. The ones of Rincón are apparently most famous because of their exquisite texture and flavour. I have nothing to object to that evaluation.

As far as Puerto Rico's cultural traditions go, one element, as predominant as it is bizarre, consists of various Protestant sects, the services of which, on account of the terrible singing that goes on for hours in their chapels, is just as much a torture to the musical ear as the ubiquitous reggaeton. At the opposite end of Puerto Rican piety, which in spite of its primitive forms of worship seems sincere enough, one finds MTV-inspired vanity. Since Puerto Rico is richer than Cuba or the Dominican Republic, people dare to flaunt gold crucifixes on heavy gold chains without running the immediate risk of being decapitated for them by *ladrones*. Add to this that a surprisingly large number of young men (gay or not) actually shave and wax their legs and arms (and the armpits, that goes without saying), have meticulously tailored beards and even enhance their peeled eyebrows with black makeup. Their preferred clothing is the rapper's uniform: far too long shorts dangling half way down their butts, sneakers that look like modern Hi-Fi systems, voluminous sports shirts hanging down to their knees and a baseball cap. And yes, Puerto Ricans do play baseball, one of the country's legendary heroes being the baseball player Roberto Clemente who, while still in the midst of his career, was tragically killed in a plane crash off the Puerto Rican coast.

It thus seems to me that the Spanish heritage, in spite of a tenacious religious bigotry and a language that, at least officially, is some kind of Castilian, is not very prominent. Still, the famous Spanish cellist Pablo Casals had a Puerto Rican mother and he was the driving force behind the creation of the Casals Music Festival, still taking place every year in the island's capital. In contrast the modern Caribbean lifestyle involves very little folklore and tradition. To most Puerto Ricans it seems quite enough that a super showbiz star like Ricky Martin counts as one of them.

To be fair to both people and the landscape, however: although my lingering impression of the island's population is that it has ended up in a sort of no-man's land between two cultures — the old autocratic albeit more charming Hispanic and the more recent and intensely consumerist North American — Puerto Rico also is a very beautiful island. The two smaller islands just off its east coast, Vieques and Culebra, are very attractive too with a staggering display of colourful tropical waters and coastlines. In particular Vieques has for the longest time been spared excessive tourism because half of the island was military terrain. I believe this has now changed, opening up what was earlier almost a wildlife refuge to real estate investors and other merchants. But even during its military tenure (and my only visit to the island so far took place as early as in 1996) it proved virtually impossible to find a decent hotel for less than at least a 100 dollars a night. The one I stayed in was called Hacienda Tamarindo and literally had a big living tamarind tree in its midst.

I said a 100 dollars a night, right? Well that was back then. After a short Internet survey, I found that as of the year 2015 you'd rather have to come up with twice that amount for a single room at the Tamarindo. Solid breakfast is included and apparently there still is a well-stocked 'honour bar' to the benefit of hotel guests. Since I had to make up my own mind as to what honourable would be, I decided that whatever I had paid for the room would give me substantial leeway, and acted in accordance with that assumption.

The view from the hotel is most enticing. I particularly remember walking down to the nearby rocky beach with its stunning array of rainbow coloured waters. As I passed over the cattle ground I came across the corpse of a horse. It was in an advanced state of decomposition. Impossible for me not to make the association to Charles Baudelaire's famous sonnet 'Une charogne' (A Carcass), in which the poet compares the future of his beloved muse to the putrefied mass, utterly invaded by maggots and insects, at his feet. It was Baudelaire's way of confounding (not confronting) ideal beauty with horror and disgust that announced a ground-breaking novelty in contemporary poetry, paving the way for the extravagant poetics of Verlaine and Rimbaud and, even later, the Surrealists. To me Baudelaire is, and has always been, the only French poet I can truly say that I admire and relish. I feel irresistibly attracted to his aesthetics and I believe I know why:

although his choice of poetical themes is quite restrained, his formal treatment of even the most appalling subjects is invariably classical, consistent, lucid, elegant and poignant. His musical cadence is impeccable to my ear and his mastery of not only French, but also of English, is rare in French letters of the era. Well known for his congenial translations of Edgar Poe, I'd like to also point out his masterly 'imitation', as he himself calls it, of Longfellow's majestic *Song of Hiawatha*. Just to give the reader a sample, here the opening of the poem in its original:

> 'On the Mountains of the Prairie,
> On the great Red Pipe-stone Quarry,
> Gitche Manito, the mighty,
> He the Master of Life, descending,
> On the red crags of the quarry
> Stood erect, and called the nations,
> Called the tribes of men together.'

And as cross reference, Baudelaire's Imitation called *Le calumet de la paix* (The Peace Pipe):

> 'Or Gitche Manito, le Maître de la Vie,
> Le Puissant, descendit dans la verte prairie,
> Dans l'immense prairie aux coteaux montueux;
> Et là, sur les rochers de la Rouge Carrière,
> Dominant tout l'espace et baigné de lumière,
> Il se tenait debout, vaste et majestueux.'

It was only seven years ago that I spent ten months in Puerto Rico, but my memories of them, like the carcass above, have begun to decompose. In retrospect I certainly don't regret having pitched camp there for a while. I did indeed have a very personal motif to choose this location, but since I have decided not to bring the more dolorous aspects of my past into this account, I can't give to the reader the more precise circumstances pertaining to my choice of location at that point in time. I thus remain true to the admonition given to us high school students by our British, gentlemanly teacher Owen Lee — who passed on to the happy hunting ground many years ago — that our essay to be composed and presented a few days later in class, might well be 'personal, but please not too personal.'

A sailing trip in the Gulf of Honduras

Since we're still in the Caribbean I'd like to seize the opportunity to tell the story of how I ended up meeting a German professor of mathematics on his way to a conference in Oaxaca on the topic of 'how to prove that something is impossible', as well as an American-Canadian yacht skipper who had been dumped by some Australian hayseed and — now in need of both a new crew and a therapist — invited me to join him for a sailing trip from the island Útila off the Honduran coast to Rio Dulce in Guatemala.

Beyond the craggy northern coast of Honduras there are a number of so-called bay islands, most of which are tiny, but three of them substantially larger than the rest. These three are really the peaks of a long coral reef laid out on a northeast axis along the coast. The smallest, most southwesterly of these, as well as the one closest to the mainland, roughly 16 nautical miles distant from the town of La Ceiba, is Útila. To get there by public transportation one has to board a marine construction that looks like some hermetically sealed amphibian landing vessel used at D-Day and offers about the same level of comfort to its passengers. Luckily the ride over the channel only takes about 45 minutes. But this was enough time for me to realise that my co-passenger (there were not many of us on board that floating trough) with big curly hair and beard, sturdy sandals, and something of a sullen regard, must by all criteria known to me to be a German.

After having impassively observed one another we struck up a conversation as the vessel was about to dock. My assumption that he was German turned out to be 100 % correct. Since we were both looking for a hotel, it came naturally to walk down the main street of Útila town together. Close to one of the many diving shops we found accommodation in neighbouring rooms on the second floor of a guesthouse. For several reasons it's often preferable in tropical countries to opt for second floor rooms if available. For one, the mosquitoes are usually less of a nuisance, second, they usually offer more privacy, and third, the view is usually better.

The view from behind the second floor balustrade over the bay and the open sea beyond it was indeed very inviting and conducive to further conversation. Fritz von Zweienhalb, as his full name spelled (and I here omit the title 'Herr Professor' because Fritz didn't like to be called that way, no doubt considering it too formal in the relaxed setting we happened to find ourselves.) Nevertheless, academia was never far from Fritz' mind and after some initial research I managed to find out that his areas of special interest and competence within the vast field of mathematics were algebraic complexity theory, parallel computation, finite fields, computer algebra, and cryptography... As for myself and my technical knowledge of math I can't even remember how one proceeds in order to carry out a division operation of multiple numbers on paper. But though I have some general understanding of the principles of mathematics, I can only hold my ground in argumentation with other generalists. With a specialist such as Fritz I couldn't even get out of my starting blocks before he would disqualify me with a drawn out and tired: 'Nein, Nein, Nein!'

Very soon I found myself cornered and had to throw my last trump card on the table. The second last is $\sqrt{-1}$, which is unsolvable (the answer is called 'the imaginary unit' by mathematical convention, read:

embarrassment), and in my view just another proof of the absurdity of negative numbers. As a matter of fact my last trump is in the same suit as the $\sqrt{-1}$ and consists in questioning how a multiplication of negative numbers can possibly yield a positive result, for example -2 x -2 = (+) 4. To which Fritz of course replied that it really is terribly simple to demonstrate — I think you can imagine the rest. I believe he lost me already at the very first transition: 'this relationship can also be expressed as'.... whereby mathematics, that to my simple mind should only consist of numbers, starts to look like an alphabet haphazardly put together without sentence structure, grammar or meaning.

After having thus exhausted my by all means very limited mathematical repertoire I wisely turned to asking the question what it was that had brought him to Útila. His answer was that his father had been there many years earlier and been so impressed with it that he had encouraged him to go there as well. That had been almost a promise on the son's part, and considering that Fritz had since travelled to almost every corner of the Earth, Útila, apart from being a father's preferred destination, was also a remaining white spot on Fritz's inner map. It seemed to me that Fritz had applied the superlatively German virtue of *Gründlichkeit* (thoroughness) to his travels as well, because he had practically been everywhere, while at the same time being an appointed Professor at various highly prestigious institutions around the world. But research is research and Fritz, in his younger days, had taken his wife and their young children on a trip in the iconic Volkswagen van of the epoch from Alaska to Cape Horn, which even involved shipping the car from Panama to Colombia, since the Pan American highway simply ceases to exist north and south of the Darién, which is the name given to the wilderness connecting, or perhaps even more to the point: separating the two states.

I left Fritz with his bottle of red wine, his pipes with fragrant tobacco and his books that, as far as I was concerned, could just as well, and rather, have been written in Chinese. After having had dinner I strolled for a while along the Main Street. In spite of being a small island with very limited motorised circulation on the boardwalk that runs along the bay, it's far from secure to walk there because of all the motorcyclists who feel they have the right to drive as fast as they can on what is otherwise, by necessity, a narrow pedestrian zone. Fritz had made the interesting remark that it was typically Anglo-Saxon to let house façades line the beachfront instead of letting the promenade pass in front of it, which he assured me was the more Latin way of arranging such things. There could be some truth to this. In spite of being administratively part of Honduras, the racially diverse population of Útila is primarily English speaking and even has its own jurisdiction, meaning for example that their police force is independent from that of the rest of the country — which perhaps contributes to explain why its members are so fond of wreaking havoc among the tourists from the top of their motorbikes. More importantly, though, this potentially sets up the island's tiny and idyllic-looking airport as a strategic hub for drug trafficking.

It is well known that all three of the Honduran Bay islands, including their surrounding keys, offer convenient storage and transit point for various drugs, notably cocaine originating in Colombia, destined for the Cayman Islands and the US market. According to a recent *El Heraldo* newspaper report, a staggering 85 % of the population of Guanaja, the easternmost and least developed of the three islands, regularly uses crack, cocaine and/or marijuana. But although Guanaja, because of its lack of tourist infrastructure, is the number one spot for narco-trafficking, frequently involving fishermen and other members of the local community, both Roatán and Útila have their fair share of drug trade as well. These islands are often the first ports of call for drugs passing via the Colombian islands of San Andrés and Providencia off the coast of Nicaragua, before being transported to Belize and Mexico. Now, this is not something the average tourist to for example Roatán (and I recently spent three lovely weeks there myself) would notice or even be aware of, but it's a fact to keep in mind for anyone wondering how many of the poor in these island enclaves actually get by on a day-to-day basis.

Anyways it wasn't drugs I was after, but rather the calm of a little seaside bar with decent and, above all, not too loud music. This is how and where I found Barney. He was sitting alone in a comfy chair by the water with a rum drink close at hand. He invited me to join him and this is how our joint venture came about. In telling it I shall skip the whole initial story of his allegedly falling in love with an Australian woman 20 years his junior (their final break-up was preceded by some argument concerning her lap dog), and just take it from the point where I entered the action.

Like Fritz, Barney is unusual among travellers in that he's actually not only an intelligent man. He also has a lot of imagination — which he's fond of referring to as his 'female side', sometimes making it slightly hard for me to decide whether or not I should believe everything he says or use my common sense to filter the information. I wouldn't go as far as to imply that he has some of the characteristics of a con man, but he's definitely, like myself, an opportunist and I think that's why we immediately came to recognise and appreciate one another.

The dance on roses having reached its grand finale on Roatán, Barney had pulled out of its French Harbour and brought his stately 42 feet yacht, Teleportation, to the bay of Útila in the hope of either selling it right there or bring it to the marine trailer parks of Rio Dulce in Guatemala. From this night onwards we began to hang out, and not only during the evenings. We did some snorkelling together, taking the Teleportation's dingy to some preferred spots. It was on Útila, with its gorgeous coral reefs, that my passion for this kind of aquatic activity was awakened for real. Ever since I love to float on top of the sea and look down on the landscapes, mountains and valleys, teeming with life, below me. The species of fish, the prehistoric looking plants, the colours; it's just fabulous, and in addition it's good exercise — just remember to put your T-shirt on before going into the water. The sun is relentless!

Finally, and even though I could indeed foresee what the result was going to be, I introduced Barney to Fritz. As expected it was like trying to unite fire and water, whereby Barney was the frustrated fire trying to light up easy-going jokes, mercilessly extinguished by Fritz' innate seriousness. As a matter of fact, Fritz every now and then became quite irritated with people around him and then withdrew into a kind of sullen aloofness that I would *a priori* consider quite inappropriate for a cosmopolitan traveller, supposedly used to deal with a lot of random trouble and annoyances. How he was going to deal with the inevitable problems connected with a planned trip in the near future on motorbike through Central Asia I can only imagine, but I suppose he finally went there and also lived to tell the story.

As a happily married man with two daughters, Barney had spent many years of his life on an island in western Canada. At that time he also worked as a technician within civilian aviation. Later he again lived life as a single in Hawaii. At the time of our encounter, however, his playboy self-assurance had been ever so slightly singed by the edges, and he clearly felt lonely and abandoned. For this reason, he was also visibly content to have me as a conversational partner, even exaggerating my crucial role in helping him to overcome his loss. He slept in his yacht while I remained in the hotel until the day we decided to heave anchor and set sail for Guatemala. But though all provisions had by now been securely stored on board and we were ready to rock, a series of nasty squalls from the southeast, exactly the direction in which we would be headed, promised to make our first leg 'diabolical', as Barney was always fond of putting it. So we stayed put on board, had beers and rum, grilled lobster tail on the barbecue and enjoyed what was to become our last evening meal in the tranquil bay of Útila.

In the morning the wind, still from the southeast, but without the rains, promised a nice voyage, even though we would have to beat against the wind for most of the day to reach the Laguna el Diamante on the Honduran mainland. It was a beautiful day and the ship initially took us past the keys east of Útila and then out onto the open sea. Barney the Skipper had carefully plotted our course and told me, the designated helmsman for that day, to just hold steady on a starboard leg for a good three or four hours. This I did. The breeze was reliable but the sea variable, here and there surprisingly choppy, as though the wind's direction had just recently shifted and left the waves undecided.

Towards noon, the coast of Honduras had disappeared to the south and didn't come into sight again until later that afternoon, after we had changed board to port. We reached up to the height of the spectacular rock formations forming the high cape west of the town of Tela as the sun began to set behind us. As a precautionary measure, Barney told me to keep well off the coast at this point since the reefs dotting it are treacherous. Also we had to prepare for an absolute precision entry into the lagoon itself. This, provided the engine worked, would not have been that much of a risk, but Barney had warned me that it just sometimes would break down. He also said he knew how to fix it, but that it would take him up to five minutes to do so. If the engine fails us, he instructed me, you have to turn the rudder and go back out into sea, and we shall have to spend the rest of the night sailing.

I didn't like that prospect very much, but of course, as we approached the 50 metre narrow strait, separating a craggy islet from the land making up one arm of the lagoon, the damn thing ceased to run. Barney, once again repeating his mantra: 'This is diabolical!' dived headlong below deck into the engine room and began to operate on the recalcitrant motor, meanwhile probably expecting that I would follow orders and turn round. But with the wind now coming in more or less from the aft, this would have been even riskier than to stay on course and I just shouted to Barney: 'We have the wind to make it Captain!' And so we did. As the engine reassuringly came on again, Barney, peeking out from the engine room with greasy hands and oily stains on his forehead, found himself in a completely new environment. We were right inside El Diamante, a natural harbour protected against all winds set in a 500 metre wide, almost perfectly circular, lagoon in the midst of the wilderness of the Punta Sal National Park.

There was only one other yacht swaying in the tranquil lagoon and as we furled the sails and threw our anchor silence descended on the scene. Well, apart from all of the monkeys howling in the verdant density and the incessant chatter of the birds. Through the strait we could see the sun set behind the coastline, illuminating the ochre-red rocks while prolonging their shadows. Before we knew it the night was over us. And what an unforgettable spectacle that was. Blessed with clear skies we could discern thousands of individual stars in the galaxy against the background of the millions and again millions making up the Milky Way. It was a rare feeling of comfort to be so close to nature without actually having to share any of its inconveniences — such as all the little bloodthirsty animals crawling on the ground. We had dinner and afterwards moved up on the deck with our red wine box, inebriating ourselves under the stars. It was an incredibly intense experience of our place, if not in the universe as a whole, at least in the Orion arm of our own galaxy, in turn a tiny seashell in the cosmic ocean, measuring a mere 100,000 light years across… But this time I'm not even going to try to convey in words the magnitude of a starry night under tropical skies unperturbed by the lights of civilisation. Please just try to imagine the impossible: a perfect, invisible hemisphere above and the enigmatic, undecipherable sounds of the likewise invisible jungle along its rim, like an infinitely convoluted, five dimensional Morse code, sent onwards into the universe by two humans tapping on the Teleportation!

In the morning it transpired, not altogether unsuspectedly, that I had spilled some generous quantities of red wine onto the deck (yes, it was my fault). This is every yacht skipper's nightmare in broad daylight because red wine, as we all know, so easily and stubbornly stains white plastic. However, Barney had a detergent product we could use to remove it. Even so it involved quite a lot of rubbing before the surface was satisfactorily restored. He also got the engine up and working. After bidding our only human neighbours, and the monkeys, farewell, we heaved anchor and motioned towards the strait. Having passed it we felt reassured that the morning would henceforth be as tranquil as the sea, a light breeze filling the sails just enough to take us along the coast down to Puerto Cortéz in a couple of hours.

So Barney turned on the outdoor barbecue on the aft of the ship and started to make us bacon and eggs for brunch. It smelled lovely, but unfortunately not only to us. We must have been at a distance of at least two nautical miles from the coast when we were suddenly attacked by a swarm of hungry bees, setting out from land like a squadron of jet fighters. This was, to once again paraphrase Barney, another 'diabolical' event. I was at the helm while he tried to fight the beasts off with a towel, whereby they became really irritated and started to also attack me. In the process of trying to fend for myself I again had to sacrifice a pair of Ray Ban Wayfarer II's to Neptune (can't even keep track of how many I have lost in this and similar ways over the years), but it's very possible that it was a small price to pay for finally getting rid of these molesters — luckily it doesn't seem to have been the entire hive on an outing but only a special unit. Even so fifty angry bees can be very annoying too, as we came to witness.

Without further disturbances we arrived in Puerto Cortéz in the late afternoon. This industrial town has a busy commercial port and we cautiously circumnavigated the enormous cargo ships that were waiting to load or unload outside it, to seek sufficient shelter in an adjacent wide bay beneath coastal mountains reaching an impressive altitude. Once anchored we managed to hail down a smaller boat with locals to get to shore and from there a taxi to the supermarket to replenish our provisions. Apart from that, and the store, I don't remember much more from that evening and believe we must have hit the bunks quite early.

Only to get up fresh and perky in the morning and cross the comparatively shallow waters of the Bahía de Omoa, and where the coastline too is flat. Apart from ensuring that the water depth would always be sufficient, there was almost no need for Barney to plot the course since the distant cape Punta de Manabique in Guatemala, which we were aiming for, could be discerned as a glistening Prussian Bluish speck on the horizon, growing more and more tangible as we neared it. In a matter of just a few hours, on a very agreeable downwind, we made it across, rounded the cape and its lighthouse in order to throw our anchor below Cambalache, which is the name of the narrow peninsula separating the Bahia de Amatique to the south from the wider Gulf of Honduras to the north. This time we could almost, but luckily only almost, sight another busy port of the Caribbean, Puerto Barrios, set in the southeastern corner of the Amatique Bay. I said lucky because I sincerely hold that there is nothing there to see. The only phenomenon worth observing in Puerto Barrios is the legacy of the United Fruit Company, which once held something like a third of Guatemala, but only used some of their land to grow bananas. This was back in the days of the Cold War. When a Guatemalan president of the epoch named Arbenz tried to alleviate the hardships for the poor of his country by nationalising the land that United Fruit had allowed to fall fallow and abandoned, so that it could be leased and cultivated again by the peasants, the mega corporation pressured the United States government and the CIA to intervene and oust Arbenz in a staged military coup.[15] The reason I mention this here, is that although United Fruit no longer exists as such, its previous presence in Central America can still be felt, notably in Puerto Barrios from where nowadays the *Fyffes Bananas* are loaded and shipped around the world.

---

15 I read about all this in an interesting book called *Bitter Fruit: The Story of an American Coup in Guatemala*, by Stephen Schlesinger and Stephen Kinzer.

It was a hot afternoon and we had been working pretty hard to beat against the wind to get as close to shore as we dared to. Once we had found a good spot to anchor, I decided to take a dip and was suddenly, while just swimming around the haul, surrounded by a school of dolphins playfully jumping and diving through the water as they passed by. Some of them were so close that I could see their eyes staring back at me and I found that very exciting — as though they were curious to find out who I was and what I was doing on their 'turf'. During the course of the afternoon some clouds rolled in and we could no longer make out the contours of the Guatemalan mainland across the water. In the morning there were some mists, but this of course didn't prevent us from making the short distance over to the small town of Livingston, located at the embouchure of the Rio Dulce, Guatemala.

Here we had to get our passports stamped. Barney, additionally, had to pay some transit fee for his yacht. Waiting for the Captain's office to give us clearance — there was a customs inspection of the boat and its cargo as well — we hung out in this rather incredible place where, apart from more Hispanic Guatemalans, Indians and Garifunas co-exist in what seems to be a peaceful symbiosis. The Garifunas are originally Africans. Legend has it that some of them were considered so impossible to domesticate for slavery that an English slave ship set them ashore on Roatán to fend for themselves. I know there are still Garifunas there because I have visited their village Punta Gorda on the eastern flank of the very oblong island's northern coast. Another legend says they managed to escape from slave transports and in this way ended up populating coastal areas and the archipelagos of today's Honduras, Guatemala and Belize. Whatever the truth is to these claims, the Garifunas themselves are convinced that their ancestors were never subject to slavery and fiercely maintain their freedom and relative independence from modern national governments too.

Their language audibly, and as can be expected, is a bewildering mix of old African tribal dialects and some European tongues, such as Spanish and English. There might also be elements of local Indian dialects in it. However, not only their language, which apparently is not similar to either Belizean or Jamaican creole, but also their traditions and spiritual practices set them apart from many other African communities of the Caribbean. I'm personally a great fan of their music, which I find successfully combines the best of West African folklore — not the least the music and lyrics associated with the traditional African lute, the Kora — and music styles with a more Caribbean vibe. Above all, their music is easy-going, not violent and brutalising as so much of the contemporary urban music of Latin America. Theirs is a more traditional, laid back beat, which alone would be reason for me to like it. On top of that it's also very harmonious. While waiting for Barney at a café I recognised one of the ambulating Garifunas (this was actually my second visit to Livingston) and I managed to buy a few records from him containing some traditional music. It later proved to be an excellent purchase.

By now it was time for us to head upstream on the Rio Dulce, which for me turned out to be a revelation akin to that of opening the first page to God's *The Illustrated Book of Creation*, perusing the illumination next to the passage describing how Paradise was initially created and then, in all its pristine glory, presented to Adam and Eve. The greenery of the river banks here comes all the way down to the water, making the interface a privileged area for fish and fowl. There are cranes and egrets leisurely walking the water edges, while a constant swirling of birds in the air seemingly announce a more eager hunt. The sun, vibrating in the hot afternoon, dives in and out of narrow valleys, sometimes hinting at the diffuse contours of human settlements tucked away in the jungle. There we were, in the midst of the winding river itself with the infinite blue sky as our canopy. I was sitting upright, my head covered by a straw hat and my back propped up against the mast, a soft drink at hand, watching the river bends unfold as Barney calmly steered us up towards the lake system making up much of the interior of this waterway.

As the river opened up and transformed into the lake El Golfete, the landscape too appeared to change character. In reality the banks are probably not that much less steep, just farther away. In principle, and on a good downwind, one can sail these waters, although we found little reason to question our acquired level of comfort. So we continued to motor up the lake and in due course made it to the Texan Bay Marina, thus called on account of its then Texan ownership (I believe it has now changed name to La Laguna Marina Lodge, although the amenities are presumably pretty much the same), where we docked at one of their piers after Barney had finally decided to make contact with the management over the shortwave (he waited until we were just outside of the bay to call.)

The Rio Dulce with its adjacent lake system is not only a place of spectacular natural beauty. From a practical point of view it offers yacht owners an extraordinarily safe haven during hurricane season, which in the Caribbean runs from June to November. Having one's boat anchored in one of its many marinas is like seeking shelter in the womb of Mother Nature herself. This is the primary reason why the Rio Dulce inlet is teeming with sailors from all over the world. Some of them just hang out in and around their boats for much of the hazardous season, leading an aquatic trailer park existence. Others leave them there to go north during summer. By all means, arriving there in the second half of April, as we did, is to witness the marinas slowly fill up with ships, captains and crews. There is a constant talk about comings and goings, and of spare boat parts, especially engine parts, that need to be ordered and shipped from far away and arrive there before a specific vessel can take to the seas again — and it should all preferably happen before June if you're heading towards the Pacific or the North Atlantic. One meets with all kinds of sailors as well: everything from professional yacht captains making a living from delivering boats halfway round the world on behalf of their owners, to grandpas and grandmas who have decided they don't want to spend the rest of their days staring vacantly at each other across a flamingo decorated balcony of a Florida condominium. There are also, and quite a lot of them, lone sea wolves, who will occasionally welcome a deckhand or two for a trip down to Panamá and the San Blas Islands, but are more than capable of handling a ship by themselves along an indefinite stretch of nautical miles. In addition, there are the gringos and Europeans, some of them dedicated landlubbers, running the hotels and marinas catering to all the sailors.

Barney was happy to charge Teleportation's batteries with fresh electricity and to even get his air conditioner working — indeed it can get hot to sleep inside such a cabin under tropical skies. Meanwhile I began socialising with the crowd of this maritime melting pot, still not quite part of the conglomerate of marinas to be found further south around the town of Rio Dulce and its busy bridge — an important link in a heavily utilised transport system connecting the northern Petén region with Puerto Barrios and Guatemala City. The Texan Bay, inversely, is located on the upper reaches of the El Golfete and because of this is an integral part of its peaceful natural surroundings. Although the lively people visiting this marina get together under its thatched roofed restaurant for barbecues, card games, quizzes — and God knows what else — their sounds are quickly absorbed into the primordial night, leaving one with the impression of a party island for mature people happily lost in time and space (the amount of weed fed joints in this place is quite impressive — oh no, the hippie generation is not yet quite extinct!)

During our entire trip Barney and I had discussed and made plans — more in jest than in real earnest for sure, but all the same — to open a bar once we got to the town of Rio Dulce. Its most popular waterhole, frequented by sailors and straying tourists alike, is the *Sun Dog*. It's run by a very sympathetic Swiss guy from Basel, and in addition to drinks also has a small menu. Barney told me that right across the street from Sun Dog there is a property that has housed a bar in the past; it was just for us to get it up and going again. My suggestion to name 'our' bar *Copy Cat* immediately won Barney's favour and we had a great time speculating about what would happen if we ever came to turn our plan into reality. But I think we both knew at heart that our intense planning was more in the nature of a pastime during long days at sea, and as we both have plenty of imagination we were the owners of an establishment in Rio Dulce long before we even arrived there. Needless to add that as soon as we were on the actual premises we quickly abandoned the idea.

In Rio Dulce too Barney had some friends at a lakeside hotel—as a matter of fact, due to Barneys' extraverted nature and apparent need to implicate even innocent bystanders in his amorous escapades, everyone in Rio Dulce, since it was here that his fling with Karen had kicked off, seemed to know about his recent romance. Barney was happy to provide them with some details of the denouement and after that everything returned to normal. He docked his boat and accepted my invitation to sleep in the double room I had rented for some days to come. Our trip, and an unforgettable experience for me, thus came to its natural and calm end.

We spent some nights hanging out at Sun Dog and this is where we both ran into Bruce, a professional Australian skipper about to set sail to a boat bound for New Zealand on behalf of a client. Bruce, though not intrinsically unsympathetic, made quite a choleric impression and was easily annoyed if one didn't always agree with him. So although I knew that Barney was eagerly looking for a way out of what seemed to be both a financial and a geographical rut, I was a bit surprised to see that he immediately accepted the offer to become one of two mates for such long voyage on board a 38-foot yacht. Wow, I thought to myself, how are these individuals going to get along in such a reduced space, and for so long?

Many months later I had to piece together my own version of what subsequently took place based on Bruce's and Barney's independent testimony (hence I don't really know in how far it coincides with a more or less objective truth, if one such is even imaginable in human relations!) As I left Rio Dulce in late April to visit Antígua and, eventually, Lake Atitlán, Bruce was still waiting for some spare part for the boat engine to be properly installed, while Barney had found himself a local lady to distract himself from the painful memory of Karen. Apparently, Bruce, Barney and a third male crew member, finally set out from La Ceiba on the Honduran coast for a voyage that would take them through the Panama Canal, over the Galapagos, the Marquesas Islands, Tahiti, etc. all the way to New Zealand. According to Bruce, Barney — and I wonder why that doesn't surprise me! — had declared that he had no money at all. In response Bruce offered to pay for food and drinks whenever they made landfall (food and drink on board for the crew was already budgeted and paid for by the yacht owner). This may not sound like such a big deal, but then one should keep in mind that even a can of beer easily costs seven dollars on any one of the Polynesian islands, so that expenses, given a certain level of consumption, quickly add up.

So Bruce keeps paying, which Barney assumes to be part of the deal, until the day they reach the Samoa Islands when, just as suddenly as unexpectedly, Barney spots another lady, a Kiwi, who immediately captivates his attention. As a consequence Barney hits it off with this new acquaintance and moves into a hotel together with her. He's also seen together with her in bars and restaurants, whereby Bruce, assuming that Barney has simply been lying to him throughout the entire trip about being broke, gets furious. As a consequence of this, in its turn, Barney signs off from the mission, or is being sacked — which amounts pretty much to the same thing given the circumstances — to instead follow his instinct and accompany the Kiwi woman to New Zealand, by plane this time. When I asked Barney about the possible veracity of Bruce's allegation, he said that it was the lady who had possessed the money and that she had agreed to pay for some of their mutual expenses and forward him the rest to be paid back on a later occasion. I guess that might have been true, but I also knew that Barney had a small pecuniary as well as emergency backup (money he didn't want to touch for sure) that he never considered important enough to inform Bruce about.

Judging from the colour of Bruce's face, as well as the tone of his voice, when telling me his side of the story (this happened on my re-visit to Rio Dulce at least a year later) he and Barney are not risking too soon to become best friends again. As far as Barney is concerned I met with him on several occasions in Florida before I even heard Bruce's version of their mutual trip to New Zealand. Afterwards, Barney had sailed Teleportation from Isla de Mujeres off Cancún (or perhaps someone else did it for him, I don't quite remember) and had it docked along a pier outside some friend's house in Fort Myers. Here it was struck by lightning while on sale, right after the visit from a prospective buyer. In the end, though, Barney managed to sell the boat, and then took off to New Zealand again. When I last talked to him he had acquired residency there and worked as a skipper for tourists off the South Island. He described his present relation to the Kiwi woman as friendly rather than passionate. In contrast, New Zealand as such seems to suit his character and temperament just fine. Good wine, good food, beautiful nature and like-minded people to hang out with, as he once summed up the situation in conversation. From our last telephone conversation, no too long ago, I got to know that he was in a state of convalescence from an operation in the knee but nevertheless enjoys very much living and working over there.

Another thing Barney told me some months after we had sailed through the Gulf of Honduras, was that only weeks after we had anchored overnight in Laguna el Diamante, some Honduran pirates attacked a yacht right inside that tranquil bay, killing its captain while, for some unknown reason, sparing his daughter's life. Also, Barney's former girlfriend Karen had apparently found herself in the wrong place, at the wrong time, and been both raped and robbed and then thrown out of a car somewhere outside the town of Rio Dulce.

As for myself, I have a keen memory of being invited, in the middle of the night, into a small motorboat to continue the celebrations of some local girl's birthday. Our party sets off down the river. But no later have we reached the middle of the lagoon than the birthday child gets hold of a loaded gun. Comprehensively drunk, as well as hysterically laughing, she starts to discharge bullets into the water and up into the air. Two of the gentleman standing at the aft of the boat, while helping the girl to aim (I'm lying down in the prow with no chance to move anywhere) seem to notice that the event has made me ever so slightly uneasy, so one of them says: 'Don't worry Senor Lorenzo, he's a lawyer and I'm a hydro engineer. Everything is cool.' I suppose this declaration was meant to assure me that since he and his friends belong to an educated class of people, a stray bullet dispatched from a drunk woman's hand would never dare to err in my direction. But how they could be so sure of that to this day baffles my mind, still capable of reproducing the sound of a gun magazine being emptied as we drift down a stream of pitch-black water, paradoxically named the Rio Dulce.

Antígua

Antígua, the ancient capital of Guatemala, is a colonial town in the heart of Central America. It is therefore also one of the must-go places in the country and frequented by tourists all year round, with usual peaks during the holidays. I too had been to Antígua a couple of times when I finally decided this might be the best place for me to improve my Spanish at one of the many Spanish language schools offering courses to foreigners. To this end I had rented for three months a rather spectacular apartment at the southern end of 5 Avenida Sur. It was one of five apartments in a complex that had once been a *finca* built by monks in the 18th century. Its present owner was, and to my knowledge still is, the gentleman, doctor of microbiology and enthusiastic horticulturalist Miguel Torres. The apartment itself, like the four others in this building facing on one side the avenida, on the other the interior courtyard and garden as well as the Doctor's own villa, was composed of two very spacious rooms. The one at the bottom served as a combined dining room and kitchen and had artful arches and niches made from ancient bricks. There was a huge lustre hanging down from the high ceiling over a rustic looking kitchen table and iron bars to protect the likewise high window from unwelcome intrusion. A tiled staircase with railings in wrought iron led up to the bedroom, spacious enough to accommodate ten double beds if necessary. But it only had one, and one TV set, initially located so far from the bed that one would have needed a telescope to clearly discern the images.

There was an adjacent bathroom that looked like a boudoir taken out of Snow White's castle and transposed to Latin America by a time machine. The shower, including the bathtub, had warm water provided by yet another one of these potentially lethal electric appliances connected straight to the plumbing. The whole apartment was permeated by a very characteristic scent. Once I got used to it, it wasn't unpleasant, but something quite characteristic, like the fragrance and taste of Proust's Madeleine biscuit. It was rather a scent of the past, of the long history of the building itself, a mixture of humidity and Earth slowly impregnating the brick walls and then again exuding from them, the smell of wooden beams, of oiled furniture and the wax used to shine the floor. I'm sure that if I ever entered the premises again the feeling I had while living there would return to me and reconnect me with a period of my life in which I was still wrestling with the question of how to have the cake while eating it, not yet fully realising that there is no way one can feed all the needy in this world and still have enough bread for oneself. Unless one is as good as Jesus of course, effortlessly turning stones to loafs and water to wine.

One of the things I did bring to Antígua from Europe, or perhaps from Miami, where I had had yet another stopover, was a tenacious flu that soon after my arrival in town sent me to bed, where I remained for a good week, only gathering enough force to go the grocery store from time to time. Even as I began to recover I was very tired and would preferably spend many hours in bed. I also mustered enough energy to attend Spanish classes. As though Spanish grammar is not complicated enough as it is, in my feverish state the verbs and their conjugations began to heave in my brain like the ingredients in a boiling broth.

Speaking of grammar, I should at least mention my formal Spanish learning experience with a few words. The classes took place in a wonderfully secluded and tranquil environment. It was a garden next to an old church and the racking of the poor students' brains over the proper use of the two (2!) forms of *subjuntivo pretérito pluscuamperfecto* was accompanied by chirping birds and colibris relishing the nectar of wide open flower cups. My female teacher was very patient with me and I really tried to be a good student. With hindsight, and after having taken language lessons from other people educated by the post-colonial school system, I do have some objections to their method though. It is based on a rather inflexible curriculum where one is supposed to go through all the different forms of conjugations that exist in the Spanish language, which is extremely hard to learn by heart even in the case of the regular verbs, and a living hell as far as the irregular, and of course more prevalent ones, are concerned.

What I have come to realise, as my Spanish gradually improved, is that it is perfectly OK in everyday situations to stick to a few past tenses and not try too hard to find the one which would be the most appropriate one to use in formal writing. But the frequent interchangeability of for example *pretérito imperfecto*, *pretérito perfecto simple* and *pretérito perfecto compuesto* in everyday language is such that everybody will understand what you mean if you just use one of them. As a beginner in learning a new language you're as little served by a dazzling array of grammatical possibilities as a person ignorant of the art of cooking benefits from having a hundred different ingredients. Let us for the sake of illustration take one of no less than two Spanish verbs signifying 'to be': *Ser*.

In first person singular 'I am' is 'soy'. In *pretérito imperfecto* ('I was') it's 'era', in *pretérito perfecto simple* (another variation on 'I was') it's 'fui' and in *pretérito perfecto compuesto* ('I have been') it's 'he sido'. Now, once you finally master the subtle difference in the application of these — and this normally only happens after long and assiduous conversational practice — you can of course begin to try to play around with them. But I don't think it's really helpful to an intermediate level student to know in how many ways he can actually go wrong when speaking.

To make the situation even worse we also have the other verb for 'to be', which is 'estar', and where 'I am' (estoy) is conjugated in the above mentioned past tenses as 'estuve', 'estaba' and 'he estado'. All these forms are frequently used in both spoken and written Spanish, but for the relative newcomer to the language it's bewildering having to choose between the following translations for 'I was': *era, fui, he sido, estuve, estaba and he estado*. And we haven't even started to talk about the other cases (you, he/she/it, we, they), about future tenses or past tense conditional variations such as 'If I was (were)'...

The problem with the Spanish education program, as I have encountered it in several Latin American countries, is that it begins with an extensive introduction to all forms of conjugations and expects me to be able to digest and integrate it with my intellect. Meanwhile, my capacity to actually understand what the man or woman in the street actually says is rudimentary and my vocabulary restricted. To make a long story short, sweet and to the point: I sincerely think the near-religious insistence on grammatical completeness in the earlier stages of Spanish training is counter-productive and apt to discourage many people from pursuing further studies. Although I am, with hindsight, grateful that someone had the patience to guide me through the grammar jungle — it has indeed paid off over the years — I still believe much more emphasis should be devoted to actually teach the student colloquial phrases and example sentences. Special, very special and close, attention should also be devoted to how Spanish words and phrases are usually pronounced as opposed to how they're written. The general tendency of any native Spanish speaker is to eliminate a number of consonants and vowels that people with Germanic mother tongues would consider indispensable for clear pronunciation. To Hispanics it isn't, and it's my pleasure to present in the following a representative list of words as they are written on the one hand, and as they might be pronounced by a Latin American person of average education — although I have had ample opportunity to confirm that supposedly better educated people too often speak in this general manner.

In my continuous and permanently ongoing research of the mysteries of Spanish, I have come to the conclusion that as far as consonants go, only the very hard core ones, such as t, r, p and c (when pronounced as k) are strictly indispensable as initial letters to make a spoken word or phrase comprehensible to other native speakers, whereas consonants such as b, d, f, l, m, n and v not only are frequently interchangeable but often just dropped.

First of all, of course, there is no noticeable difference in the pronunciation of b and v. Second, m and n too are notoriously confounded (hence Jerusalén — no problem!). A third instance is the phonetic resemblance of d and l. The letter s, if it doesn't happen to be the first in a word, is simply cut out whenever possible. Thus, what we foreigners would believe to be *buscar* (to search) — because this is how the word is written and according to rule is supposed to be pronounced (buscár) — instead becomes *bucar*.

The list also includes many foreign, predominantly English words associated with the modern world of computation, and how they are likely to appear in 'traditional' Spanish pronunciation. By studying them, a lot of confusion can be avoided and you will hopefully find yourself actually understanding the language and its colloquial use much better. By all means, they will amuse you. In the left column you'll thus find the words and phrases correctly spelled (English translation, if needed, within parenthesis) and in the right column how they are sometimes likely to verbally come across in several Hispanic countries.

Investigar (investigate)	Inbetigar
El celular (cell phone)	El cedular
La Internet	La internes
Un e-mail	Un emelle

El Golden Gate (the bridge in San Francisco)	El golengay
Nueva York	Nueva yor
Washington DC	Goasinton dece
El Wi-Fi	El guifi
El whisky	El wicki
El vodka	El bolka
La estatua (statue)	La estuata
El monument	El menemento
Verdad? (really?)	Beldá?
Vamos para allá! (Let's go there!)	Vampaya!
El teléfono	El teléjano
El Skype	El eskipe
El YouTube	El yutuve
Las fotos	Las afotos
La camera	La carama
La moto (motorcycle)	La amoto
Donde vas (where are you going?)	Chondeva?
La escuela (the school)	La ecuela
Despues (afterwards, later)	Depué
El Facebook	El fejboo
La television	La pelevision
El futebol	El efutevol
El espaguetti	El epagetti
El Twitter	El twister
El coctél	El chotél
Los pancakes	Los panekekes
Amor	Amó
Mi amor	Mi mó
El sandwich	El sanduiche
Esta bien	'ta bjeng
Mister Muscolo (Mr. Muscle, detergent symbol)	Mitte Muculo

Ensalada	Salada
La pelicula	La pejicula
El Western	El bestern
El aguacate (avocado)	El guacate
El spa	El esplá
La gaseosa	La gaciosa
La hamburguesa	La emburgesa
La piñacolada	La piña de escolada
El cheese cake	El cheské
El Google	El gogle
Googlear	Goglear
El G-mail	gamajl
El apanado (breaded food)	El panádo
El Hotmail	homell
La Aroba (@)	La erova
Entonces (thus)	Entonce
El WhatsApp	El guasá
El vino	El bino (but of course!)
Harvard (the university)	Arbar
La SIM	La TIM
El bestseller	El beseller
La frontera	La fontera
El traductor	El tradutor
El baseball	El veivol
El basketball	El vackevol
El español	El pañol
El blue jean	El bruyean (I have actually seen it spelled like that!)
El Weekend (weekend)	El wiken
Los tennis Nike	Los tenes niki
Los tennis Puma	Los tenes epuma
La espuma (foam)	La epuma

El gourmet	El goumé
La Coca-Cola	La hoca-cola or even hoha-hola
Un ron rum	Un guon
El desayuno (breakfast)	El desatjuno
Los frijoles (beans)	Los frisoles
Los camarones (shrimp)	Los caramones
La cerveza (beer)	La chebesa
El langostino	El lagotino
La lasagna	La lagagna
La hamáca	La maca
Las alcaparras	Las caparras
El jugo	El fugo
El s?	No el f! (sounds exactly the same!)
El hotel	El chotel
El cepillo (comb)	El cepollo
El papel higienico	El pepel ifienico

Lake Atitlán

It was also during my stay in Antígua, and alongside with my Spanish studies, that I brought my historical novel on the fall of Constantinople to its conclusion. As mentioned, I had previously visited the Ionian island Corfu to get the local colour and atmosphere right for the final scene of the book. It features ex-state secretary George Sphrantzes as he, having taken the monastic vow on the same island in the 1470s, thinks back on his life and wonders if that which actually did happen had been predestined by God and therefore was unavoidable. This is the so-called epilogue of the book; an imaginary account, rife with poetry and feeling, of what might have transpired through the old man's mind as he readied himself to rejoin his beloved emperor and see his maker.

Once finished, I was for a while reluctant to busy myself with another script, and over New Year's I even made a short visit to Texas at the behest of the same woman who the previous summer had so graciously helped me to a whole bottle of gin at the sumptuous colonial hotel El Convento in San Juan. This trip was notable, not only because it allowed me to experience an authentic, albeit a bit shocking, side of contemporary life in redneck country at a ranch where wild animals had been brought in and kept corralled, waiting for tourist hunters to come along for a weekend of organised slaughter around the feeding grounds, inevitably luring the animals to their demise. There were literally piles of dead boars rotting in the sun, and as far as the coyotes were concerned their killers would suspend their corpses from the fences running for miles through this dry country, proudly advertising that another one of this loathed scavengers had been eliminated. The deer on the other hand had been disposed of in a different manner since their hunters were proud to put their taxidermied heads above a mantelpiece and boast of how excellent their aim had been: 'One clean shot, and he came down as though he'd fallen straight out of the sky'...

I myself fell out of the sky, back into the street grid of Antígua, in early January and was henceforth intent to wrap things up there. I had been in town since late October, and although I had initially entertained hopes that it would be able to captivate my interest for several months to come, I now felt this not to be the case and decided to move on according to my initial plan. By this time, I knew pretty well what the various streets and their establishments had to offer. Initially I had been quite impressed by the variety of cuisines on offer in such a comparatively small place, but even the existence of a really nice French restaurant no longer exerted an irresistible attraction on me. On the other hand, there was a place called JP's Rum Bar on the premises of yet another Spanish school. It used to attract a slightly more eccentric clientele than the usual tourist crowds. To go there for a couple of drinks and some pseudo-philosophical chit-chat was one of my preferred diversions, but as usual, wherever conversation is decent in public, the girls shine with their absence, and JP's own blond girlfriend behind the bar was not only off-limits but, if I remember correctly, pretty flaky too. Last time I was in town JP and his female companion had evidently packed up and left town, perhaps for good, since the rum bar was gone and the edifice formerly housing it sombre and silent.

There is also Café Teatro run by a Swiss called Alan. He was always friendly towards me and the food was very good, but for some reason — I was never badly treated or so — I never felt quite comfortable sitting at the bar (probably because at the time I could not participate in discussions in Spanish as much as I would have wanted) and eventually stopped frequenting it. Further down the 5 Calle Poniente there is a restaurant in typical Guatemalan style but with a gringo couple as owners. I have forgotten what the name of the place is, but you can't really miss it since there is always a guy out in the street trying to shove a menu down your throat. But fear not! The restaurant is pleasant. Apart from attentive service it has good steaks, brochettes and, rather surprisingly, the best chocolate mousse I have ever tasted — having lived in France for many years I do have some experience of this national dessert. I don't know how they make it, but it's simply delicious and you can even eat the receptacle because the bowl containing the mousse is in itself made from chocolate.

The town in itself is famous for its chocolate shops and pastry chefs, and I'm sure it must be one of the latter who is responsible for the mousse. If I were the Michelin Guide for Gourmets off the Beaten Track I'd put the restaurant up for 'well worth a detour' alone on account of the restaurant's chocolate mousse. Another thing that adds to the ambiance here is that the owner has a past as a studio percussionist in Memphis, Tennessee, and every other night joins in on the congas together with native Paco and his orchestra of Pan flutes for some Andean entertainment, traditionally peaking with the local theme song always on demand: '*Volcán de Agua*'. Nonetheless, the arguably best restaurant I had the privilege to dine in while living in Antígua is the Panza Verde, conveniently located just a few blocks north of my abode on 5th Avenue. Its interior is both elegant and rustic at the same time. Prices are slightly at the high end, if I remember correctly, but the French inspired cuisine, run by an excellent Swiss chef, is consistently top-notch, so there is never a deception to be feared. And the service is impeccable.

Apart from the steady stream of tourists — everything from backpackers in striped pyjama pants and hay coloured Rastafari curls on a shoestring budget to wealthy Americans in khaki shorts and Hawaiian shirts frequenting ancient monasteries converted to luxury spas — and apart from the many foreigners running hotels and restaurants here, the population of Antígua remains predominantly indigenous and the town has a large stationary artisan market. I bought a very beautiful handmade bedspread there and only regret that I subsequently gave it away.

The presence of many Indians in turn means that people of my height (roughly 6'2") and nothing whatsoever to boast of in Holland, not to speak of in the NBA, where I would have been the token pygmy) come across as veritable Gullivers among the Lilliputians. There might be some pretty Guatemalan girls throughout this native population but in all honesty, I'd have to walk on my knees to meet them face to face. And they really are too traditionally raised and dressed to normally come into question as prospective mistresses, or even wives, to the visiting Westerner. Notwithstanding, I have met at least one tall gringo married to a *guatemalteca*. I also remember a hotel and restaurant owner from former East Germany who had knocked up and married another one in Flores in the Petén region. And then there is of course the sympathetic Swiss owner of Sun Dog Bar and Restaurant up in Rio Dulce — he too is hooked up with a local girl. But none of these girls, on the occasions I met with them, were traditionally dressed.

The real Indians on the other hand keep to themselves and seem content that way. Their general standard of living is rudimentary enough to most of us, used to at least have floors and window frames in the places where we live. Antígua, on account of its influx of tourists and the money invested in its maintenance, is quite an exception to this rule of deliberate primitivism. But wherever the indigenous element predominates (such as is the case not only in Guatemala, but in many parts of Ecuador, Peru and Mexico as well), the more houses seem as though they had been completely abandoned, in milder cases midway into construction but mostly right after the rebars have been put in place and the casting plate defining the first floor has hardened.

But that is a deceiving appearance. To most Indians a slab of rough concrete is a very good roof keeping almost everyone beneath it dry, and they soon move in under it, unconcerned about such trivialities as doors and windows, since anyways the house will never, ever, become what we palefaces, applying even the most lax standards to the concept, would call finished.

Antígua, with its long straight boulevards lined with colourful (lots of red!) colonial buildings thus remains the beautiful and interesting city in the country. From the 16th century until mid 18th century this highland sanctuary for birds and flowers, blessed with an all year-round mild climate, was the regional capital. At that time the Province of Guatemala was a vast dominion of the Spanish crown comprising the better part of Central America, including the Mexican state of Chiapas, to this day largely unexplored. But then, as so often happens along the edge of the Pacific, there was a series of earthquakes, of which the one in 1773 prompted the authorities in Madrid to eventually issue an order to evacuate. Although the new capital was subsequently built, and also has remained the administrative centre of the independent republic, the evacuation of Antígua was only partial. Over time it was repopulated even though it never became so densely settled as during its heyday.

Culturally speaking it nevertheless is the Capital and a testimony to the religious zeal of its once Spanish masters; the town is literally crowded with ancient churches and monasteries. Most of the churches are in a ruined or semi-ruined state and no longer in service. This partly gives Antígua the character of a Hispanic pendant to the historical Maya sites. In some aspects it really is a ghost town where the pious whispers, tolling bells and shuffling feet inside the Christian temples have long since dissipated, the walls become overrun with ivy and the cracks invaded by grass, lizards and nesting birds. Centuries of heavy rainwater running along the once white-washed facades have created long dark patches working as inkblot tests to the receptive mind. In this sense the town is its own graveyard, with its own monumental tombstones, and has something eerily haunting about it. This is especially noticeable at night when the long avenues and side streets become almost interminable and the streetlights run into vanishing points, eventually ceding to darkness.

Since I lived at the very southern tip of 5 Avenida Sur, I would have the town's iconic arch disappear at a distance as I headed home. I had of course been recommended to use the mototaxis — cheap and reliable as they are — to shake me home over the notoriously cobbled streets in the wee hours, but somehow I nearly always felt that I was a big enough boy to make it home on my own. However, the further south I descended my avenue, the more deserted it and the side streets became, making circumspection mandatory while crossing them. Nothing evil ever happened to me, but the last 150 metres before my solid gate didn't have any street lights at all, and I had to rely on the ones quickly fading into insignificance behind my back, as well as on some dim driveway lights surrounding select properties. Just before reaching my haven I had to pass by a gated community with a vehicle barrier and an illumined station normally containing an armed guard. In between that and my house there was just the darkness outside the botanical garden to be negotiated and then I was home, pushing the wooden door inserted in the huge wooden gate inwards and again entering the peculiar scent of centuries past.

In the end I missed not having a balcony or terrace that could be reached straight from my bedroom. Only the apartment next to mine had one and it already had tenants. The reason I felt my own balcony to be indispensable was of the view it would have offered of the *Volcán de Agua*, taking up a huge portion of the horizon to the south. Once again I had to conclude that in the long run I don't like too much to stay in places where I feel that the landscape dominates me. Antígua is located at the bottom of a flat valley surrounded by volcanoes and mountains. For me to enjoy such vistas I need to have an elevated point somewhere from which I can contemplate the grandeur of *la naturaleza*. It could be a balcony, or a roof terrace, but it generally needs to be something above ground or, if it's on ground level, it needs to have a free view ahead, preferably ending with a slanting bluff. My apartment didn't have that and even though I knew the iron bars, even on the windows facing the interior of this old complex, were there to protect me, I began to feel imprisoned. It was time to break free and make a leap for *Lago de Atitlán*. The essence of that experience in turn is perhaps best conveyed in a travel letter that I sent shortly afterwards to my spiritual brother and most poetic colleague Kenneth Geneser. By all means the impressions recorded below possess the non-negligible merit of having being formulated in connection with my first visit to this wonderland, and so have the freshness of a recent inspiration, as opposed to the memory archaeology invariably associated with the digging and evaluating of a more distant past. Without further ado I thus invite the reader to feel included in my envoy and its ensuing enthuses:

Dearest Brother,

This was most certainly meant to be a letter reminiscent of the good old days when epistles took their epic time to arrive at their destination. Temptation, however, was too great. Instead of waiting, like an Alexander von Humboldt, for the enduring Indian to stick the letter inside one of two leather bags straddling the mule, and then embark on the arduous trek up and down steep and narrow gorges, only to arrive in the capital a week later, where the letter would be reloaded on to the stagecoach and, after another three days, reach the Caribbean coast; instead of subsequently waiting for the wind to turn and allow the heavily loaded ketch to weigh anchor and set sails for Aruba, its first port of call on a journey that doesn't end until in Cádiz two months later; instead of waiting for the next ship to take the letter over stormy Biscay to Rotterdam, and then for the schooner to carry it onwards, past the Friesian islands and the treacherous Borkum Reef, arriving in Copenhagen on an unusually cold day in late April; instead of waiting for the mail boat from Copenhagen to finally dock in Rønne after the ice has melted in its port, and for the postman to reassume his Wednesday run to Arnager in order to hand over the stained, but still sturdily sealed, document to the stunned artist in his atelier, I said: instead of all this, which would have been the only way to go about these things two hundred years ago, I hereby expedite this travel account by the speed of light, via Boolean algebra, electrons, positrons, neutrinos, corpuscles and other unimaginably small and fleeting things, in order that thou mayest, suddenly and unexpectedly, nay, virtually simultaneously, receive it in your own electronic magic box!

Imagine a Persian style paraideza *as described by Isidore of Alexandria, as a Garden of Eden bereft of its divine children, in the centre of which a source has sprung up. Over time this source has turned into a lake. Its banks are lined with trees bearing all kinds of fruit; on one slope grows the Tree of Life itself. The climate is neither hot nor cold, but an eternal flowery spring. The lake feeds four rivers simultaneously indicating the four cardinal points. All is surrounded by ridges crowned by a Ring of Fire preventing illicit entry.*

This, dear Brother, is what I, sitting on the balcony of my own hotel room, presently have before and around me. I can thus confirm the old hermetic rumour claiming there really is a Paradise on Earth — for artists and poets. Lago de Atitlán *is its name and it so precisely fits Isidore's description that it can no longer be any doubt about it. 'The journey to Atitlán' — doesn't the title alone sound like some kind of initiation? — and surely some will be tempted to associate to the illusive Carlos Castaneda and his encounters with the legendary Don Juan. But in fact there is not just Don Juan and Tirso de Molina here.*

For the sake of illustration: imagine throwing the English romantic poets pêle-mêle *into this magic cauldron — a Keats, Shelley, Byron, Coleridge, de Quincey, as well as the challenging German team with Kleist, Hölderlin and Novalis in the line of attack, backed up by pic-*

torial symbolists such as Caspar David Friedrich, Eugen Bracht and Arnold Böcklin, in turn garnished with some French poets following in Chateaubriand's footsteps. My bet is that they would never manage to crawl up and out of it. Not that it is physically impossible — even if the slopes are steep they are not insurmountable — but because they simply wouldn't ever want to leave! In short: this is Xanadu! Toteninsel! Der Gestade der Vergessenheit! The Island of the Damned! The Island of the Lotus Eaters! L'isle des Bienhereux! *You will find the fata morgana of them all at some time of the day, in the light playing around the vanishing point of a distant cape, in the shadow of three giant fire-breathing monsters towering high above the aquatic expanse: the volcanic cones of San Pedro, Tolimán and Atitlán.*

In scientific terms this body of water is the consequence of a gigantic volcanic eruption that took place some 85,000 years ago — an hour on the geological time scale — spreading pumice and dust that are present in the fossil and stratigraphic records from Florida to Ecuador. In the process the massive crater imploded, creating a caldera that subsequently filled with water, transforming the scene of violent primeval creation into one of serenity. Because of this — and you don't really need to accept theories of energy meridians, spiritual vortexes and other pyramidal miracles two believe it: here the moment of creation is ongoing. The Earth still vibrates, because underneath one's feet hot lava is fermenting and the great Toliman himself had his last known eruption as late as in 1853, geologically not even a minute but a fraction of a second ago.

A 'ring of fire'? Yes, indeed. The lake, situated at 1500 metres above sea level, is ringed by mountains which in theriomorphic formations dive into the lake's unfathomable blue water (there is no actual reliable measurements of the lake's maximum profundity, but so far depths of up to 600 metres have been estimated.) Although I would never contemplate taking a swim in its water (primarily because of the agricultural fertilisers that are washed out there with the rains) local children certainly don't hesitate to do so. And just as Isidore said, the water, regardless of is *depths, is neither too cold nor too hot because it is heated from underneath by magma.*

Over the shorelines waterfowl hover all day long. Grebes and seagulls you may see around Bornholm too. However, add to these the archaic looking pelicans, descendants of the flying dinosaurs. Finally the clouds, as always in hypnagogic formations, are also coloured by the lake and the eternally verdant mountains. At dawn, as experienced from Hotelito el Almanecer *(Sunrise Hotel)* the fishermen can be seen hoisting nets into their kayaks — it's rather like watching the Mayan culture itself hail 'the place from which the rainbow takes its colour', allegedly the exact linguistic meaning of the single word Atitlán!

The atmospheric light is infinitely seductive, refracting in the finest nuances and shades in the course of a single day. Some sunsets offer a firework display of flashpoints that wander over the mountainsides following the sunlight as it peers through clouds and canyons, and descend on mountain passes. And it is during these 'Zauberberg' hours that the Isle of Death and the Beach of Oblivion suddenly rise out of the mist, engulfed in a supernatural, timeless light that slowly and mysteriously fades, like a vision, a visitation, a waking dream…

Venit nox: The Zodiac lights up in its zenith. Orion and his hunting dog solemnly proceed; the Pleiades wave and flash like the seven days of the week, of which Monday is the smallest and sometimes invisible. Heavenly diamonds, observed with a glass of cold white wine or a whisky at hand, in a deck chair on the hotel's wide Earthen terrace. Above the skies shine in their infinity.

I arrived at the village of San Pedro, located on a promontory on the lake's western shore, four days ago, and have since not felt a desire to seek another residence on Earth. It feels like I've come home. Maybe I'm already dead? But in that case, an unusually living death! I am excited and inspired. Like a fish in water, a bird in the air, an artist in his fifth element. I send no photos, partly because I do not have a working camera, but quite especially since all the photos I've ever seen of the lake and its *surroundings make the mountains look both flatter and lower than they actually are. Similarly, the camera can't reproduce the subtle light shifts that give the incredible depth of perspective to the mountains.*

Contemplating all this artistic subtlety, I begin to find it a bit surprising that contemporary Maya painting so often insists on interpreting Guatemala's magic landscapes in bright monochromes squarely dressed against each other. As far as I can see, the use of that colour-scale can only be justified in the last trembling minutes of twilight, when the mountains turn into blue-grey giants, the sky into a purple streak while the laundresses are seen gathering their clothes beyond a foreground of yellowish-white water lilies. In other words, it seems to me as though Atitlán is still waiting for its artistic interpreter. Dear Brother, it's time to start packing the travel easel!

With that laconic exhortation, I embrace you and wish you a great, rich, abundant, fertile and lush new year.

Always yours

Lazarus

The Bus

Traveling in so-called developing countries certainly has both its rewards and its fair share of hardships. One of the latter is the inevitable, and at times even hazardous, bus journey. One sometimes hears about terrible bus accidents occurring in the mountainous regions of the Earth. The only thing that surprises me in relation to these is that they don't happen more often. And I'm not here talking about the absolutely deadly passages over for example the Hindu Kush, where encounters with another vehicle can result in a literally abysmal catastrophe, or where landslides may make the road disappear altogether, necessitating, in the best case scenario, days of excavation and restoration before circulation can be resumed. No, I'm just talking about the regular bus trips over good to decent to almost satisfactory roads that take place, every minute of the day and night, in every nook and cranny of Latin America. Here, in the overall absence of railways, buses are by far the most common and economic means of transportation.

In every town and city there are one or several bus terminals accommodating a steady stream of arriving and departing coaches. These terminals are by their very nature bustling places. A bewildering array of bus companies have their ticket booths inside them; outside exhaust fumes of diesel engines blend with the coarse voices of ticket collectors attracting potential passengers by loudly announcing destinations, while passengers are eager to get on or off before everybody else. There are food stands, porters, pickpockets, security personnel and taxi drivers. The ambulating vendors are not content with offering their merchandise through an open window but must enter the bus — sometimes there are four or five of them yelling inside one at the same time. Add to this the sound system of the bus itself *pumping* out, at max volume, everything from vallenato and cumbia to techno and reggaeton. Sometimes the existence of air conditioning is a blessing, sometimes not. Often it too is set to maximum, with the consequence that it gets so cool inside that you may consider yourself lucky to get away from your travel adventure with only a cold and torticollis.

With the possibility of opening a window, on the other hand, one stands a chance of being able to maintain an agreeable temperature in the cabin. It also provides a partial escape from the sound of rattling machine guns and crashing helicopters in the action films presented as part of the on-board entertainment. Needless to add that this sound too is a strong competitor to any attempt at conversation and that sleeping during long night trips becomes difficult, not only because of the constant tossing and turning, accelerating and breaking of the bus on interminable mountain roads, but quite especially, I should say critically, on account of the general sound level. The only merciful purpose the sound system occasionally serves is to partially block out the crying of wet babies — and on average there will be several of them on board. The frequency of screaming babies in the buses generally stands in inverse ratio to the poverty of the region: the poorer the country, the louder the bus. Sometimes the whining and heart wrenching cries of these babies go on for hours while their teenage mothers — too young to already be the mother of three, one would think — play with their cell phones. Because, yes: you might think that if these mothers are that poor, how can they even afford to have expensive cell phones? Well, I don't know how, but they all have one. It's possible that they haven't had the money to replenish the credit, but they'll still have access to the games software — alright! So here we go:

The bus is filling up with local passengers, all used to bump into each other in the streets for no apparent reason, and even more so inside the restricted space of a bus. If it's rare for a passenger, once seated, to get up and allow another one to reach his window seat, to help a senior citizen to place her luggage in the overhead compartments is practically unheard of. Since the use of deodorants and colognes to further personal hygiene is not all that prevalent, an exotic blend of scents, adding to the ones already being part of seat and curtain fabrics, soon permeates the atmosphere. Some passengers also find that the sound system isn't playing exactly their kind of music and thus open cross fire from their own playing devices. Since the internal sound system is quite loud, they need to compensate for this by turning up the volume of their machine as well. Excuse me? Head phones? You gotta be kidding! Our newly arrived, and presently comfortably installed passenger, can't even imagine that it could be a nuisance to you having to cope with more than one sound source at once. Or to be more precise, it neither occurs to him, nor does he care. The only way to make him stop his music is to firmly tell him to do so. But even if he grudgingly consents to this, he will never have understood why his freedom was curtailed in this irrational and random manner. As a male westerner of some physical stature, or otherwise of authority, you might just get away with telling him to shut up. But don't take my word for it!

At last, the bus full and the vendors gone, one hour after scheduled departure, it backs out from its platform — already here one will have ample possibility to admire the incredible manoeuvring skills of the otherwise autistic drivers — and hit the road. Or at least that's what you hope for. In reality you have chosen to travel on the eve of a major weekend, and to just get to the outskirts of the town takes another hour accompanied by abrupt stops involving the loading and unloading of merchandise, boxes and plastic bags, as well as the delivery of some documents to a policeman on guard at a roadside café. Simultaneously more passengers enter the bus straight from the streets. These remain standing and usually get off within the greater urban area, but the frequent stops take time, especially since the ticket guy will not always have money exchange ready at hand. Normally, you have been told, the trip should take three-and-a-half hours, but since after two-and-a-half hours we're just about to enter the countryside, you realise that a total of five-and-a-half hours under the circumstances would be a near miracle, six-and-a-half something to wish for, and a full eight hours the most likely.

This, however, is of no concern to the indigenous driver or passenger, who both have a completely fatalistic approach to the vicissitudes of traffic, weather and wind. You too soon realise that you can do absolutely nothing to change the situation for the better. The only thing you can positively do is to work on your own attitude and try to be as comfortable as possible, which, for example, involves pushing a firm knee into the back of the seat in front of you so as to prevent the person seated there from reclining into your lap. Since nobody will ever ask you if you think it's OK to have a ponytail in your mouth, this is the most discreet and efficacious way to ensure your own comfort zone. Often the passenger ahead will conclude there's something wrong with the reclining mechanism, and you're more than happy to endorse that belief. If, per chance, he does insist, he will at one point or another be forced to turn around to find out about your role in this quandary, and that will give you a welcome opportunity to more or less politely discuss the matter, explaining that though Procrustes certainly had no scruples in this regard, you are not willing to cut off your own legs in order to comply with even his most ardent wish.

I mentioned that some of the bus drivers, apart from a stamina enabling them to sometimes drive for eight hours straight, seem almost autistic, or at least awkward as far as social interaction is concerned. By all means, they bother minimally about the comfort of their passengers and for the most part entertain a capricious driving style. I'm not saying that safety is none of their priorities, because to some extent, and insofar as they too would like to reach the destination unharmed, I think it is. But hardly anyone in Latin America, regardless whether they're cab or bus drivers, ever tries to drive smoothly. A public transport is just as much part of the general race towards the next traffic jam as all the other vehicles in the road. The driver will thus only step on the breaks when he absolutely has to, that is, in the very last instance and only to avoid an imminent crash. The immediate consequence of this is that you're shaken around as if inside a tumble dryer — and sometimes that is exactly how it feels when both heat and humidity are on. One, two, even three hours that way are still endurable. The real tests to your own character, strength and stamina occur on the long runs, preferably involving one or a couple of national border crossings. These, in combination with bumpy, heavily trafficked or winding roads — or all at the same time — can be absolutely gruelling.

The worst I have ever experienced in this regard took place quite recently on a bus trip from Playa Máncora in northwestern Peru to the city of Cuenca in Ecuador. Two weeks prior I had been forced to conclude that Immigration from Ecuador to Peru was extremely slow. As I arrived in a taxi one afternoon to the Peruvian side of the border the customs agents there couldn't process my passport because allegedly they had no access to their own database. The only one who had this access at this time was the Ecuadorian border station. I had to take a cab back to where I had come from and line up in order to even get out of Ecuador. This alone was a 1½ hour procedure with hundreds of people waiting in line for two customs agents to repeat a mysterious bureaucratic ritual before they could stamp each passport. The process was very slow and painstaking. After finally having had my own passport stamped, I had to join another line and wait for the improvised Peruvian customs office on Ecuadorian soil to carry out the same convoluted procedure. As I said, this took about two hours in total and I really thought that was bad enough. However, crossing the same border two weeks later was an even worse experience.

The bus for Cuenca had departed around midnight, one and a half hours behind schedule from Máncora, arriving at the border station in the small hours. This time there was only one customs officer in each boot, one Peruvian and one Ecuadorian, whereas the people waiting in line were even more numerous than last time. I consequently had ample opportunity to study the immense interior walls of the waiting area covered with proud publicity and photos of happily smiling faces. It announced in both Spanish and English that the facility had been thoroughly modernised and provided with a number of amenities for the benefit of the passengers, such as toilets and shops. It also boasted of its transparent, efficient and state-of-the-art processing services. Yeah, right!

The toilets, for one, were unbearable to visit because there was no water to flush human waste down the drains. Since the only little shop available was closed at this time, there was not even a vending machine where one could get a bottle of water — and mind you: the night was stifling hot! The bus itself was locked up so one couldn't even return to it before all passengers had been cleared by customs. As usual there was nothing else to do than to quietly acquiesce. This time such acquiescence involved three hours of waiting in double lines until the bus was ready to hit the road. Or so we vainly hoped, because in the middle of nowhere something went wrong with the engine and the bus stopped for another 45 minutes. Luckily no malicious vagrants seemed to be around as the ticket collector managed to get the engine up and running. Then, at 4 AM, to the great joy of all overtired passengers, the sound system came on at full blast with Latin Metallica, one and the same atonal pattern mercilessly repeated until the bus reached full stop in Cuenca four hours later.

If this border station thus is the modernised and hyper-efficient version of Latin road customs, what would then a regular old fashioned one be like the reader might wonder? Strangely, in my experience, they are to be preferred in all respects compared to the one described above. I once embarked upon a bus journey that took me from Lake Atitlán via Guatemala City (where I had to change buses) to Managua, and eventually all the way to Granada in Nicaragua. This 24 hour trip involved crossing no less than eight border stations (both sides of four border lines). They're located along the asphalt cattle track pompously baptised Pan-American Highway, and you'll note that you're approaching one by looking out of the window. If suddenly there's more than a usual amount of roadside junk, meaning even more apparent poverty, plastic bottles, dirty cesspools, tin cans, hovering vultures, skinny cats and stray dogs, chances are you're getting close to a national border, habitually the most neglected area of even otherwise somewhat neglected countries.

The actual border facilities are in only marginally better shape than its surroundings. But they do have ambulating vendors at all times of day and night, stands selling refreshments and nutritive tidbits, as well as officials apparently less burdened by detailed protocol than their 'modernised' colleagues. It's even easy to slip through borders without even showing a passport; although it's not to be recommended. Usually, if one doesn't have a valid entry stamp allowing access to the country, getting out can become a problem to which money might in the end be the only solution. Nevertheless, this did happen to me once, and before I continue to describe my onward journey to Granada, I'd like to invite the reader to follow me from Flores in northern Guatemala to Belize, where my encounter with the local officials might have taken a turn for the worse.

It was early afternoon, the rooftops basking in the hot sun while every living being, except mad dogs and Englishmen, tried to stay out of it. For me, however, the time had come to say goodbye to the idyllic Flores Island in the Lago Petén Itzá which had been my home for almost a week. A taxi had been ordered and my strapped bag gone before me into the cockpit as we took off. The driver brought me to the local station for minibuses where a rustic Mayan family, indigenous to the strange borderland sharing territory with modern day Belize, took care of me. They swiftly brought me to the border station where I had no reason to expect a problem, especially since I had deposited my bag with magic herbs from Lago de Atitlán as a gift to the next passenger in my roof terrace hammock (one of my very few principles in life is precisely to never have 'anything on me' when crossing a national border). I even looked forward with a rather unmotivated self-confidence to the imminent customs ceremony.

At first everything seemed to run ever so smoothly. There were smiling female faces, goodbyes and stamps about to be sealed in my passport when, suddenly, the inhuman computer refused to give final clearance. After much puzzled investigation it transpired that I was apparently in Guatemala without having been formally admitted to the country. My passport showed that I had recently left Guatemala for Honduras but it contained no evidence of my re-entry. I explained that this must be due to my recent two-day visit to Copan, located just on the other side of the Guatemalan border. My continued plaidoyer ran as follows: 'What really happened at that border control I'm not quite sure about. It's possible that I managed to unknowingly ignore the booth where I was supposed to get a stamp. It is also possible that in the general turmoil and confusion of documents, (not at all as unlikely as it may sound) the officer simply forgot to mark the re-entry in my passport.'

Though it's perfectly true that a typical Latin American border station leaves it almost entirely up to you to find or not find the appropriate counter in order to obtain your stamp, and that you might in principle cross back and forth between two countries without ever being noticed by the authorities, I was nonetheless detained awaiting further investigation. Not in a prison cell, for sure, but seated opposite a Guatemalan senior customs officer who amiably went over the details of my recent confession. But not for long, since the Father himself was only all too eager to get inside the confessional! He soon had me introduced to his wife, appearing from nowhere, and then shared pictures with me of the rest of his family members. As a final gesture of confidence he extended an invitation for me to visit with him and his family in their home. After an hour of absolutely delightful small talk over coffee and cookies, I was released and not even obliged to pay fiscal fees to the Republic of Guatemala, since these only apply when you leave the country by air.

On the other side of the border control, however, the customs officers were more than eager to have me paying. Entrance and exit to and from Belize territory is a frontier business, the authors of which don't find it below their dignity to even charge for the issuance of a surprisingly expensive 'One Day Transit Permit'. The whole thing is carried out pirate style, with a touch of unsentimental Anglo-Saxon expediency. After this legally enforced robbery, the taxi driver waiting on the other side seemed friendly and cooperative in so far that I mentioned what I thought the trip from the border to the town of San Ignacio should cost, and he consented.

But where was I? Oh, yes, on my way from Guatemala City to Managua. Although the border controls between Guatemala, El Salvador, Honduras and Nicaragua did take some time, the bus passed through them during the hours of daylight, which is considerably more comfortable to handle than being forced outside in the middle of the night. Of course we had in many instances to carry our own luggage across the frontier and then make sure it was reloaded again. But sometimes this walk was mostly symbolic and only involved carrying the bag from one corner of the room to another. The hassle was really nothing compared to the ordeal described above. It also considerably helped to blunt the edge of hardships that the bus made a full stop in San Salvador at a hotel offering decently priced accommodation.

I managed to sleep well and horizontally for a couple of hours before regaining my bus seat at seven in the morning.

The most picturesque of the border stations mentioned is no doubt the one between Guatemala and El Salvador, the Aduana Terrestre las Chinamas. The borderline between the two countries here coincides with the course of the river *Paz*, which I think is a pretty good suggestion to both sides — let's not forget that in 1969 the Lilliputian state El Salvador actually went to war with neighbouring Honduras, a brief bellicose event triggered by the outcome of a soccer game between the same two nations. El Salvador also had a civil war on its hands during the 1980s in which an estimated 75,000 people lost their lives before a peace treaty between the government and the guerrillas could finally be concluded in 1992. Guatemala too, during the same period, had its own share of military and civilian atrocities.

It may have been in my imagination only, but the lively clear waters of the river, where the women stand up to their waists doing laundry while their colourful dresses float like lotus flowers all around them, and where naked children frolic in the natural cascades, evoke the image of an untouched Indian Eden; yet, at only 100 metres distance above them on both sides of the bridge, the representatives of two armies are present. There is a steady stream of trucks, buses and cars in both directions waiting to receive clearance but, naturally, leaving Guatemala was of course easier than entering El Salvador. Before we could continue towards the capital of the latter the bus was searched repeatedly and everybody asked to identify his luggage, both the one travelling in the compartment below deck and the ones brought inside the cabin. However, after about an hour in total we were on our way, enjoying the spectacular sight of the, for the time being, peacefully smoking volcanoes dotting the plains.

Less interesting than the nature scenery is the metropolitan area constituting the country's capital San Salvador. But it does have one of the most beautifully located modern airports in the world; close to a long sandy beach framed by vegetation. The adoption of the US dollar as the national currency in 2001 predictably has been a thorn in the side of the political Left, since it effectively means that the country can't carry out any monetary policies of its own and instead has completely placed its faith in the hands of the Federal Reserve. Low interest rates, allowing people to take cheap loans to buy private property, have on the other hand triggered inflation with surging prices on everyday commodities as a consequence.

In spite of the temptation, there is actually to my knowledge only two Latin American countries (apart from Puerto Rico which really is almost a part of the United States) that has adopted the US dollar as their official currency, and that is El Salvador and Ecuador. In Guatemala the national currency is the quetzal, which is a very apt name since it designates a swiftly flying bird. In Honduras they have the lempira, and in Nicaragua it's the córdoba. Notwithstanding, a greenback is pretty much welcome everywhere in Latin America, whatever local governments and political parties try to say to the contrary.

The bus arrived in San Salvador in the evening and I managed, as mentioned above, to get a room for the night in the hotel from which the bus would depart again in the morning. That was all fine. But why had I even embarked on this long trip all the way down to Granada? The principal reason might sound odd enough. The truth was that I was going to see 'my' dentist, Dr. Leo Grant. I guess it might seem a bit exotic to travel 24 hours in order to visit a dentist in Nicaragua of all places, but I knew Dr. Grant from before and had reason to be satisfied with his work. I'm not the only one in this position. There are for example quite a lot of elderly Americans who travel to Nicaragua to have their dentures taken care of at a fraction of what such interventions would cost in the US. In addition, other expat gringos combine their trips abroad to renew their Costa Rican visas with a visit to a dentist in Granada. It really is a bargain. If you're in the region and need to have some dental work done, this is the place. I know only Leo Grant by personal experience, but there are several other highly professional dentists and I suppose both their prices and services are comparable to those of Dr. Grant's.

In order to string all this together I had consequently made sure that my return ticket to Florida would be from Managua and not from Cancún, which had been my point of entry to Central America a month earlier. There was not only foresight and convenience behind this decision. In order to emulate US immigration laws, several countries that ought to be more than grateful that tourists come there to spend their money have implemented laws stipulating that foreigners must be able to show proof of a return or an onward ticket to be admitted to the country. To be honest, upon arrival in a Latin American country by air I have never been asked by any customs official if I have a return ticket and I don't really think they care if you do. Unfortunately, however, it's the airline companies that cause the problems. Although I, along with many other passengers, know them to be in the wrong as far as most Latin American countries are concerned, they routinely state you won't be allowed in to this or that country unless you can show the airline taking you there that you have a return ticket. Apart from not being true, this is highly inconvenient for any traveller who is planning to go from point A to point B, C, and D without returning to point A, but instead flying out of this part of the world from point E at some so far unspecified date, and this simply for the reason that he hasn't decided as yet for how long he's going to be travelling and where. The airline companies never seem to have given a second thought to the fact that there are travellers with open schedules, preferring to go about the world in an impromptu way.

In other words, if you can't or don't want to return from your point of entry and alternatively prefer to choose another airport to fly back from, you often have little other choice than to eventually end up buying two separate tickets for more or less the same return trip. Perhaps this weird regulation, upheld only by the airline companies and not by the custom authorities of Latin American countries, is part of the plan, since it forces you to spend more money than would otherwise be necessary on your flights. To this end changes in budget round trip tickets are either impossible or very expensive to make.

Most recently, in connection with a trip back to Europe from Colombia, the patent absurdity of airline corporate policies came to unabashed light. Having prolonged my stay in that country, I had had my return ticket from Medellín changed twice through the travel agency responsible for its initial issuance. These procedures of course cost me substantial sums of money. Still, it was cheaper to make these changes than to pay for a new ticket. As the day of travelling approached I nonetheless happened to be back in Miami, several weeks ahead of the rescheduled departure from Medellín. But it was from Miami that my second flight out of a total of three eventually was going to leave. Being familiar with the intricacies of airline policies, I thought it advisable to at least inform American Airlines, (head operator of the flights) that I wouldn't use the first leg of my trip. In other words: they were free to use and sell my seat from Medellín to Miami a second time (well actually, with all the previous changes taken into account it would have been more like a fourth time!) To this end I went to the Miami Airport, seeking out their reticketing office hidden in the remotest location of the terminal area. As I began to explain what I thought would be a very straightforward matter of just taking me off the passenger list from Medellín to Miami, I could see on the face of the female representative that this was not going to be a merry waltz in the rose garden.

Sure enough, though it was still possible to cut out one part of the itinerary it would incur a 330-dollar fee. I tried to talk some sense into her but there was simply no way round this obstacle as monumental as it was arbitrary. In AA's perspective, my joining the flight sequence in Miami — and although the flight from there was not with AA but with Iberia a full seven hours after the scheduled arrival of the AA machine — my change of departure city would qualify my shortened itinerary as a 'different journey' altogether, hence subject to the rates applicable at this point. She assured me that in view of this, the 330 dollar rebooking fee 'was not bad at all' for the proposed change. I on the other hand was appalled, especially after learning that any luggage taken from Medellín to Miami would all the same have to be brought through customs clearance and then be rechecked in at the appropriate Iberia counter. I left the airport without having made any new reservation with the 330 dollars still at my disposal.

Calling up AA's Customer Service a couple days later I had to spend nearly an hour waiting on the line for the agent to find me pertinent information. Some of the delay was attributable to the hopeless task of trying to convince an automatic voice responder/decoder to accept my correct (Hispanic) pronunciation of 'Medellín' as the city of departure: 'I'm sorry but I don't understand what you're saying', the robotic voice repeatedly stated before finally transferring me to a human representative. The only gain in finally talking to a supposedly living person was that after 45 minutes of my holding the line, she returned with information that I could indeed check in my luggage at the Miami instead of at the Medellín Airport free of cost. Now this may sound like a very marginal concession on AA's part, but it was essential to the plan fomenting in my brain ever since I had been confronted with the prospect of the 330 dollar rebooking fee.

To make not only a long flight but also an otherwise long story short: the music event at which I participated in Miami was held on a Sunday evening. The following Monday morning, I returned my rental car to Fort Lauderdale to hop onto the Spirit Airlines flight to Medellín, allowing me to once again briefly meet with my beloved travel companion for a single special evening in connection with her impending birthday. I wouldn't say that the whole thing came out any cheaper than the 330 dollars mentioned above, but it sure was a great satisfaction to know that the money was spent on traveling, champagne and a festive dinner instead of ending up in the pockets of corporate bosses, just sitting there on their fat asses doing absolutely nothing!

Tuesday morning the AA plane on which I had a reservation left for Miami, allowing me to eventually check in to my subsequent Iberia flight from Miami in concordance with corporate requirements of a complete journey. However — and here comes the second reason for my seemingly convoluted manoeuvring — before I left Miami this time, I would pick up another rental car for the hours necessary to collect my luggage left inside Mike's tranquil lakeside townhouse (where I had been residing for the last ten days) and return the violin I had rented from Manuel at the Allegro Music Store. Finally, although the staff at the Iberia check-in counter was arrogant, they wouldn't refuse my luggage because it hadn't been previously checked in at the Medellín Airport. And no matter how annoying explicit rudeness can be, my share of inconvenience was in the end minor. True, it was and is still is absurd to me, that my luggage could join the trip in Miami for free whereas I couldn't. But one should perhaps, for the sake of mental peace, compare such an annoyance to the simultaneous lot of 150 passengers and crew blown to smithereens in the French Alps as a consequence of a psychopathic German pilot's decision to distinguish the day of his 'suicide' as a truly memorable occasion. The regional Iberia air shuttle from Madrid passed in the vicinity of the crash area only hours after the disaster. But instead of going insane, the pilots of the aircraft safely brought us down on the tarmac in Nice, where the promise of a Provençal spring seemed to just be awaiting my arrival to be fulfilled.

So much for the malpractices of airline companies. Leaving Fort Lauderdale for my impromptu visit to Medellín, I indeed had to produce proof of my return ticket with AA to Miami. Apparently there is nobody to disprove this assumption, although it should be none of their business to control where a passenger goes after having ordered and paid for a one way ticket to any destination. I have on a previous occasion personally spoken to the very helpful local manager for Spirit Airlines in Managua, and he certified in situ that you can indeed fly there without having proof of a return ticket. I later tried to make this point at the Spirit Air US counter in Fort Lauderdale, only to hear them stubbornly maintain that I need proof of a return ticket to even go there. Some years ago there was still a way to get around all this by buying a full price ticket and then have it refunded at the airport upon arrival. Now they have of course made sure this possibility no longer exists.

*

After this digression into the various horrors of flying, let me return to Granada in Nicaragua, where, as the reader may recall, I had arrived by bus more or less straight from Lake Atitlán in the highlands of Guatemala. The reason I didn't fly from Guatemala City to Managua in the first place was not only because it would have deprived me of the pleasure of seeing the landscape along the route, but also because of the unforgiving prices that Latin American airlines habitually charge for even very short international flights — inversely domestic flights can sometimes be very cheap, so it's always a good thing to be on the alert for national sales and promotions.

The town of Granada was founded by yet another one of these indefatigable Spanish conquistadors (in this case Hernández de Córdoba) in the early sixteenth century, and named after the famous eponymous city in the southern Spanish region of Andalucía, at this time only recently reconquered from the Islamic Moors. In many ways it's a pendant to Antígua, Guatemala. But although it lacks some of the cultural romance and noble nostalgia of the former, it's a more open and spontaneous town located on a plain with only one volcano as a visual backdrop. The climate too is different and sometimes, for example in March and April, so hot that one thinks twice about trotting the streets during siesta hours. Inversely, evenings can be absolutely delightful, especially on the broad pedestrian Calle La Calzada, stretching all the way from the eastern end of Parque Central down to the ferry terminal on the shores of Lago Colcibolca (although to go all the way down there after dark is not highly recommended.) There are bars and restaurants along this pedestrian street offering in- as well as outdoor service — the latter something one will never come across in Antígua, not even in the loggias surrounding its Plaza Mayor.

As anybody who has visited early Spanish settlements in the New World knows, all its colonial towns are variations on one and the same theme: a central square or rectangular tree-shaded plaza, in some cases adorned by an elevated, roofed, wedding-cake-like music pavilion in its midst, surrounded by the most important official buildings and private mansions as well as the city's cathedral. If there is no pavilion the probability is very high that there will be a statue of Simón Bolívar or some more local libertador at the geographical midpoint. Judging from the staggering amount of roads, streets, and plazas named after Simón Bolívar throughout South America, one can only conclude, without even being familiar with his career and itinerary, that he must literally have been everywhere. As a professional revolutionary with dictatorial ambition he has since been intensely admired and emulated by self-styled 20th and 21st century Latin American dictatorial leaders, such as Fidel Castro, Hugo Chávez, Daniel Ortega, and Rafael Correa, to just mention some of the more colourful of them. He might even have inspired William Walker, a physician and professional filibuster from the United States, who in 1856 proclaimed himself President of Nicaragua, only to put the city to the torch as the locals refused to acknowledge his authority. He was executed, not by the Nicaraguan but by the Honduran government in 1860.

Typically, the central plaza of Granada houses market activities along with soccer playing youngsters, a representative selection of dogs, cats, horses and birds, old men gathering under the panoply of trees, protected by their sombreros to watch the younger generations criss-crossing the park to and from their schools and work places. No such plaza would be complete without its crew of shoe shiners and food stands. Nor would it be authentic without commercial megaphones announcing everything from ripe avocados to children's shoes.

A square not surrounded, or crossed by intense motorcycle and scooter traffic, would be another anomaly. During festive days and hours, music comes out of every corner while adjacent restaurants and bars offer large TV-screens showing sports event, notably European and Latin American soccer games. Many towns take pride in the variety of trees and bushes in their public gardens and the central plaza should have its fair share of trees springing into bloom at various times of the year. Beyond the perimetre of the plaza cobbled streets parading colourful one- or two-storied haciendas, relentlessly absorbing heat and light, stretch out in a straight grid pattern. Behind these walls and barred windows, just like in the ancient Spanish haciendas, there are shaded galleries, tiled loggias, gardens, fountains, flowers, chirping birds and butterflies.

Nicaragua's Granada, here being the example under scrutiny, is no exception; the central park, with its tall trees, vending stands and water kiosks, is particularly spacious and inviting. Along the street in front of the Hotel Plaza Colon (what other name would be possible for the town's flagship?) the horse carts so characteristic of the street picture are lined up waiting for tourists. From this plaza the town reaches out uniformly in all directions with the nearby Calle Atravesada as its always bustling market street. Here the commerce is so lively that it's hard to blaze a trail through it. Sometimes the best thing is to just follow behind a car trying to make its way through the human thicket. Surprisingly, or typically, vehicles are an integral part of this pedestrian market place, so the honking of horns is a sound background as constant as the vendor's a million times repeated mantra: '*A la orden!*' (At your service).

Over the years I have become acquainted with some of the local hotel and restaurant owners in Granada, although I can't say that I ever had any real friends there. Moreover, a local owner here is often a person of European or North American extraction, some of whom I have briefly met with before dispersed by the capricious winds of destiny. There was for example the Dutchman of rural background (I did once meet with his peasant parents) running the locally prestigious *Hotel el Club*. During his tenure, disco nights were still organised on the premises of the hotel but there was no price reduction offered to the hotel guests who had to put up with the noise until early morning. Nonetheless I often stayed in one of the rooms on the second floor at the very back of the hotel, since the noise could be held at bay there by the closing of a door in the corridor. I liked the place, even though the young girls staffing it were a bit inexperienced, not to say simpleminded. But the Dutchman sold the establishment and nowadays the disco nights, according to the hotel website, take place in another though nearby location.

Then there was Jimmy Threefingers who had ended up in Granada with his two Harley Davidson bikes for reasons unclear to me. He was the rather bohemian owner of another hotel/restaurant/bar in town, and would happily join his guests at the bar for cocktails. His bikes were parked, day and night it seemed to me, in the street outside of the hotel and I naturally asked if he wasn't afraid that somebody would knock them over or steal them, but he answered 'They wouldn't dare'. I said: 'You'd kill them, eh?' To this day I have a hard time believing the assurance that followed: supposedly he had never in his life owned a gun and never laid his hand on anybody…

There are people you could actually believe their saying so. But although Jimmy Threefingers — apart from only have three fingers on his right hand and two Harleys, was indeed a romantic, perhaps even a poetic soul — I was never able to overcome the sensation that part of the explanation for his hiding in this small Nicaraguan town was that he must have been doing time back in the US and now needed a little timeout. This assumption might be completely wrong, even insidious, and I have to say that in his dealings with me he was always kind and generous. Consequently, in connection with my latest trip to Granada, I tried to look up both him and his hotel, but they had vanished so completely that I couldn't even find the entrance to the building where it had once been located.

Personnel at a laundry facility further down the street eventually told me that he had gone back to the United States without leaving a physical forwarding address. I tried to send him e-mails to the address he had given me previously, but to no avail. It seems Jimmy again wanted to disappear for a while. But if I know him right, (and I'm not talking about knowing him intimately, only about knowing the impression he made on me) he's got to be somewhere else in Latin America right now, because that's where I think he belongs, and I certainly wouldn't mind running into him somewhere and again shake his three fingers. Besides, his spare ribs and other meats were excellent and I remember him reproaching me, as I wanted to order French fries to go with my my steak: 'Fries, that's for kids! You can do better than that!', where after I ended up with a large portion of *haricots verts*, prepared with butter and garlic in classical French style.

Last but not least it was from Jimmy that I learned the background to one of the more melodramatic events taking place during one of my visits to town. Opposite the Centro Cultural Convento San Francisco, in the corner of Calle Cervantes and Calle El Arsenal, there is a gringo style breakfast place called Kathy's Waffle House, named after the owner's young and vivacious wife. Since she was in charge of the place all regulars would have met with her and been duly impressed by her beauty, energy, and charisma. In connection with my breakfasts I also frequently met with her husband, an expat Jew from New Orleans with a remarkable marital record. Kathy, not even thirty years old, and thereby fifty years his junior, was his eighth or ninth wife. His last one before Kathy had been a *tica* (Costa Rican woman) and it was also in Costa Rica he had allegedly spent some time in jail for the possession of marijuana.

As for now, he would typically sit at one of the terrace tables at Kathy's, amicably chit-chatting with his guests while always managing to either boast of his wife (her whereabouts or actions) or making sure we were overhearing his telephone conversations with her. I can understand it flattered his ego to have such a perky young woman at his side, but I also felt that he overstated his pride ever so slightly. Like so many men in his age and situation, he seemed to have fallen prey to the common idea that the love and affection of a young woman is not only a natural thing, but something based on a mutual physical and emotional attraction rather than on the attraction that money exerts on beauty. This fatal misunderstanding really was at the root of subsequent events, though I still have a hard time understanding why she had to make the outcome so irrevocable.

One morning, as I approached Kathy's Waffle House to have brunch, the building had been cordoned off with black ribbon. Knocking at the door to find out what happened, I was told by an employee, peeping through an ajar door, that there had been an accident. The official story varies slightly depending on whom you listen to. But it's agreed that Kathy had been found dead by the police in the couple's bedroom with a big bullet wound in her chest (others say it was her in in her head), fired from her husband's Taurus Magnum, calibre 357 (another source states it was a Colt). The husband was questioned, but any suspicion of homicide was soon written off as at the time of her death the bedroom door had been locked from the inside and Sandy (the husband) together with somebody else had tried in vain to gain access to it. Also the police only found gunpowder residue only on Kathy's clothes and not on Sandy's. Everyone was duly shocked, Sandy apparently more so than anybody else. Nobody seemed to have any idea whatsoever what could have moved this exuberant young woman, a legend in her own time and town, to take her life.

Sandy's and Kathy's marriage, as well as their joint business venture, had all seemed such a perfect illustration of the tale that love knows of no limits and can make even vast differences in age between two lovers immaterial. Then this. It was literally a lightning from a clear blue sky. Kathy's funeral was held in the Cathedral, her coffin carried to its final resting place by the city's largest horse carriage adorned with flowers and surrounded by mourners. Her beloved black stallion Lucero, draped with her riding boots and with her sombrero hanging over the saddle, took part in the procession. Kathy's father, who had organised and paid for the funeral, was heartbroken repeatedly crying out: 'Kathy, mi hija, mi angel!' Sandy reportedly shook with deep grief, despairing over his terminal loss. The whole town was on the move, paying her last and enduring respects.

As said, this is roughly how the drama was presented by some eye witnesses and in the press. Jimmy Threefingers, though, gave me some inside information that helped to explain to some extent why this tragic event had occurred in the first place. According to him, Kathy had entertained a lover during her marriage. She had let him understand that all they needed to do was to wait for the old man to either kick the bucket, or preferably sign over the business to her. After that she could file for divorce and they could get married with some money put aside to provide for future children. As it turned out Sandy unfortunately got wind of Kathy's illicit relationship and promptly let her know that he had cut her out from his will and transferred ownership of the waffle house bearing Kathy's name to his daughter, also living in Granada. This draconian gesture apparently so shattered Kathy's hopes that she saw no other way out of the conundrum than to commit suicide. Whether or not this is the truth, and the whole truth, I can't guarantee. But Threefingers said — and I do believe him since it was Sandy who on several occasions emphatically had recommended his restaurant to me — that after the funeral, during which Sandy had appeared inconsolable, he and his daughter had spent the evening at Threefingers' restaurant, eating, drinking, laughing and cheering.

So much for the old man's grief. Perhaps having had nine wives had turned him into something of a Knight Bluebeard character, (figuratively speaking) relishing in the fact that every buried wife had been laid to rest in rooms to which only the Knight himself had key and access. Perhaps he was relieved that he never would have to explain to his customers why and how his wife had turned against him. In this way he also freed himself, without the threat of any legal backfire, to seek a tenth wife, unsuspecting of the darker shadows looming in his past. By all means Kathy's Waffle House, still apparently operating under her name, has changed ownership since. Whether or not the widower is still living in Granada I don't know. Somehow it would surprise me if he did. My bet is that he was quite happy to get out of there.

Assuming Threefingers's story to be largely consistent with truth, I nonetheless find that Sandy could and should have acted differently in order to avoid triggering this melodrama. Being a realist, he could simply have cut his losses, divorced Kathy and reached an agreement. That he took her off his will is understandable. But there really wasn't anything to prevent him from trying to reach a settlement on mutually acceptable terms. I guess his pride was too hurt for him to consider behaving benevolently towards her. This in turn, as my theory goes, can only be explained by his exaggerated belief in the enduring strength in his own virile powers, whereas he should in my opinion have been old and mature enough to realise that she would never have married him for less than money. As the French moralist Chamfort once stated: female actions directed against males are often the result of vile calculation. In poverty-stricken areas of the world, such as Nicaragua, it doesn't even take vileness to make the calculus, just a simple will to survive. Unfortunately, that's exactly what Kathy didn't, and so there must have been some irrationality in her response as well, perhaps a sense of utter abandonment that she couldn't handle, although she must have understood that her prospects in life were not entirely ruined just because the old geyser didn't want her any longer. Conclusion: human emotions are a mystery, perhaps not always one that fascinates or merits to be solved, but a mystery all the same.

Hotel del Pacifico[16]

Playa Azul, a stretch of almost-deserted beach some twenty miles to the west of the industrial town and harbour of Lazaro Cardenas, lies at the end of a primitive road on Mexico's sun-drenched Pacific coast. To the uninitiated eye it seems forlorn. Its thatched beach cafes have something sombre about them, a morose intransigence that says 'Here we are, here we stays; we'd rather die than change our ways'. In short, there is not very much in the village at Playa Azul to welcome the foreign tourist. When I first alighted there, after a five-hour bus ride through the rough and forbidding hills of the Sierra Madre, I felt like a discus newly released from the hand of a spinning Atlas.

---

16 Although it's perfectly true that I have in the past lifted material from my book *Dionysos* to substantiate some of my more recent works, notably *Homo Maximus*, and now again do so by here reintroducing gently edited versions of 'Hotel Pacifico' and 'Boca del Cielo' from the above mentioned opus, I do so with a good conscience. That book is a storehouse of fertile ideas, and these travel reflections — albeit the imprint of a slightly younger myself still at loggerheads with his tenacious romanticism — are nonetheless thematically and stylistically affiliated with the present text. Since the Dionysos book, released in a very small edition, is furthermore long since out of print, I'm actually welcoming the opportunity to have them reproduced here, happily verifying that they seem captivating enough to enjoy a better fate than to be forgotten without a trace. Last but not least there is also an esoteric reason for all this: in order for the god Dionysos to be resurrected to eternal life he had, (according to the myth) to be dismembered by the Titans. Now let's assume I'm one of the Titans and Dionysos is Dionysos. What's this book then? Hmm… a resurrection?

Although I was the only foreigner here, there was not a single hotel bed to be had in town. All of them had been booked by Mexican holidaymakers intent on spending New Year's Eve at the seaside. A persistent campaign on my part in one of the hotel lobbies did secure a room for the night, but only on the condition that I vacate it the following day.

By the time my negotiations were over it was dark outside. Although I had already passed by the Hotel del Pacifico several times, I had considered it only as a last resort. As soon as it was brought home to me that even a last resort was precious, I entered and asked for accommodation. The man at the desk shook his head, and said, reassuringly and with a becoming smile: 'Come back tomorrow'.

Tomorrow is too late, I thought, not yet realising the depth of my naïveté. But the next day, when the sun had begun to hammer on the thatched roofs, the palm trees swaying in the gentle breeze, I found myself retracing my steps to the hotel's plain wooden desk. Again I saw the clerk's bright smile, as he handed over the keys to a couple of rooms. 'These are free today', he said, 'Take a look around. See which one you like best.'

I settled for the room nearer to the street. Its window had probably been quite low when the hotel was built. Now, as a result of earthquakes, the building had sunk further into the sand, so that my window was now practically on a level with the pavement. From the small window of my shower and toilet, I could hear every word spoken in the street, and by now the laid-back tones of people's voices had begun to seduce me.

There was a ceiling fan in my room, and I took a close look at it. It was encrusted with shells, coral and salt. At first it didn't work — considering its appearance, it would have been a miracle if it did. Its thick dusty cables, like obscene intestines, were visible through a hole in the low ceiling and at their far end was a very rusty box with six buttons to regulate the fan's speed. I pressed one after another. Nothing happened. I hammered on the box with my fist. At first the movement was hardly discernible, and it could have been the breeze outside which made the fan's vanes turn. But soon the rotation became so regular that I was able to rule out this possibility. By the time I turned the speed up to the third level the fan had become an absolutely lethal weapon, furiously circling one and a half inches above head-height. I resolved to turn it off whenever I was moving about the room — one false move with the hand, and...

The fan went round and round. I opened the window so that there was only the mosquito net between myself and the street. I turned the fan's speed to maximum, and went outside, leaving the key on its big wooden tag at the unmanned desk. I crossed the street. The sand was sizzling hot, and as fast as I could I got myself into the shade of the canopy of palm leaves. From there I went down to the water's edge, took a few steps out past the immaculate sand into the warm sea, and was hit by the first enormous wave.

As I stood on the shore later, feeling the water drip from my hair and face, I saw the façade of the Hotel del Pacifico in its true, immutable aspect. It was perfect: the concrete structure with iron scaffolding on its unfinished roof, vacant windows and patches of sun-bleached turquoise paint. In front of it there was the unbroken row of palm-trees, the tall radio mast, and the road facing the beach lined with buildings in various states of disrepair.

Later, walking eastward along the beach I noticed that the road was coming to an end. Beyond the turning area there were stagnant pools, lizards and a hotel abandoned in mid-construction and never completed, its windows and empty rooms gaping as the rays of the afternoon sun passed right through them. Beyond that point there were no more buildings to be seen. Lazaro Cardenas' monstrous factories hovered ominously in the distant haze. I continued walking in that direction for some time, but seemed no closer to the city, so decided to turn back before sunset. I found the hotel, went into my room and showered in blissfully tepid water. The fan had already become dear to me, not only because it did its job, but because of its fantastical, encrusted, deep-sea look. It was as if every turn it made told of countless days and nights at sea, stories brought into the room by the untiring winds, an image of the planet itself circling around its moving centre, held in vertical mode by an unimaginable force.

I put on some comfortable clothes and went down to the beach to eat shrimp and have a couple of Coronas in a restaurant luxurious enough to be lit after dark by a single bulb. With coffee I moved to a chair closer to the sea. And there, in the faint violet and rose light of dusk, the revelation began.

In the wake of one the most magnificent sunsets I have ever witnessed, bright Venus was drawn toward the horizon by a crescent Moon — the barque of Sinbad. Mars and Jupiter were in conjunction in the vicinity of the constellation of Orion. Although it was by no means the first time I had observed the stately passage of these celestial bodies from east to west, I was spellbound. Then, suddenly, everything assumed another dimension. As I watched the planets move majestically from the zenith down toward the horizon, it struck me most forcibly that not only was I seeing the phenomenon in the way I was used to — that is, from the geocentric aspect — but that I could also visualise the imaginary disc which keeps the planetary orbits at their predetermined distances from the sun. This flexible disc containing the solar system was tilted at about a forty-five-degree angle to the horizon and projected outward over the ocean. Thus for the first time I found myself able simultaneously to envisage both the geocentric and the heliocentric models of the universe. And as if this were not wonder enough, I was granted a second vision. I imagined the dark and just barely visible outline of the rest of the Moon (in reality the reflection of Earth's own reflected light) to be the centre of a gigantic dome, a natural Saint Peter's cathedral in the terrestrial sky. It seemed that there was an intense light on the outside of this dome, and that the subdued shimmer which showed within it was so faint because it was the only bigger opening in the vault of heaven letting light into our sublunary world.

I found myself calculating that if with an immensely long ladder I could climb to the Moon herself, I would be able to look through the hole and see the bright light of the lunar day, which my eyes had already dimly observed from the Earth. And from the Moon an even longer ladder would convey me up along the vault and orbit of Venus to an observation point of the lunar dome. The Moon's steady and intense light adumbrated an enormous dark vault around her, within which Venus emitted a faint light, as from the far end of a tunnel. The ladder reaching up to this level would have to be many, many times longer than the one that led up to the Moon. And once I had reached Venus there would be another endless climb to Mars, and from thence yet another to Jupiter and Saturn, with corresponding levels pertaining to the tower of vaults. Beyond the last planetary dome I would, a million years hence, finally gaze straight out at the fixed stars, and would be delivered at last from planetary forces and the laws governing human destiny. As my gaze became lost, penetrating further and further into the uttermost void, I lost all faculty of orientation and fell like a parachutist into a swarm of diamonds spiralling in the trough of galactic space.

In commemoration of this extraordinary experience I spent most of the following afternoon building a kind of Babylonian ziggurat in the sand, with a road running spirally round it from base to top. The children playing on the beach became interested, inciting their youngest siblings to walk the spiral stairway up to heaven. The thought of their reaching for the stars was a beautiful one, but all the same their game threatened to ruin my creation. I had placed a white conch lined with pink mother of pearl at its apex to suggest the continuation of the spiral ad infinitum. But the shell was of course 'stolen' as soon as I turned my back to it. I then replaced the conch with a beer can, and since the beer's brand name was *Modelo*, I named my ziggurat 'Model of the Universe'. But in inverse ratio to my own philosophical subtlety, the compulsion grew among the kids to destroy the tower. They could hardly wait until dark to attack it without incurring the wrath and vengeance of its architect. Next morning the once so proud structure had been reduced to a formless heap of sand, crowned by a dog's turd.

It was the last day of the year. Hotel del Pacifico cruised on its daily tour with the sun over the ocean. The sea pelicans had gathered for their evening meal; the wife of Ricardo, the hotel owner, hung clothes over the balcony, from which the Sierra Madre could be seen in the distance, clothed in a froth of white cumulus clouds blown towards her by the sea. It was about four o'clock, the time of the day when the heat culminates, shadows lengthen and colours become deeper. The sun still shone white over the clouds, the palm trees rattled gently, and the sand away from the water's edge was still terribly hot. In short, it was the writer's idle hour. I could see him sitting on the terrace of the hotel, waiting for the sun to seek him out from under his tin roof and summon him to duty. Soon the small bars and restaurants would shrink to lonely points of light glimmering here and there among the dark palm trees, while the beach was metamorphosed into the bridge of a dark ship, infinity-bound.

When the sun set, mercifully, as it always will at the end of a labouring day, I went below decks and lit up a good pipeful of the local herb. Feeling inspiration gradually seize me I went out to the beach to witness nature's incomparable evening performance. The colours of dusk were of a particular subtlety. Not only were there nuances of tones, but nuances of nuances, and then fractional nuances of them in turn. The Moon's foetus had grown noticeably since the previous evening, and had moved closer to Venus. The juxtaposition of the two heavenly bodies, further and further descending, was a spectacle beyond words. The waves were illumined, and began to assume whatever shape the inspired fantasist wished. A black cloud came sailing from over the horizon; the planets donned their darkest clothes.

Like the poet who, (unfortunately disturbed), forgot much of the poem that came to him in his dream, and remembered only fragments — the stately pleasure dome, the caves of ice, the Abyssinian maid singing of Mount Abora — I can recall little of that wonderful transformation today. But I do remember that the recurring theme of these hypnagogic visions was a huge wolf, one of whose eyes, (the Moon), was large and mild, and the other, (Venus), was no more than a small glistening point of evil portent. It was completely dark when I finally summoned the energy to fetch myself another beer from under the canopy which, served as the roof of both home and restaurant as I met the former marine warplane technician Jerry.

He was in his seventies, and had come down to Playa Azul for no particular reason that I could discern. He had served on aircraft carriers most of his life. On demobilisation he decided to seek out some place of retirement other than his native Oklahoma. Although he had money enough to live practically anywhere in the world that he wished, he had come to Playa Azul, more or less by chance, just like me. He had stayed in the Hotel del Pacifico for five weeks before finding a villa to rent.

He explained to me how a jet engine with an afterburner works, and said, in a tone that made me believe him completely, that if someone were to take a helicopter to pieces and spread it out arbitrarily on the floor, he could 'Goddam put the whole sucker back together'. One reason I believed him without question was that he was meticulous to the point of obsession about his Cuba Libres. Once — we were firm friends by this time — he fetched from his home a cooler full of good (as opposed to bad) ice, cans of Coca-Cola and a bottle of rum. He asked the bartender for a glass for me. When the right (eight-ounce) glass proved to be unavailable, he became annoyed because it simply wasn't it. I said it didn't matter, but he wouldn't have any of that and was very much put out that there weren't the right glasses in this 'godforsaken place'.

Eventually Jerry gave up trying to find me the right glass, and taking the cooler with us, we moved up to two chairs closer to the sea and poured ourselves a few tall ones. After a while conversation between Jerry and myself, initially punctuated with crude jokes, turned more philosophical, hence more to my liking. I found myself delivering a lecture on the impossibility of ever making physical contact with other planetary systems within our universe. My argument, which I hoped would stimulate his technical curiosity, was based on comparisons of size and distance.

If we think of the sun as a balloon one metre in diametre, then the Earth, proportionately, is a pepper corn at a distance of more than a 100 metres from it. A nearby star to us, on the other hand, may be represented by a second balloon some 350,000 kilometres away, just about the real Moon's distance from Earth. 'The first thing that amazes me', I said, 'is that a glowing balloon can be seen at all at such a distance'. It gives us an idea of how intensely luminous these objects really are if we consider that there are other balloons ten, or a hundred, or a thousand times farther away from us than the sun, which are still visible to the naked eye. 'This is a verifiable fact', I added, with a wide gesture towards the stars above us. 'Add to this that the rays from these luminous balloons travel at a speed of 300,000 kilometres per second. How would it ever be possible for an infinitely small object on the sphere the size of a pepper corn to attain a velocity sufficient to convey it to the Moon and beyond? A travelling air bubble in a piece of solid glass would be a lightning compared to the fastest rocket man could devise.'

I had the feeling that Jerry was inclined to agree with me. Who, if not an aircraft technician, would know how much fuel/energy it would take to accelerate a material object to the speed of light, or very near it? It was, and he knew it, unimaginable. It would probably take more fuel than the totality consumed in the history of aviation. Billions and billions of tons of fuel! And this was just the beginning; a mere prerequisite!

In addition, nobody knows whether or not material objects can be accelerated to velocities approaching that of the speed of light and still remain material objects. Nobody knows what happens to time encapsulated inside an object moving that fast through space. It has never been seen, and never experienced by humans; the great Einstein himself hypothesised that material objects would put up an ever increasing resistance to further acceleration as they approach the speed of light and thus behave as though they possessed infinite mass.

The speeds of material objects (as opposed to the light they might emit) within a galaxy or our own star system can be measured using the same parameters that apply to the measurement of rocket velocity, that is, they can be expressed conveniently in thousands of kilometres per hour. The Earth, for example, moves through space in its orbit around the sun at approximately 108, 000 kilometres per hour; the solar system itself moves through space and around the centre of the galaxy at an estimated speed of 720,000 kilometres per hour. At present our fastest space-probes are capable of speeds up to 80,000 kilometres per hour, and can reach even the outer planets in a matter of years. But even if we were to succeed in accelerating a spacecraft up to say 100,000 kilometres per hour, it would still be more than 10, 000 times slower than light, travelling at a speed of 300, 000 km *per second* (1,79 billion kilometres *per hour*!). It would consequently (and provided that my mathematic extrapolations are accurate!) take that probe 10,000 years (roughly the time that has elapsed since the latest ice age drew to a close) to reach only one light year out into space, and more than 40, 000 years to make contact with our very nearest stellar neighbour, *Proxima Centauri*. A one way trip to *Sirius A*, the brightest star in the night heavens and like Centauri another star in our immediate 'vicinity', could be reached in just little more than 80,000 years — 'Welcome on board!'

Even if it were technically possible to build a spaceship with an enormous self-supplying nuclear power plant aboard capable of bringing about an even higher acceleration; even if man learns how to more efficiently use the gravitational pull of our solar system's planets to maximise centripetal acceleration, yes, even if man could survive travelling at speeds close to that of light (at the speed of light it would theoretically take a spaceship just slightly more than a second to get from the Earth to the Moon), he would thus have to travel for decades to reach stars in our neighbourhood. And these stars don't even have planetary systems and so would not provide conditions suitable for life as we know it.

Unless someone in the future were to invent a technique of transmitting human beings by telekinesis, any exchange of ideas between us and the 'intelligent' inhabitants of planets in other solar systems than our own would require decades to centuries to millennia to make a single round trip — and I deliberately abstain from here referencing the highly hypothetical discussion of so-called 'worm holes', allegedly capable of creating short cuts in the space-time continuum. If we thus remain within the framework of a more conventional and empirically verifiable understanding of the physical universe and organic life, the spaceship itself would have to resemble a planet, capable of producing all the prerequisites of biological survival — including artificial starlight — because although it crosses the universe at the speed of light, it would be very dark and empty around it. And so it would be for many, many years...

What passes through the minds of human beings who know that they will never be able to return to Earth? Can we even begin to imagine their nostalgia for a paradise forever lost? It would not take many years before the generation that remembered life on Earth becomes extinct. If there were any survivors — clones of the ship's original population, perhaps — they would never themselves know what sunsets were like, because they have never seen that glorious celestial light.

O, melancholy of men lost in absolute nothingness. O, inconceivable melancholy of sitting at a window throughout a lifetime with nothing to do but to watch the eternal, immutable cosmic night.

But all this is, of course, science fiction. 'The truth is,' I said, 'that it is never, ever, going to happen. The only way to reach other worlds, other life-forms, will be to invent telekinetic means of transportation. If we could transport our souls to other stars and other galaxies, and then come back, then we would really have achieved something.'

Perhaps this is exactly what human beings at a level of technical expertise supposedly lower than our own have already done. Perhaps the gods and monsters of ancient mythologies were in reality images, if not actual creatures, from another world? And perhaps primitive human beings were completely in the right to identify planetary bodies with men's faces and destinies. The modern obsession with the technical and material aspects of the problem may have eclipsed the fundamental concordance between travel in space and the ancient cult of the dead. Perhaps our 'science' is just another myth propagated and maintained as a more credible attempt to solve the problem of death, and is in reality no more and no less efficacious than the work of the past?

The cult of, and passionate interest in, the realm of death was revived in the 19th century with the birth of Theosophy. Although its claim to objective truth is ridiculous, the longings and the desire that sustain it are as old and as real as the human soul itself — we should remember that one of the most fervent admirers of Madame Blavatsky and Colonel Olcott was the technological pioneer and ingenious inventor Thomas Alva Edison, who gave us among so many other things the light bulb. The man who conquered the night was also intent on finding ways to communicate with and to record visitors from the spirit world. The light bulb worked all right, the phonograph as well, but the spiritual Dictaphone wouldn't say 'Mary had a little lamb', like the early recording, because it was made of solid matter, and the spirits are lighter and as such perhaps even faster than light itself.

If it were simply a matter of statistical probability, life would abound in the universe in the same way as certain nuclear particles in the sun constantly collide with each other, thereby feeding the nuclear process transforming hydrogen into helium, although the statistical chances that any two such particles should collide is a phenomenon occurring on average once in four billion years. However, the amount of these elementary particles within the sun is so enormous that billions upon billions of such collisions occur every fraction of a second. In other words, if we had evidence of life on one other planet in the universe, life must exist everywhere, and in such abundance that we couldn't even begin to estimate how many inhabited planets there may be in only those parts of the universe explored by our telescopes. Just try to let the following sink in for moment: in the now visible universe there are at least as many stars as there are grains of sand on every beach and desert of the Earth. Just try to imagine: our sun as a single grain of sand in the Sahara. For comparison: take just a handful of sand in your palm and try to count the amount of grains contained therein...

In the extremely unlikely event that life is *not* a statistical probability, and that countless planets in countless galaxies meet the requirements to support organic life, without actually doing it, then our predicament here on Earth in theory takes on a new aspect. Suppose that life could not exist anywhere other than on our planet. If we could be sure that life exists here and here only, we would also find it impossible to escape the religious paranoia which singles us out as unique and chosen by the Creator. It would be impossible for us to accept that life is the product of chance. Its uniqueness forces a metaphysical significance upon us. Everything we do is observed by the mute overseer responsible for this unique biological experiment. The notion of God's existence then becomes axiomatic, and the eternal question remains invariable. 'Why the spark out of nowhere that doesn't seem to be going anywhere?' He for whom God is dead in such a universe is lonely beyond all imagination. Perhaps God himself is this person; or perhaps, insofar as we have assumed the responsibility for his creation: *we* are?

So long as we keep looking outward, into space containing the most dilute disposition of matter and light, we will never know. We will never be able to communicate effectively through deep space, unless the messages we send or, per chance receive (I must insist on the distinction), will be transported telekinetically. We might just as well turn inwardly to find the questions to our unavoidable answer. In physical terms, the universe is sealed off and is for all eternity inaccessible. The Earth's spiritually-awakened inhabitants are condemned to live on their planet as Robinson Crusoe lived on his desert island, with the difference that Robinson stood a reasonable chance of discovery and rescue, whereas Man on planet Earth probably has none.

Open a human skull and look inside. The brain is lodged in the cranium like a big cloud in the celestial sphere. As we see the thoughts and fleeting sensations of the giant brain in the sky, the old saying attributed to Hermes Trismegistus comes to mind, 'As above, so below'. Bishop Berkeley's question then imposes itself, 'Would the universe exist if there were no one to perceive it?' And the unavoidable answer is: 'No'.

The universe so far as we know it exists for us and for us only. We are at its centre because there is nobody to tell us otherwise. When the Aztecs sacrificed warriors and screaming babies to the rain god in the belief that this would appease him, there was nobody to tell them that what they did was morally wrong. Indeed, their experience told them it was the right thing to do, and they knew more about the workings of stars and planets than their conquerors, who ordered them to put an end to such barbarous practices. Similarly, whatever we do here on Earth, there is and will be nobody outside it to tell us if we are in error. Our solutions inevitably become the words of God, and we are obsessed with the idea that our existence must have some kind of meaning beyond evolution alone.

The Hermetic proverb invites us to regard all things made by human beings as mirrors of a universe which we have projected onto the concept of space. There is the same immense loneliness inside us as there is in the universe we extrapolate from the cold expanses of intergalactic space. And there are the same fantastic forms and spiritual detours within us as there are out in projected space. Any thought or sensation is in itself a putative universe. When man tries to see beyond the stars, he peers into the dark recesses of his own mind, and just as he can see so little of himself beyond the reflection of his mental mirror, so it is as impossible for him to transcend his universe.

And why should he? The demiurgic imperfections in it may be annoying and our mortality and our suffering appalling, but still, it is our world, the only one we will ever know, and the only one we are free to populate with our gods, angels and chimeras. If only we could open the gate to the realm of death as the divine watchmaker opens the safe of the universe by turning one after another the immense tumblers round the infinite lock, we would have no reason to believe ourselves inferior to the Demiurge in any way. So far the master has kept this enigma locked inside his immense construction, and has ensured that any attempt to break his code and enter the world which runs parallel to ours, the world of the dead, is of the utmost difficulty and danger.

'Only a monster', the austere Gnostic philosopher Emil Cioran said, 'would be capable of seeing reality as it is.' One possible implication of this statement is that we are sheltered from the horrors of the universe by our own ineradicable will to illusion. So ingrained is this habit of mind that we will always replace one shattered illusion with another. It may even be that the ultimate illusion, as invincible as death itself, consists in the idea and incarnation of a contradiction in terms — in the man without desire, the Buddha of ultimate wisdom. Perhaps such an individual, attaining Nirvana, really has seen through the veil of

Maya into the realm of death, and perhaps knows that even if he were to reveal to the uninitiated its secrets, they would understand him as little as a blind man would a verbal description of colours? Whatever the breadth of his knowledge and insight, so long as he breathes and is mortal, he remains subject to the illusion of being. And he should be. The sage is not here to show us the impossible, but to make the act of transition from here to the unknown a path for us to follow. It is not his task to disappear and liberate himself from the shackles of this world, but to reveal the Way as far as it goes. 'Where we are death is not; where death is we are not'.

I am myself still too much under the spell of fallible instinct not to be drawn to the primordial perversion of the human mind as manifested in the unlimited cruelty of great civilisations. Whenever I fly over the Earth at night, I see the city lights form strange and enigmatic patterns, whose original meaning and design go back to the dawn of civilisation, and perhaps beyond. At the same time I see galaxies and stars below me, as well as the tower which the Mesopotamians began, and left to us to continue.

Over millennia the levels, departments and connections inside the tower have become like an architectural nightmare engraved by Piranesi. Nobody has the overall view; nobody sees the building plan; nobody knows where the whole thing is heading. Both beginning and end have vanished. The dimensions of the early ruins remain to serve as a reminder of the original impetus, but it is now possible to walk a lifetime through one room of one section of one of the many hundreds of levels, and still not see the nearest door.

Not all of us yet understand how grand and monstrous the edifice of the human spirit is. In the past century literary mystics like Kafka and Borges were able to hint at it; Kafka in his unfinished novels and horrifying short stories; Borges in his description of metaphysical space, as for instance, in his *The Library of Babel*. And in *The Aleph*, of course, the mystical point at which all the lines of the universe meet, time and space are annihilated and everything, past, present and future, converges.

I had begun to wonder if that fan in my hotel room was actually such an aleph. One possibility for its being so was that the philosopher's stone, according to alchemical lore, reveals itself only in the most unlikely, unexpected and commonly disregarded of places. The Aleph, or the philosopher's stone, is actually the disregarded thing itself. And there it was. The hypothetically immobile centre of the fan in my room allowed me to see worlds come and go. The progression from the achievements of Neolithic man to modern technological miracles was inscribed in fugitive patterns in the sand, faithfully recorded by the concentric movements of the fan. The rhythm of the sea still bore witness to an era when the continents had not yet emerged from Earth's primeval oceans. The sound of the sea's endless swell was sometimes heightened to a roar in lunatic nights and by furious hurricanes, and if sometimes it quietened to a distant murmur, it was nevertheless always there, always and immutably there. Cosmic history was written and erased again with every succeeding wave coming to rest on the miles and miles of the fine white sand spread before an unbroken line of palm trees, brooded over by the distant Sierra Madre.

The ocean was another and even more tumultuous *madre*, breeding monsters in her enormous belly. Unfathomable as the universe itself, she could be perceived and interpreted in the turn of each wave, yet she would always remain essentially unknown. Jerry obviously saw her as peaceful, and said that he wouldn't mind being out there, just floating. 'I wouldn't be able to swim for long', he said, 'But I could just float for a couple of hours'. 'And then?' I asked. But he didn't answer, thinking that I would understand anyway. As I made no sign of understanding, he put an end to speculation by saying, 'You know, I think I have come here to die.'

I looked at him. His face expressed no particular sadness or resignation. It wasn't that he was expecting to die the next day — it was just bound to happen sometime. I realised that he, who had been living at sea most of his life, was longing to become at one with her amniotic waters again. I looked up into the starry night and out over the sea, and remarked that he could have chosen a worse place to do it in. He laughed and nodded in agreement. We then changed the subject, I believe.

*

The following day was the last day of the year, and I was determined to make it memorable. After having spent most of the day in and out of the sea, I pulled myself together towards late afternoon and began to build in the sand what was to be a far larger castle than the one I had made before. This time I planned on a grand scale. I began by ramming a huge and heavy palm trunk vertically into the ground, and poured sand from a bucket over it. Moving in a circle I made an artificial depression around this fixed point. This time my sandcastle was not in the shape of a ziggurat but was a kind of truncated pyramid — though it turned out to be impossible (for me, anyway) to make really good sharp edges in a sand construction of this size. The whole thing became circular instead of square at each level. There were seven of these levels, one for each planetary sphere (in accordance with ancient cosmology).

The construction stood about two metres high and four in diametre when completed. I looked upon my work with some contentment then threw myself into the sea to wash away the sweat and sand sticking to me. I didn't let the pyramid out of my sight for more than seconds at a time, but still, as I walked out of the water and up to it I saw that someone had been able to sneak up on its rearward-facing side and to destroy part of its fragile terracing. Realising that I could not leave my construction unattended without risking its prompt demolition, I bribed with Coca-Cola one of the younger and more docile-seeming boys to look after my creation while I showered and dressed. That worked. The boy obviously took pride in his new office as guardian of the temple. I was happy to give him his Coca-Cola and took the next watch myself. I now saw, with some surprise, that some of the Mexican children — not local children but those who were on vacation with their parents — had, under the supervision of one of the women, an architect by profession, begun building, not a copy of my sandcastle but a replica of the Temple of Inscriptions at Palenque — I was later able to confirm the accuracy of their 'imitation' when I saw the temple in its jungle setting.

The children kept diligently at their work, and were able to finish their construction before sunset. The temple was very neatly done, not very big, perhaps, but perfectly shaped and precise in all its detail. For a while we all stood in contemplation of its formal perfection, and I went so far as to suggest that, if my temple was dedicated to the sun, theirs should be to the Moon. There was no time for abstract inaugurations, however, for before the sun had fully set, the children threw themselves on their pyramid and rejoiced in its utter destruction. I stopped them from doing the same with mine because I wanted to draw a line along the very last shadow cast by the tree trunk before sunset all the way to my point of observation under the canopy.

This I did, and later that evening I drew the line of the shadow cast by the pole, which was clearly discernible by the light of the setting Moon. In this way I recorded the bearings for the sun and the Moon on New Year's Eve. I thereafter decided that the tower had served its cultural and astronomical purposes and could now be abandoned to the natural elements, e.g. curious dogs and wilful children.

I no longer had any intention of preserving my ephemeral creation, and remained in my chair for a long time, enjoying the view of the ocean and of the towering shadow below the darkening vault, revolving under the window of the pole star. A sense of being privy to the primitive beginnings of a civilisation haunted me.

Soon I even began to feel that I was being watched. In itself this was not surprising. Jerry had already warned me that no matter where I moved about in Playa Azul, I would at any given time have at least one pair of eyes fastened to the back of my neck. The presence I had sensed, however, was not a real person. It was more like a wraith, an insubstantial entity flitting silently and in an instant from one end of the beach to the other. When I heard sudden shrill laughter right behind me I spun round, panic-stricken.

There was nobody there, but I had the impression that the shadow, faster than a flash of lightning, had moved again. Although I had no wish to remain under its spell, I made myself stay seated. The figment of my paranoia was no doubt a significant epiphenomenon of the psychic energies I had invested in my tower, and I reminded myself that to have the courage to confront my fear was the only way to make contact with the demon. The apparition was not alien, it was an integral part of myself. I knew it, but could not avoid feelings of discomfort and fear. So I stayed where I was, and forced myself not to keep looking over my shoulder. The one apparently constant feature of this mysterious being was that he was discernible only at the outer edge of my field of vision, in this way marking the unsubstantial frontier between the realms of the dimly seen and the altogether unseen.

The apparition had its existence at the edge of the shadow of night, which continually sweeps over the planetary sphere as the Earth spins around its axis. It lived on that indefinable line that separates the known and the unknown. It was an inhabitant of the twilight zone, and its primal trait was that maddening laughter, audible and recognisable only to those who were themselves on the verge of possession, or even madness itself.

I interpreted it as the original demon of creation, the primordial fear of the void which so haunts the human mind that it would rather face mortal danger in a concrete form than succumb to this horrifying ambiguity — eerie laughter that tears the veil of illusion and leaves nothing behind. Perhaps it is this laughter that animals are deaf to, and only we human beings are fated ever to hear. We can never dominate it, never become its masters. It is the eternal companion of loneliness, the *Doppelgänger*, the madman. It has no reason to exist and needs no reason to exist. It is the heart of darkness in the midst of the light.

The fanatic anchorites of the Egyptian desert seem to have been familiar with this demon. It was known in the Greek vernacular as *acedia*, the demon of midday, bringer of mortal lethargy to some, of mysterious panic to others. It was sometimes seen as an approaching figure which seemed never to arrive, until, suddenly, it was there, right next to the hermit in his cell.

My demon had not appeared at noon, however, but at its opposite pole, midnight. True, my paranoid tendencies are sometimes extraordinarily reinforced by weed. One might consequently be justified in interpreting the psychological oddity accompanying my night-time session on the beach in strictly biochemical terms, leaving the demon out of the equation for at least as long as he remains superfluous to the correct assessment of my mental profligacy. Very well, but I still feel compelled, though, to ask myself why I seek out singular incidents such as these, and the drugs to go with them, if the outcome is no more than a gratuitous paranoia?

My answer is that the sense of being haunted in this way is only one side of the coin. The exciting side of paranoia is that it encourages me to place myself at the centre of the universe and to identify with a divine purpose. To be psychologically more precise, I magnify my intentions to a point at which they lose their familiar connotations, and assume the significance of a cosmic adventure. This is what the positive side of paranoia is all about for me, and I have so far been willing to accept its negative aspects because of the intensity it adds to my perception of self. Then, the purport of the 'opiate' is to diffuse logic and reason, to dissolve the whole of life into a waking dream.

Who am I? If the climate is cold, I am obliged to admit that I am here and am doing what I must in order not to freeze to death, and until I am dead that is no dream but stark reality. (One of the most important disciplinary exercises practised by Tibetan Buddhist monks is to learn to endure excessive cold.) If the climate gives me a perfect sense of balance between outside and inside, I can more easily identify myself with all that I see and sense around me, and look upon my actual self as an emanation of a nebulous macrocosmic being of which I am, along with a thousand other microcosms, an integral part. The philosophical conclusion that this particular state of mind adduces is that individuality is an illusion: everything is in the *Prana*, the universal breath of life.

The temperature of Playa Azul's air and water was such that it allowed me the perfect illusion of being at one with the cosmos. There was, after all, no one behind me except my fear of myself, and as this particular fear seemed as old as Methuselah, there was no more reason to worry about it today than there was yesterday or would be tomorrow.

The conclusion thus presented itself: there is a profound unity in the cosmos, from microcosm to macrocosm, and there is endless variety also. Within the overall monotonal universe, inconceivable as an entity any way, all kinds of heavenly bodies are imaginable, even if in reality they do not exist. In fact, the universe, my universe, is nothing but endless possibility. The human mind is identical with this universe, because the things it cannot experience will never be revealed to it. This does not prevent them from being possible, just as a mad and utterly alien idea is still possible, even though inapplicable to any known and existing order.

But then again, I believe that there is just as much order as there is chaos in the cosmos, and that the depressing symmetry and regulation of atoms, as revealed by the electron microscope, conceal another infinity of chaos, in which all is possible and all indefinite. Einsteinian physics has taught us that 'matter' and 'energy' are interchangeable terms, and that there is in theory nothing to prevent worlds from coming and going in and out of different states of aggregation: gas, solid, super-solid, or spiritual. Perhaps the visible universe is in the last instance no more than that part of the universe which resonates on our mental wavelength. That the visible universe represents but a very limited part of the whole spectrum of existing physical wavelengths is already a known fact.

The only thing not possible is that our cities, religions, arts and sciences differ from the universe — in the particular way, that is, that it reveals itself to us. The universe we see when we look into the sky is the same as the one we see when we look into ourselves. The two are interdependent, and a city can be compared to a galaxy just as a galaxy can be interpreted as a city, or a hurricane, in space. The galaxy may be a million other things as well, but we will never know, so long as we have to look upon the world as human beings look upon the world. In other words, our human universe is a perfect blueprint of the universe in the particular way that it is accessible to us.

As I write this I feel a sudden shiver along my spine. It all sounds so assured and rational, as if we were confident that of course we do understand ourselves and each other, and are not simply, as it were, fumbling for the light switch in the dark. But perhaps you and I, dear reader, in spite of all our mutual goodwill, are metaphorically light-years apart, and my words will never in a lifetime reach you? Perhaps we really are as far apart from each other as the stars? Perhaps, although we keep sending messages to one another, we know that they will never be received? And if, impossible though it is, they were received, they could never be opened. And if opened, which again is impossible, they could not be converted. And if converted, which is impossible, they could not be deciphered. And if deciphered, which is impossible, they could not be interpreted. And so on, for ever and ever...

I again recall my acquaintance Jerry sitting next to me under the canopy of stars saying, 'You know what, I think I have come here to die'. But his words did not reach me then. They are still travelling, and the farther they go the lonelier they become. Indeed, words like these can travel for a very long time.

Boca del Cielo

Before leaving Playa Azul I was intent on witnessing a full Moon in some spectacular setting further down the Pacific coast. About a week later I found myself winning closer to my goal. In Boca del Cielo — which one reaches by taxi from the town of Tonalá off Carretera Federal 200 — Sierra Madre de Chiapas comes writhing almost all the way down to the sea. Its pointed crocodile's head doesn't quite reach to the water's edge, but stops just short of the broad lagoon which separates beach from mainland. The beach itself is a strip of unspoiled Eden set between two hostile entities: the relentless glittering ocean on the one side and the rugged and no-less-relentless mountains on the other. The shores of the lagoon are fringed with palm trees, the hills rising toward the plateau of Chiapas covered by jungle-growth.

Lodgings here are of the most primitive kind, and unless you are content to lie in the sand in the company of stray dogs, or on a veranda besieged by swarms of mosquitoes, restricted to a hammock suspended between the sand and a corrugated tin roof. But there was no room for discussion here, for only the very western tip of the beach, where the stretch of water connecting lagoon and ocean is located, accommodates a few scattered sheds and houses. Others may be hidden in the jungle where the beach broadens toward the east, but as I began walking in that direction I soon found myself the seemingly only occupant of a deserted beach.

The sun sank down towards the sea: a giant drop of ruby-red glass along a stretch of shallow water finally engaging with the land. The pelicans spread their wings for a final reconnaissance flight along the line of the breaking waves before returning to the shelter of their lagoon. The purple of evening rose up to the zenith in the shape of a fan, and from deep down in the east a dark-blue curtain was drawn toward the same point. Minute by minute it covered the sky, until the purple had become a thin line of ruby and gold on the rim of an enormous deep, deep-blue glass chalice.

Returning to my point of departure I went into the modest little bar where fishermen were knocking back one beer after another. I sat down and invited them to drink whisky with me while we awaited the full Moon. We waited a good hour longer than I had expected, but as the great and good make a point of never arriving early at a party, I wasn't surprised that the lady took her time. And when finally she peeped over the mountain top, even those fishermen could not hold in check a sigh of admiration. Arrayed in perfect amber, in which fossilised leaves and insects could be seen, as perfect as if they were still living, she made her entry on the back of the giant crocodile, throwing her silvery cape ahead of her into the lagoon, and shyly arranging a few glittering diamonds in her hair, while her shawl, in mother of pearl, reflected the depth and colour of her dress. The higher she rose up the palace steps, the more brightly glittered the scales of the crocodile at the foot of the staircase below her. His eyes turned yellow, his smile all the more ingenuous as he shed shimmering tears the size of coconuts into the lagoon.

After the formal introductions of her guests, staged behind soft curtains, the Moon moved into the great ballroom, where the orchestra began to play. Along the white chalk of her limitless beach stood dark palm trees in military formation. From the far end of the great glittering room, Lord Orion caught sight of her and hurried to her, to kiss her hand and claim the favour of the first dance. The Moon made a discreet sign to her two attendants, Jupiter and Mars, who stood aside as she was led out onto the ocean floor by the noble huntsman, who proved to be a most accomplished dancer, unashamedly requisitioning the floor for himself and his chosen lady. At the far end of the great room glistened the jealous eye of Venus, enveloped in the last rosy hues of the western skies. She, much against her will, had been assigned the role of Cinderella on this occasion, and would have to leave before midnight a stage which in the past had been the scene of so many of her conquests. Venus was vexed, but there was nothing to be done, and, swollen with fury, she mounted the lofty stairway at the end of the ballroom, and was gone.

I must assume that Lord Orion kept company with the Moon for most of the evening, as I myself took refuge from the mosquitoes and the continuous din of a drunken Mexican singer, by climbing into a hammock in a tin-roofed bamboo shed. But I did not get very much sleep. The doleful Mexican was singing far too loudly, and as soon as the first faint light of the false dawn touched the eastern curtain, I stood up and began walking around aimlessly, waiting for the sun to rise. Children whom I hadn't noticed before were soon up too, and the mother of the family, cheerlessly attending to their needs, handed me a cup of coffee. I accepted it gratefully, and took the opportunity to walk out onto the beach again. Knowing that the sun had to rise somewhere in the east, I set off in that direction while the Moon, pale and tired after the ball, prepared to leave by way of the same staircase Venus had climbed long before.

Suddenly, the King Sun was there again, gradually effacing the trace of his Queen, spreading the cards he had been keeping at the gaming table while the others were dancing (aces and trumps only) one by one on the sand. The crocodile discreetly backed up against the mountain ridge, and the sea birds rose into the air, eager to fill their bellies.

There was one last moment of grace and perfect balance between the monarchs of day and night. Before the Moon, dimmed and weary, turned to retire to her chambers, she gave her husband a long poignant glance across the length of that interminable beach. 'Don't ask me the question to which you already know the answer', she seemed to tell him. In his generosity and discretion, he did no more than to watch her pale into insubstantiality, and retire to bed behind the first cumulus clouds to appear on the western horizon.

I felt compelled to walk towards the sun, whose turn it was now to gain power by the minute. The air became pleasantly warm. I sank to the ground, and must have slept awhile. I woke up feeling hot and dizzy, as if my previous unconscious state had been closer to annihilation than to sleep. The sea glittered magically, turquoise and all shades of blue, and I threw myself thankfully into it. After that sudden resurrection I was no longer inclined to dress myself again, so, in splendid isolation, among wildlife and exotic trees, with the one open yellow eye of the crocodile of Sierra Madre upon me, I strode down the beach as God and other countless good things (ambrosia and nectar!) had made me.

In passing I emptied my waste straight into the ocean and even made an ecstatic offering to mother Earth from my reproductive organ, which, by the way, had started to assume a strange oceanic aspect. The testicles no longer wore their familiar aspect, but looked more like some kind of sea urchin: a leathery, firm pouch armed with countless sharp protective barbs. This alien creature, to which a no less curious looking snail was attached, had apparently made its nest right in my crotch!

Its thorny carapace had rubbed against the inside of my thighs, which became somewhat irritated and inflamed. There was no way, however, that I was going to take notice of a minor inconvenience when I was about to merge, body and soul, not with a sea-urchin alone, but with the whole of nature. In fact, the presence of the urchin was probably no more than the first sign that I had begun to turn into an animal myself, some semi-aquatic mammal, and host of other species!

While the sun continued to climb it grew hotter still. Ahead of me, at the water's edge, stood a white crane, his slender body and legs motionless in the water. I approached him slowly and came so close that I could see his eyelid blink from time to time. But when I got too near he hoisted himself into the air and flew off in the direction of the sun, settling himself, still at the water's edge, a little further up the beach. I amused myself by running after him and making him repeat the manoeuver, but though I ran as fast as I could I never quite caught up with him, and after a while he got tired of the game, made a wide turn over the sand dunes and disappeared. I was gradually coming to my senses when, through the white haze of midday, I saw something odd at the far end of the beach. It looked like a tree from this distance, but this was unlikely to be the case, as trees don't grow that close to the water. Curious, I moved nearer to it.

As its shape became more distinct, it looked more and more like a human being standing erect and immobile on the beach. This was uncanny: where had he come from? Slowing down, I nonetheless continued to move forward, though somewhat apprehensively, until to my relief, I could see that it wasn't after all a person. A few minutes more, and I saw that it was an upright hollow tree trunk, the same height as myself and shaped curiously like a human body. There was a hole in the top where a man might place his head, and two smaller holes at the sides, through which he could push his arms. It was too tempting not to try it, so I stuck my face in the oval and my arms through the two smaller holes. Standing inside the hollow trunk in this position I raised my arms until they crossed over my wooden chest. I was about to utter a prayer to the sun in this sacerdotal position, when the whole trunk, as if hit by a bolt of lightning, simply fell to pieces, leaving no more than a few dark wooden fragments scattered on the sand around me.

In that very same instant I heard it again — the laughter. It ruptured the silence as if someone had ripped heaven into two parts. And then the light went out. For a fraction of a second the light drained out of the Pacific, the Sierra Madre and the sky. It all happened in the blink of an eye, only I know for sure that I did not blink. The moment passed, and it was as if nothing had happened, except that the trunk had disintegrated around my body, and I was as cold as one seized by a tropical fever. After that both the laughter and the instant of total darkness were gone.

The sea still glittered, the fishing birds hovered and swooped over it while the sun climbed to its zenith. Strangely enough I had neither the time nor the energy to give the incident much more thought. I had left the tavern early in the morning without eating, and without bringing water with me. I really hadn't planned to stay away so long; it simply happened as I have said. But now it was high time to head back to base. I put on my shorts and the shirt I had worn like a turban on my head, and walked westward again. Two hours later I met the friendly Mexican who had given me shelter for the night. He had begun to worry about my prolonged absence, and set out to find me. He didn't say as much, but there was no other reason for him to walk the length of a beach he knew to be deserted except for crazy tourists and the odd louche native element. He, more than anybody, knew that there was always some risk in walking the beach alone, no matter what the time of day. At least, that's what I think he had in mind, or if not that, that I had drowned through venturing too far from the shore. It was good to see his face break into a broad smile as we met, not far from the bar.

I drank two litres of water but ate nothing. I wasn't hungry, or didn't know I was. The fishermen had been drinking beer all morning, and were thoroughly drunk. One of them asked me to come over and inspect their catch. There was a very ordinary open boat with an outboard motor; on its bottom boards lay five sharks, each of them longer than I am tall, three hammer sharks and two grey sharks, their magnificent teeth covered in blood.

It didn't occur to me to fetch my camera. Instead, when I had summoned the energy, I asked one of them to ferry me over to the opposite shore. I bade them all farewell, especially my host and his gloomy wife, who probably understood only too well my wish to take a hotel room for the night.

When the fisherman had taken me across the river, I gave him what coins I had, and sat down under a bougainvillea tree to wait for the local taxi. At last it came. I threw my things into the trunk and got into the car. The driver and I spoke of many things during the journey to the village by the lighthouse, but still, throughout our conversation, I overheard an inner female voice intoning the haunting melody to *Hotel California*. Only the text was slightly different:

> Welcome to Hotel del Pacifico.
> Such a lonely place, such a lonely face.
> Nobody else stays in your room.
> It's there for you, it's there for you.
> Once checked in you'll never wanna leave.
> Once checked in you'll be here forever.

While moving in to another modest hotel room along the Pacific coast — with its incrusted ceiling ventilator, trickling cool water shower, two sheets (one to lay on and the other for cover) a pillow, a towel and two small pieces of soap — it dawned on me, as it has always dawned on me facing the Pacific, that this is where all roads, not just the ones leading here, end. It's the vastness of the universe itself presented in terrestrial terms: waves of unimaginable amplitude permeating the expanses of space, breaking over the peaks of Earth as the Pacific crashes onto the Ring of Fire .

Taking to the heights

On a continent characterised both by man-made pyramids and natural ones, notably volcanoes, the adventurous tourist can't really stay away from the challenge to hike some of the latter. I'm in no way an alpinist and have never wanted to be one. But since childhood one of my great passions has been to contemplate nature, not the least its panoramic vistas. To this end I sometimes embark upon more or less strenuous mountain excursions, all in the modest hope of being able to conceive in my mind, and in the course of a single day, the poetry of the universe.

One such event was my walk over the lava field to the volcano Paricutín, located about 20 kilometres to the north of the city Uruapán in the Mexican state of Michoacán. I had spent a tranquil day sightseeing Uruapán. It's a sympathetic enough town with a pleasant climate, though I must confess I liked the state capital Morelia, its central square and cathedral, even better, and was now ready to move on. A short bus ride brought me from Uruapán to Angahuán, an indigenous community offering no more than basic tourist amenities. On the contrary it has the indisputable advantage of being the human settlement closest to the actual volcano. The population here leads a traditional existence, meaning for example that families will tend to sit on the floor in their humble abodes and use horses as taxis. Because of its elevation — roughly 2,300 metres above sea level — nights get quite chilly. There was only one tourist facility in the village and a pretty rustic one at that. I declined to sleep alone in the enormous dormitory that seemed designed for a legion of Boy Scouts. The only option left under the circumstances was a ten person room with a fireplace so small I had to sit right next to it to get any warmth at all. Since the beds were part of the permanent fixtures I eventually had to cuddle up under a mountain of coarse blankets and nonetheless freeze sufficiently through the night to gratefully hail the sun when it finally rose.

As agreed previous evening the manager of the hostel sent a young boy to guide me through the woods to the beginning of the lava field. That guidance was quite useful as there are hardly any beaten tracks between the village and the volcano. But the boy of course knew the way and after about forty-five minutes walk he pointed towards something that I took to be some darker patches in between the trees. Coming closer I realised the darkness in between the trunks was a ten to fifteen metre high wall of solidified lava. We had reached the outer edge of the once moving lava stream. Here the boy, having done his duty, was happy to leave me. I paid him and he waved me off only to soon disappear in among the trees. I was now on my own.

Paricutín is not one of those volcanoes that have been fuming slowly and majestically for the last couple of million years, every now and then throwing a tantrum. It was literally born in February 1943 when its first alarming eruptions forced locals to realise they were longer no safe. Over the coming weeks and months the Earth continued to spew out lava and pyroclastic clouds with the consequence that the village of Paricutín, (now entirely buried in lava) and its neighbour community San Juan Parangaricutíro had to be evacuated. Luckily this could be done without casualties. However, everything that couldn't be moved was lost forever. Over the coming weeks and months the cone of the volcano grew at a staggering speed. Within a single year it had almost grown vertically to its final size, towering at a respectable four-hundred metre above the surrounding terrain. Then, in 1952, its seismic activity came to a sudden halt. Being what the seismologists call a *scoria*, or *cinder cone*, type of volcano it's not expected to have another eruption ever and has consequently become something of a trekker's wet dream. Because although the volcano is now considered inactive by geologists, there is still enough fume and vapour seeping through its cracks heating and colouring the ground in a vast spectrum.

Although half a century has passed since the last eruption took place, the lava field has acquired very little vegetation. It thus fits the cliché description 'like on another planet' perfectly. The rock is as black as tar and still looks like it was delivered from the bowels of the Earth yesterday. But it's not glowing any longer. On the contrary. I had to conclude I wasn't really fully equipped for the task at hand, realising too late that my tennis shoes with soft rubber soles were at best condemned, at worst would be ripped to shreds leaving me barefoot in the midst of razor-sharp coagulated crests. A critical thing would be to keep my physical equilibrium no matter how craggy the petrified seas grew.

It was a splendid day: pitch-black rock set against a radiant sun and a crystal-blue sky. I set out confidently over the lava and had surprisingly little problem reaching the volcanic cone, avoiding every temptation to fall and badly wound myself. Since I was approaching the volcano from the north, where the lava flow had been the most intense, the ascent had been slow but steady, so that finally climbing the actual cone and reach its ridges was a piece of cake. Once up there, after two hours of hiking from the village, I unexpectedly ran into jovial tourists dressed in Hawaiian shirts with cameras dangling over their bellies. It turned out that there was a paved road all the way to the backside of the volcano. There was even a parking lot, enabling tourist parties on organised excursions easy access to what I had hitherto considered one of the last vestiges of wilderness. That was an anticlimax, but I soon found my bearings, confident in the conviction that these day visitors would never come to experience the lava field in the way that I had. And that was true. After a descent into the bottom of the volcano, where the ground was still warm, I readied myself for the return trip. It went faster as it was largely downhill. As my point of orientation I kept the old church tower of the otherwise obliterated village of San Juan, and happily arrived there in one piece.

This particular church has not become famous because of its architecture, although it too is worth noticing. Its lasting claim to fame is that only its roof and the upper part of its tower have remained above Earth; the rest is buried in lava. However, while the lava relentlessly moved on, the church walls resisted the pressure and didn't cave in so that today one can actually descend into the interior of the church through its tower. Walking the floor of this abandoned temple is like treading a man-made piece of Heaven locked in a permanent embrace by Mother Earth. There are places in nature that do look like churches or temples, and there are churches, notably Gothic cathedrals, the columns and vaults of which look like stylised nature. But to see nature and human art combine in this unexpected and completely juxtaposed way is indeed a unique experience, suggesting a descent into Hell that inadvertently got stuck halfway. The angels and the saints were ready to accompany the Saviour on this ungrateful mission, but by a fluke of nature the Host and the wine still remain locked up in the sacristy awaiting Judgment Day, when Gabriel shall blow his horn, the earthly shackles fall from the walls and the entire church takes to the skies in a cloud of thunder and lightning!

By mid-afternoon I was back in Angahuán. An Indian invited me to mount a taxi horse with my luggage and accompanied me back to the paved road. I could hardly have refused the offer since it would have made my pale face look even paler and my figure the laughing stock of the village. Unfortunately my horse took a wrong turn somewhere in the village and I was unable to turn him right by myself. The fierce-eyed Indian, spiritual grandson of the great Gitche Manitou himself, had to turn round in order to set my horse straight. It was a rather embarrassing moment and I promised myself to try to become more of a horseman in the future. Well, I'm still no cowboy, but if the horse is not too willful I nowadays usually end up having it my rather than his or her way.

As the bus brushed past the pine forests, descending into more tropical vegetation and finally into Uruapán, my whole adventure around the Indian village and its volcano began to almost seem like a dream, albeit an exceptionally vivid one, because the images from that trip have left a tenacious afterglow on my mental screen and it sometimes still happens that I involuntarily gauge 'blueness' in general using my memory of the colour of the sky on that particular day as my reference.

Yet another ascension

Peru. After a full day spent observing the legendary Machu Picchu from all possible angles — in atmospheric conditions ranging from early morning drizzle to mysterious mists slowly dissipating in sunshine, like a dream-woman undoing clouds of gauzy cotton in front of her admirers — I had reached a state of satiation. But then there was Wayna Picchu. In practically all panoramic photos of Machu Picchu, Wayna Picchu makes up the impressive hump-like mountain in the background. Buying a separate ticket allows you to gain access to its summit. It takes about an hour to get up there from the base of the mountain, but with hindsight I admit that it was well worth the effort.

There were literally people from all walks of life on the trail. One of the more conspicuous characters was a moustached Brazilian gentleman in his 70s dressed in sports clothes that seemed to have been manufactured roughly in the same era as the man himself. An elegant cane offered extra support to his body. Notwithstanding, he was surprisingly fit — a modicum of agility being an absolute prerequisite to even attempt the steep ascension — and in due course made it to the top. The ascent really is a mixture of walking and half-climbing stairs or stair like natural structures, and is not to be recommended for people with a heart condition. About two thirds up the way I began to feel quite tired and turned round to a Chilean young man who had been trailing in my footsteps over the last twenty minutes: 'Now', I said, 'a bunch of those coca leaves would have come in handy, don't you think?' Whereupon he smilingly produced a plastic bag from his backpack and handed it over to me. It was the stuff.

For those of you who have never tried to chew coca leaves it might be useful to learn that they turn quite bitter when masticated for any length of time. But this inconvenience must be compared with the positive effect that it has on your stamina: coca leaves actually do the job! Having been at the brink of exhaustion with one third of the way still to go, the ingested substance revitalised my life spirits and fortified my legs. I wasn't even that much tired as we eventually reached the top.

There is no better place to assess the singular and enigmatic location of Machu Picchu than from its adjacent high cliff: Wayna Picchu. There is nothing to suggest that the ceremonial centre of Machu Picchu was in a practical location in terms of communications or even administrative power. It even seems to have been erected in a response to a threat primarily perceived as spiritual rather than physical. Otherwise it would hard to explain why, in spite of having being constructed in the early 15th century AD, it was abandoned well before any members of the Inca people got wind of the Spanish Crusades in the Americas. In short, both the Incas who built and those who eventually abandoned the temple site were equally unaware of the real nature of the impending threat to their empire. However, it seems as though the Inca elite had begun to suspect their days in the sun to be numbered all the same, half a century before Columbus even set sails on his first voyage to the West Indies. According to some theorists on the subject, the whole purpose of erecting the astronomical observatories, as well as the temples to the gods, at Machu Picchu, was to slow down the cosmic clock itself in order to give an a priori doomed civilisation a little more time to prepare itself for the unavoidable.

The Incas, as opposed to for example the Mayas, have left no written records behind. Most of these theories are therefore at best informed speculation based on circumstantial evidence. But since it's indisputable that the Spanish never found Machu Picchu — and believe me:

they would have gone looking for it at the faintest rumour of treasures buried on the premises — it's permissible to assume that not even the descendants of the sacerdotal elite responsible for its abandonment had any idea of the existence of this site, constructed at a time that qualifies as an industrial stone age by today's historical criteria. This to me suggests not only an exodus of priests and their assistants. In accordance with the strict hierarchy associated with all pre-Columbian religiosity, mass sacrifices and/or collective suicidal acts cannot be ruled out with any degree of certainty. Surely epidemic disease could have achieved the same result, and perhaps even more efficiently, but there is as little evidence for the one thing as for the other. Other calamities, such as earthquakes and sudden climate changes, are less likely to have produced a permanent abandonment of a site which has visibly remained intact, albeit hidden under layers of earth, since more than five hundred years.

Of course the aura of mystery surrounding this Andean sanctuary only contributes to intensifying the adventure of visiting it, and as I sat on what seemed to me the top of the world, looking down like a bird of prey on a rocky plateau dotted with ancient stone monuments, surrounded by the river Urabámba and by a near-perfect circle of higher ridges, the cry of the wilderness and the silent paw of the jaguar were not far away. As a perfect illustration to my state of mind a condor took flight from the promontory. It was, truth be told, a young condor, still only spanning a metre between its wingtips, but it was a condor alright, and I think the reader will excuse me if at this moment I seize the opportunity to conjure from the depths of his imagination all the associations — musical, verbal, pictorial, emotional, philosophical and existential — connected with the emblematic song of the High Andes: 'El condor pasa'.

The Andes are breathtaking both literally and figuratively. It takes some time getting used to walk the streets of Cusco at 3,500 metres above sea level, and to mount some of its steeper gradients presents quite a challenge. I remember initially having to take siestas every other afternoon from sheer altitude fatigue. The average altitude of the archaeological site of Machu Picchu, on the other hand, is only about 2,400 metres, but its spectacular location makes it seem suspended midway between Heaven and Earth. There are no paved roads leading to the village of Aguascalientes that serves as a base camp for visitors, only a railway track.

At the time of my visit to Cusco an international consortium was responsible for the maintenance of the line. It made sure that tourists didn't get away with paying local prices for transportation through the Sacred Valley of the Incas, today also known as the Urabámba Valley. Although normally priced trains leave regularly for the various stations along the river Vilcanota, tourists were not allowed to use them. By all means the 'rules' nailed to an inner wall of the Cusco railway station stipulated that only foreigners who could show proof of a permit of residence were allowed to share these trains with the Peruvians. For the benefit of the tourists, on the other hand, there was one expensive train with panoramic windows allowing the passengers to admire the mountainsides as the train advances through the narrow glens between them.

I opted for the only budget alternative available: the Backpacker Train. It was fine enough but not cheap either. Even though it perhaps didn't allow me to see the full extent of the mountain peaks around us, it had normal windows offering a traditional view. Besides leaving Cusco by train was a rare experience no matter which type of train one would take. It's something similar to being sluiced through the locks of a canal, with the train going in zig-zag back and forth for a good three quarters of an hour before it reaches the rim of the caldera in which the town is located. Only from there does it begin to roll forward.[17]

---

17   Today the trains for Machu Picchu supposedly no longer depart from the city centre but from some location on its surrounding ridge, and so this kind of railway sluicing in Cusco is now another part of its history.

The journey takes one past the city suburbs, the ensemble of which makes a rather gloomy impression because of the abundance of naked concrete blocks, hollow red brick, cement, barbed wire and rebars. I have never been to Bolivia, so I can't make the comparison but, among the countries I have visited in Latin America, Ecuador and Peru undoubtedly has the highest instance of what even an unprejudiced Westerner would call half- or even unfinished buildings. In addition, the climate at close to 4,000 metres above the sea is not always that inviting; evenings and nights can be both moist and cold. Nothing for me, so I happily embraced the fact that the train was gradually descending into Aguascalientes, an approximately two hour ride from the ancient Inca capital. One image, and it wasn't one of nature this time, particularly engraved itself in my mind from that trip. It was a young man standing somewhere along the railway track looking at the train as it slowly passed by. In a sense he looked like every other Indian boy in this country, except for his eyes which were sad to the point of mute despair. Whether or not I had simply caught him in a pensive mood, I can't tell, but his eyes have followed me ever since and represent to me the human sorrow that makes up the darker of the two masks in the mundane theatre. One of countless human destinies on this planet, as it appeared to one passenger, sitting inside a train, a snapshot in time, for sure, but also one of irrevocable time…

There is a good reason why Aguascalientes is called Aguascalientes: it does have hot springs! I was lucky to find myself a nicely secluded hotel at the top of the village straight above Rio Aguas Calientes, at the beginning of the slender road that runs parallel with it up to the thermal baths. The river is a silvery ribbon woven into a majestic mountainside, and it's in splendid view from the pools of the thermal station. The pools have sandy bottoms and the warm waters carries scents from Vulcan's smithy. There is, or was at least when I was there, a full bar adjacent to the pools and all I needed to do — the staff said so themselves — to order a drink was to whistle, and the waiter would appear at poolside kindly taking my order for a gin and tonic.

I remained in Aguascalientes for a couple of days, during which I visited the baths every day, relaxing and pondering my memories of the great and mysterious temple ruins at Machu Picchu — believe me, at the end of the day it doesn't matter that the monuments are perhaps the most famous and most visited by tourists in all of America. The place truly is magnificent, although its architecture, in spite of the legendary precision of the building block's lapidary joints, on close inspection comes across as more rudimentary than that of Pre-Columbian civilisations elsewhere, notably the ones of Central America. Its magnificence resides in its cosmic significance and impact. It's a speechless poem on the universe written in mute stone, testifying to the curious subtlety and artistic fancy of the very last generations of Peru's ruling elite.

For the discerning tourist, not satisfied by merely going back home with an overloaded camera telling himself and others: 'Been there, done it', there are many other remarkable sites to visit in El Valle Sagrado. For example, a twenty-minute taxi ride from the town of Urabámba in the Valley had brought me to the Inca's 'greenhouse'. It consists of some fifteen to twenty terraces propped up with stone walls, mainly concentrically and conically arranged in a big hole in the ground. Even though the difference in elevation is not so important as to allow banana and pineapple to thrive immediately below coffee, cacao, orange, and corn plantations, the temperature and light variations from top to bottom is considerable. This helps to explain how this funnel-like horticultural structure could serve as an experimental ground for the Incas to investigate optimal growing and harvesting conditions for their various crops.

As I made my way out of the 150-metre deep cone and reached the vast high plateau above it, leveling at around 3,500 metres' altitude, I met a group of Indians in traditional attire who offered me to partake in their lunch. Sitting there with some rather exotic food stuffs in my mouth, my gaze wandered across the panorama. Yes, the sky was a deep blue and the colours reflected in the thin air amazingly bright and vivid. However, over the far-off horizon I could see high cotton-like cumulus clouds gather. Or so I thought. At closer inspection these clouds revealed themselves as the massive Cordillera de Vilcanota, the peaks of which reached yet another 3,000 metres above my vantage point. Witnessing the silent snow covered peaks at this altitude, and at this unfathomable distance, is arguably one of the most serene visual impressions I have ever had, condensing to diamond clarity my memory of this ancient land, resounding of ancestral voices as humans walk hand-in-hand with the giants of the Earth and the gods of Heaven.

The village of Pisac further to the east of the Valley has a sprawling marketplace occupying its central square. This market is a veritable phoenix, rising every morning out of last evening's ashes. Incredibly, neither the myriad stands nor their merchandise remain anywhere to be seen during evening and night hours. But by the break of dawn a race of short but unbelievably sturdy people, like ants carrying five times their own body weight, has silently and efficiently dragged every item back in place. As I woke up from my sleep in one of the hotels around the plaza, it was bright morning and the market in full swing. Opening the shutter was like opening the sluices of a dam, the light instantly flooding the room, enveloping the iron lattice of the French balcony in glittering mosaics. Like so many other commercial gatherings with indigenous Peruvians, this market too is a folkloric fiesta galore sparkling of colour and bustling with life. Notwithstanding, my most important goal this morning was to reach the Inca ruins dominating the village and its surroundings from the hill above it.

The ascension turned out to be a very pleasant one hour walk along a scenic tributary to Rio Vilcanota, accompanied by my own vocal improvisations over Schubert's *Happy Trout*. The ruins themselves at the top of the hill are surprisingly well-preserved and easily stand comparison with those of Machu Picchu. But here the tourists are considerably fewer in numbers. If I remember correctly there was no official surveillance, no ticket booth and consequently no entrance fee to be paid — if there was one it surely was quite modest. From these ruins — and to have oneself photographed in the entrance to the Sun Temple is just a must — a fair stretch of the Sacred Valley can be seen meandering its way towards exotic sounding municipalities such as Urabámba, Moccopata and Ollantaytambo, giving the spectator an idea of the Inca trail and communication systems once connecting the villages of the Valley with the immense Amazonian jungle beyond the snow covered cordillera.

With this image of the ancestral territories of the Incas engraved in my mind, I returned by the asphalt road to the village, collected my belongings and hopped on the bus headed for Cusco. From Pisac it's only a 33 kilometre ride, but there are many archaeological sites along this route too. The Sacred Valley surely constituted the main artery of the Inca heartland, and it continues to do so for an indigenous population that has lived through the reign of several successive and often oppressive domestic rulers. Subsequently they acquiesced to the certainly no less oppressive Spanish crown and its Viceroy, to finally become citizens of the modern Republic of Peru. Still, life on the fringes of the Sacred Valley remains traditional and often convey timeless images:

Early morning. A deeply tanned Indian woman on her way to the market leads a fully loaded llama down a hillside. Her facial features are prematurely aged from relentless exposure to the elements. She's dressed in coloured skirts, a deep green poncho flung around her neck, while carrying an enormous load of merchandise wrapped in a textile tarp on her back. On her head sits a solid hat high as a chimney. Walking the steep gradients, she puffs on a short pipe filled with tobacco while her adolescent grandson, leading the way, entertains her with Andean airs from his reed flute.

And the sun also rises over purple mountains.

The ultimate ascension

Climbing the Wayna Picchu had been part of a birthday gift I had promised myself, to prove that I was still capable of making such an effort without actually suffering a heart attack or a stroke while doing so. Truth to tell I never expected to embark upon a similar adventure again. But Destiny, again, had other ideas on my behalf. Very recently I was thus talked into hiking the world's allegedly largest natural pyramid, the so-called *Cerro Tusa*. This remarkable mountain lies within sight from the village Venecia in the Colombian province of Antioquia, and not only from there, but allegedly from all angles, has the shape of a pyramid. The only two explanations I have as to why I accepted the challenge to mount it was that I didn't want to disappoint my dear travel companion, and that I thought that the only existing path that could take one there, though strenuous enough, would zigzag its way from the base to the top. At the beginning this was actually quite true.

The moped taxi, having brought us outside the village to the foot of the mountain, had stopped next to a brook beneath a cow pasture. This was our point of departure on foot. The advantage of having a guide with us at this point was that we would never even have found the beginning of the path leading up the mountain, since to get there one has to cross a number of fenced-in cattle fields which didn't have any beaten tracks. In addition, I don't think I would have dared to take on Colombian bulls on my own. But since our guide seemed to trust their docility we lined up behind him, occasionally crawling under electric fences as the terrain gained altitude, revealing more and more of its spectacular topography. After about half an hour's walk, we latched the last gate behind us and embarked on the path that would take us to the top. Eventually… because here the disadvantage of having the guide with us began to show. It only took me about another half-hour, coinciding with the path turning from a steep zig-zag pattern into a straight line pointing towards the sky in a 75-degree angle, to realise that though the project would have been marvelously appropriate for trained mountaineers, it presented us with the challenge of a lifetime — and one about to run out for good! Had we been alone on the trail, I most certainly would have suggested to Asíle that we turn around and try to make it back to the village as soon as possible. But our guide, mountain-fit and quite used to doing this often, would have nothing of the sort and kept spurring us on. There was nothing we could do to talk him out of it. Besides the whole thing had started to become a matter of prestige — always dangerous, sometimes fatal, when it comes to *proving* something in the face of sublimely indifferent nature.

But there we were. Luckily for us the hot afternoon sun sometimes had the idea of hiding behind a cloud. This spared us some of the worse effects of heat exhaustion. Which is not the same as to say we didn't suffer. The distance to the top from where the path turns into a straight line of steep ascension may not be more than a kilometre, perhaps even less, but since it is really more of a climb than a walk — whereby I would define 'walk' as a bodily movement where a pair of human legs primarily do the job as opposed to a more simian type of ascension where all four limbs are not only useful but actually indispensable to bring one ahead.

The latter was the case here. As we got closer to the top we did stop every fifty metres or so to drink and try to assess the compass points across an ever expanding mountain region flooded by light and shadow, overflown by darkening clouds. We could hear thunder roll like avalanches deep down in the Cauca Valley and saw lightning run crisscross over no longer so distant summits. At this point I could see that Asíle was just as tired as I was and I again deeply admired her strength and courage. As for myself I had a serious problem even keeping my legs going, since both of them were cramping from the continuous effort of bringing a hundred kilos' worth of flesh and bone up an unforgivingly steep mountainside. Even at only fifteen metres from the top I thought I had had it, but our guide rolled down to the crevice where I had ended up with leg muscles as tense as two over-engaged bow strings. He helped me to relieve some of the pressure by pushing my feet up against the legs in order to stretch the muscles back in their normal position. After a while the cramps ceded enough for me to make the final effort to the top.

Triumph! We had made it. The high plateau — and finally some reasonably flat ground — was no more than a natural shelf measuring some 60 by 20 metres. The panorama from up here comprised a huge portion of southwestern Antioquia, incidentally the most mountainous state in all of Colombia. But if overheating had been one of the problems to avoid while we were coming up, the cool rain that now began to fall from the cloud above us would perhaps had been a most welcome shower had it only lasted for two minutes. But this downpour, if not exactly a deluge, promised to become bone-chilling. It was accompanied by lightning and thunder.

Remember: we were at the top of the Cerro Tusa, where the nearest reminder of humanity was a rugged ten-foot iron cross, decorated with a small Colombian flag, fluttering in the breeze, and a couple of dangling tin cans making their modest contribution to the percussion of the spheres. The crude reality of the situation, however, was that iron leads electricity quite efficiently, and that we had nowhere to go to avoid a more and more possible lightning strike, except down the same way we had come, where the rain had begun to make the path even more slippery than before. Though we did have the time to take some heroic photos of one another, even one or two where I proudly pose with our guide, the latter, after the first lightning struck in our vicinity, was suddenly nowhere to be seen. Without telling or even advising us to go into hiding, he had, so Asíle assured me, taken shelter under some branches on the opposite side of the plateau. I realised we should have done the same, in this way protecting ourselves better from the rain, but all I could come to think of was to pull Asíle closer to me and to seek some kind of protection further down the trail, nudging us in as close as possible to a thicket of overhanging grass.

That the rain relatively soon stopped I now consider to have been our saving grace. Had it continued, the conditions on the slope would simply have been so difficult that there is no telling if I and Asíle would ever have made it. I was — of course a bit naively, credulously, not to say stupidly — wearing some Puma shoes designed to offer a decent grip on the surface of a dry indoor tennis court. Even if they hadn't been specifically designed for that, they proved extremely inappropriate for serious mountain trekking and climbing. In the now prevailing circumstances they might just as well have been a pair of skates... Yihaaaaaaaaaaaaaaaa!

Even a month or two after the actual expedition took place, my shoulder joints were still not quite back to normal after the hits they were forced to take as I hung on to every branch and root I could find in order to avoid becoming a living mud sleigh taking a leap for eternity. Asíle too had to fight very hard to not fatally go off on a tangent. Our guide, back in business, seemed unperturbed by the ground conditions, but then again he had the right kind of boots on and could give Asíle the necessary assistance. I'm quite proud, though, that during this entire ordeal we both remained cheerful, even to the point of making provocative jokes in the face of the Grim Reaper! I don't know how many times I lost balance and fell to the ground, only to be dragged downwards by the implacable force of gravity. My estimate is somewhere between twenty and thirty, and every single time this happened I needed to make sure I wasn't going to break a leg or some other bone in my body as I hit the ground — buttocks first!

I'd say there are ways to make sure you're still alive and at least not going to die from a heart attack within the next week, because if had I been susceptible to one, this would have been the moment to go. That it didn't happen was reassuring. That Asíle (who was only all too keen to take all blame on herself) and I lived to tell the story was even better. Best of all, for me at least, is the sensation of having to some degree surpassed another real or imaginary personal limitation. I don't normally feel the need to show myself brave and death defying when the necessity of it isn't even at hand. But I believe Asíle and I accomplished something important by climbing Cerro Tusa, and something that, no matter what the future holds, has created another secret correspondence between us.

Coming back to the hotel, Asíle prompted me to go into the shower first. There was at this point no other solution than to walk in there fully dressed and begin cleansing by trying to remove the larger lumps of mud sticking to the shoes. But there was so much of it on my shoes and clothes that the walls soon were covered in dirt and the drain clogged up. We had to call the cleaning maid to help us get it working again. And when that was finally accomplished there was a short circuit in the electric wiring providing warm water, resulting in a powerful explosion, the residues of which stained the white tiles all black around the faulty wiring. At this time I was nearly done, but there was no warm water to be had as Asíle went inside the shower room. Even though the short circuit wasn't really my fault, I apologised for the inconvenience I had indirectly caused her. But she would have none of it and instead went ahead without as much as a word of complaint, to take her cold shower while I was already comfortably installed on our balcony, a whisky at hand. As the warm water eventually came back on again, after the visit of an eccentric local electrician mending what had obviously been a precarious rigging in the first place, she also took care of our shoes and made sure they were cleaned and put out on the balcony to dry. When I told her I might just throw away the clothes I had been using, supposing the stains they had suffered would never come off, she responded that the clothes were already in the hotel laundry washer, and that of course the stains would come off!

I was immensely grateful for all this, but on the other hand I know that this is just who and how Asíle is, and nothing to interfere with. She wouldn't allow me to give her a hand in this as she always considers it 'her job' to do the cleaning. Now that would make the perfect housewife, right? But it gets even better. On top of being a domestic phenomenon she's also spiritually and physically richly endowed, enduring like an Indian in the face of travel hardship and a first-rate cook. She has intense big eyes, a fabulous chest, sensuous lips, and a great sense of humor; she's a famished panther in some other important respects and loves to take a deep look at everything I have to offer... Now, how could I as a man, resist her? Above all: why should I!

Epilogue

Although tempted to end my script on such a climactic note, it would be lopsided to do so. There is, and has always been, as a contrast to my spontaneous love for life and its sensuous pleasures, a poetic, melancholy streak in my character. I'm not sure all those who more or less pompously call themselves 'poets' suffer the same ambivalence, but I feel confident in saying that all poetic natures invariably oscillate between the poles of an ecstasy of the senses and the unspeakable horror in being aware of existence as such.

It's the essence of this awareness that makes up the terrifying spirit of man, hence of the mystery of life; a sense of being part and variation of a continuous enigma. I wouldn't say that the passionate melancholy and loneliness pertaining to this quest for mystery is of a morbid kind; it's more like an occasional but nevertheless habitual introversion, an illustration of the famous phrase commonly attributed to Ludwig Wittgenstein — although I believe having encountered it previously in Johann Wolfgang Goethe's writings: 'Whereof one cannot speak, thereof one must be silent.' For example: I can't speak with any certainty about the existence of extraterrestrial beings, and so I shall remain silent hereof. But I have indeed, on rare occasions, witnessed some flying objects that were and ever since have remained unidentified by me. However, one of them, perhaps the strangest of them all, I have classified as yet another close encounter with the ever illusive *Aleph*.

It appeared me to me in all its mysterious glory during a starry night over Lago de Atitlán.

I was comfortably seated in a deck chair on the outdoor garden terrace of Hotel el Amanecer in the village of San Pedro La Laguna, situated above the western shore of the lake. It was a beautiful clear night, slightly cool, but the hooded alpaca jacket I had bought at the market in Panajachél on the opposite side kept me warm in the nocturnal breeze. Though it's perfectly true that I had indeed taken a sip or two from the magic pipe, I was not in a hallucinatory state. I should say that alone the longevity of the phenomenon about to present itself excluded any psychological exaggeration on my part. What I came to behold was a pulsating yellowish light, bright and big at its luminescent maximum while invisible to my naked eye at what I took to be its minimum. At first glance I thought it was some unusual kind of satellite. But it seemed much closer in the sky than a satellite and, if that was true, also moved much slower.

Even more bizarre was that the luminous object didn't move in a straight or even a curved line. As it kept emerging and vanishing in intervals of about fifteen seconds, I found myself trying to estimate, in relation to its apparent speed and trajectory, where in the sky it would appear next. To my surprise my initial predictions were all wrong and remained so until I assumed that the light, constantly waxing and waning, was actually zigzagging its way, or, more precisely, wriggling like a snake through the interstellar medium. Once I had understood this I could quite well foresee where the light would appear next.

By this time the light had traveled from my western horizon towards the zenith and I anticipated that it would slowly but surely continue its meandering path towards Panajachél and eventually beyond the ridges of the lake, where it would become unobservable.

It would be very tempting of course to use some poetic license here, and say that the light then suddenly stopped and began to slowly rotate around its own centre to finally reveal the one point that contains all other points, e.g. an *Aleph*. Tempting, of course, since it would allow for fascinating fiction, but I would here like to remain truthful to my experience, and nothing of the sort really happened. As a matter of fact, the slowly pulsating light just continued across the sky in exactly identical fashion only to disappear beyond the eastern horizon, just as I had predicted. But although that was it, as far as my observation in relation to what seemed to be a perfectly objective phenomenon is concerned, many thoughts and feelings, notably memories, did cross my mind while the tranquil light appearance lasted. In terms of measurable and conventional time I'd say that the entire experience lasted for about ten minutes, but subjectively I felt it to be much longer.

One of the memories that came to me that night was my encounter with Dr. Henry Kesselman, an octogenarian retired dentist from North Carolina at the time travelling and photographing the poor of Mexico. He would typically appear in the main square of Oaxaca like the *Piper of Hamelin*, only it wasn't by the sound of a flute that he enticed all the children to cluster around him, but by all the small change he handed them from out of his pockets. I became acquainted with Dr. Kesselman and we used to meet for breakfast in his hotel, where he was patiently searching for the correct words in order to describe, in the local vernacular, how he wanted his eggs done: '*suave, estrellados*' (more frequently in other parts of Latin America: *fritos*) '*de un lado*', (easy, sunny side up).

During our conversations Dr. Kesselman, or Henry as he presented himself, began to ask me about my preoccupations. When he heard that I was writing he immediately retorted: 'But for whom are you writing?' A bit evasively I answered: 'For anyone who might be interested in reading what I have to say, I guess'. But that kind of vague and evasive answer did not satisfy Henry. He went on the attack and said: 'You must always have a clear reader in mind when you're writing, because you're not just writing for yourself and your own pleasure, are you?'

This was not a rhetorical figure on his part, and I began to feel ever so slightly intimidated by his inquisitive eyes, the insinuation being that I was just another public wanker. Regardless of its possible veracity, this is something a writer is not keen on admitting, no matter how narcissistic and self-conceited he might be. In return, I jestingly reproached him for considering himself such a philanthropic hero just because he had put enough dental implants in rich American mouths to now be able to walk the streets of Oaxaca and hand out tidbits to kids in need of a good bit more than chewing gum to stand a decent chance in life. But I think he felt he was doing something worthwhile, and that's all that matters in the end.

As for myself I never really enjoyed the luxury of 'knowing' my reader, apart from some friends and acquaintances kind enough to commit hours of their precious time. To me, personally, it really is a great joy to see the present text published and I entertain the (perhaps vain but nonetheless) hope, that any real, honest piece of literature, possessing some indisputable merit, over time *will* find its reader. As opposed to the slightly younger me, somewhat melodramatically stating that we can never hope to be understood (see end of the Chapter 'Playa Azul'), I nowadays lean more towards the persuasion that a text can sometimes be a ray of light travelling years through empty space before reaching a perceiving eye. The traces of real life one can extract from a series of written statements are like a stream of elemental particles, unnoticeably passing through the inflexible molecular grid of grammar and sentence construction. These particles are in themselves too small to be directly observed. But it might happen that one of them occasionally passes through this grid and collides with another particle on the opposite side of the linguistic shield. This all happens on a subatomic mental level, as it were, but the reaction can nonetheless have extraordinary consequences. A single word or phrase, appropriately launched, might thus ignite and engender an entire world.

It's now more than a decade since I met with Dr. Henry Kesselman in Oaxaca. Together we visited Monte Alban, the famous archaeological site of the Zapotec civilisation on the outskirts of town. I remember taking a photo of him there with a purple flower at the corner of his mouth. The photo has since been lost and I think I was never able to send it to him. If he's still alive I hope he enjoys being so, but I doubt he does any extensive physical travelling, since he already at the time confessed to me that he didn't feel he had the energy to keep up his philanthropic mission among the disinherited of this world forever.

In the afternoon Henry took a cab back to his hotel. I remember staying on the grounds until the long shadows dissipated. The sun was setting beyond the ridge of the Oaxaca valley, bathing in red and ochre, while silvery man-made birds silently descended towards an invisible perch. Some enthusiastic Californians performed a yoga ritual in honour of the setting star. But their music was discreet, and sitting on a stone, chiseled by an unknown Indian thousands of years ago, I could still clearly discern the wind, whispering in the temple grass.

The Island of Old Providence (Colombia), December, 2015.

Lars Holger Holm

OTHER BOOKS PUBLISHED BY ARKTOS

Sri Dharma Pravartaka Acharya	*The Dharma Manifesto*
Alain de Benoist	*Beyond Human Rights*
	Carl Schmitt Today
	Manifesto for a European Renaissance
	On the Brink of the Abyss
	The Problem of Democracy
Arthur Moeller van den Bruck	*Germany's Third Empire*
Kerry Bolton	*Revolution from Above*
Alexander Dugin	*Eurasian Mission: An Introduction to Neo-Eurasianism*
	The Fourth Political Theory
	Last War of the World-Island
	Putin vs Putin
Koenraad Elst	*Return of the Swastika*
Julius Evola	*Fascism Viewed from the Right*
	Metaphysics of War
	Notes on the Third Reich
	The Path of Cinnabar
	A Traditionalist Confronts Fascism
Guillaume Faye	*Archeofuturism*
	Convergence of Catastrophes
	Sex and Deviance
	Why We Fight
Daniel S. Forrest	*Suprahumanism*
Andrew Fraser	*The WASP Question*
Daniel Friberg	*The Real Right Returns*

OTHER BOOKS PUBLISHED BY ARKTOS

GÉNÉRATION IDENTITAIRE	*We are Generation Identity*
PAUL GOTTFRIED	*War and Democracy*
PORUS HOMI HAVEWALA	*The Saga of the Aryan Race*
RACHEL HAYWIRE	*The New Reaction*
LARS HOLGER HOLM	*Hiding in Broad Daylight*
	Homo Maximus
	The Owls of Afrasiab
ALEXANDER JACOB	*De Naturae Natura*
PETER KING	*Keeping Things Close: Essays on the Conservative Disposition*
LUDWIG KLAGES	*The Biocentric Worldview*
	Cosmogonic Reflections: Selected Aphorisms from Ludwig Klages
PIERRE KREBS	*Fighting for the Essence*
PENTTI LINKOLA	*Can Life Prevail?*
H. P. LOVECRAFT	*The Conservative*
BRIAN ANSE PATRICK	*The NRA and the Media*
	Rise of the Anti-Media
	The Ten Commandments of Propaganda
	Zombology
TITO PERDUE	*Morning Crafts*
	William's House (vol. 1–4)
RAIDO	*A Handbook of Traditional Living*

OTHER BOOKS PUBLISHED BY ARKTOS

STEVEN J. ROSEN	*The Agni and the Ecstasy*
	The Jedi in the Lotus
RICHARD RUDGLEY	*Barbarians*
	Essential Substances
	Wildest Dreams
ERNST VON SALOMON	*It Cannot Be Stormed*
	The Outlaws
TROY SOUTHGATE	*Tradition & Revolution*
OSWALD SPENGLER	*Man and Technics*
TOMISLAV SUNIC	*Against Democracy and Equality*
ABIR TAHA	*Defining Terrorism: The End of Double Standards*
	The Epic of Arya (Second edition)
	Nietzsche's Coming God, or the Redemption of the Divine
	Verses of Light
BAL GANGADHAR TILAK	*The Arctic Home in the Vedas*
DOMINIQUE VENNER	*The Shock of History*
MARKUS WILLINGER	*A Europe of Nations*
	Generation Identity
DAVID J. WINGFIELD (ED.)	*The Initiate: Journal of Traditional Studies*